AMERICA'S CHURCH

The Basilica of the National Shrine of the Immaculate Conception

Gregory W. Tucker

With Best Wishes —

Gregory W. Tucker

Our Sunday Visitor Publishing Division
Our Sunday Visitor, Inc.
200 Noll Plaza
Huntington, IN 46750

International Standard Book Number: 0-87973-700-X
Library of Congress Catalog Card Number: 99-75101

Cover and text design by Eric Schoening
Cover photos by Matthew Barrick
PRINTED IN THE UNITED STATES OF AMERICA

700

For Catherine, Olivia and Emma

ACKNOWLEDGMENTS

I wish to thank Bishop Thomas J. Grady for providing his vivid personal recollections of the years he served as the National Shrine's fifth director. His humble witness and unique perspective inspired my efforts to retell this compelling story of the people and events that gave rise to the Shrine and contributed to its completion as a monument to the faith and accomplishments of Catholics in this country. I am also grateful to Msgr. Michael J. Bransfield, the Shrine's current rector, who recognized the need for this illustrated history and ensured its completion.

I am indebted to the work of Shawn Perry, whose extensive research as the Shrine's archivist in the 1970s provided the foundations for this narrative.

A very special thanks is extended to Gerald Korson, my editor, for his reassuring and keen perspective. His many fine suggestions, patience and good humor throughout this process made for a most enjoyable collaboration. I wish also to express my gratitude to Eric Schoening for his excellent design of this book and willingness to kindly consider all-too-many recommendations from its writer. I am grateful to Vernon Geisel, who suggested a logical scheme for so many words and pictures at an early stage. Norrie Epstein likewise provided many notable improvements to the text.

Finally and most importantly, I wish to acknowledge the invaluable contribution of my wife, Catherine Gibbens Tucker. Her great love and constant encouragement ultimately made possible my own dedication to this worthwhile and necessary endeavor.

GREGORY W. TUCKER

CONTENTS

INTRODUCTION

⁂

The Basilica of the National Shrine of the Immaculate Conception stands in the nation's capital city as a remarkable testament to the faith and devotion of American Catholics in the 20th century.

In many respects, the National Shrine needs no introduction. Its massive scale and artistic beauty speak more eloquently than any guidebook or historical narrative. And yet, the Shrine's adherence to Byzantine form anchors the largest church in the Western Hemisphere historically and spiritually to the period when Christianity achieved dominance over a pagan society and appropriated public architecture as its own.

The National Shrine is far more than an impressive ecclesiastical monument or awe-inspiring example of human ingenuity, skill and artistry. In clear and simple terms, the National Shrine is the story of Catholicism in America. The many chapels and oratories that make

the Shrine a veritable reliquary of contemporary Christian art and iconography also reveal something about the very nature of the American people as hopeful, generous, resilient and united in diversity.

The origins of the National Shrine long precede architectural plans, ecclesiastical consent and fund-raising strategies. Efforts to build the Shrine ultimately collided with two World Wars, the Great Depression and resistance even from members of the American Catholic hierarchy.

While the history of the National Shrine is inextricably bound to the tenets of 19th- and early 20th-century Catholic piety and devotion — made even more interesting by evolutions within secular society upon which the Shrine's founders built their case among the American people — one cannot overlook the heroic role of the National

Shrine's principal "architects." Their names alone would serve as appropriate titles for the chapters dealing with the Shrine's earliest beginnings and the revived movement of the 1940s and 1950s that ensured its completion: Cardinal James Gibbons, Bishop Thomas J. Shahan, Msgr. Bernard A. McKenna, Cardinal Dennis Dougherty, Charles Maginnis, Archbishop John Noll, Cardinal Patrick O'Boyle, John McShain, Eugene Kennedy, Archbishop Fulton Sheen and Bishop Thomas J. Grady.

Still, theirs was a mission which had as its source the determined faith, moral conviction and spiritual devotion of a nation of Catholics. The true "builders" of the National Shrine were the untold millions of "ordinary" Catholics who gave in measures both great and small to express the deeply personal sentiments of their faith. This is their story — the story of a great love and profound devotion that continues to inspire the hearts of men and women everywhere even as it bears witness to a far greater Love made known before time began and promised to endure long after the final age.

"Unless the Lord build the house, in vain do the builders labor" (Ps 127:1).

GREGORY W. TUCKER

FOREWORD

One day in 1958, I was standing at the entrance to the Crypt Church. The Upper Church was just under construction at the time. I met a young Japanese lady going into the crypt carrying in her hand a bud vase and one beautiful rose. In the last year or two I had noticed her a couple of times but had never had any conversations with her. She explained that she had been studying at Catholic University for the past two years. Her work was now completed, and she was going back to Japan. She had been going to the early morning Mass at the Crypt Church every day, and the rose was to be her parting gift to Our Lord and Our Lady.

She had come to Washington to a culture that was different from her own — a culture she did not fully understand, and one which neither fully understood her nor grasped the reverence of offering a single exquisite flower as a prayer of thanks. Soon after her arrival, she came to the Crypt Church, and there she found peace and rest.

The Crypt Church was a low, vaulted space of exquisite balance and proportion. It was dominated by an alabaster altar, situated down the nave between the transepts. It was not a Japanese space or an American space. It was a Roman space, reminiscent of the Catacombs. In the crypt, there were 15 aspsidals, or side chapels. Twelve of the 15 were dedicated to women saints, which gave her comfort. Beyond the main altar, at the end of the north apse, was the Blessed Sacrament Chapel. The reredos, or background, of the altar was a mosaic of Christ the Good Shepherd, the one who watches over His sheep, especially the lost and lonely, with love and care.

Near the ceiling was a small ceramic picture, a copy of a fresco in the catacomb of Domitilla, depicting Mary showing her child to the Magi, the Gentiles, in depicting the all-embracing love of God — the love that said, "Go, therefore, and make disciples of all nations." The Crypt Church brought her back two thousand years to the life and person of Jesus

Christ and brought her back to her baptism and the faith in which she had been reared. Away from home, she felt a strong sense of belonging to all that the crypt expressed: devotion to God and his Blessed Mother, the Virgin Mary.

The Shrine is not just a building or merely architecture. In the mind and the heart of Bishop Thomas J. Shahan, the founder, the Shrine was a hymn in stone to the honor and glory of God and to the honor of Mary. It represents the devotion in the hearts of the Catholic people of the United States. It represents the devotion of the early English and Spanish and French colonists. It represents the memory that the first diocese in the United States was dedicated to Mary. It represents the fact that, as America grew and expanded from the East Coast toward the Mississippi and beyond to the West Coast, there were many, many churches, large and small, dedicated to Mary under one of her titles. It represents the fact that the faith of the Catholics in the early United States represents more ancient faith. A vast number of the people who came to the United States to populate it came from Catholic countries in Europe. They brought their faith with them.

The Shrine is not a story of the past. It is a living hymn. It began in the mind of Bishop Shahan as early as 1891. The first Mass was said in the Shrine in 1924. For 75 years, and as we approach the next millennium, Mass has continued to be said at the Shrine — for the first 30 years in the less imposing but stunningly beautiful Crypt Church, and since then in the majestic Upper Church. Masses are said in small side chapels by priests for their families or friends. Magnificent ceremonies are celebrated in the Upper Church presided over by cardinals, bishops and archbishops. Thousands upon thousands of people have gone to confession in the Confessional Chapel. Many hundred of priests have been ordained in the Shrine. Thousand of anonymous people have come to the Shrine to express personally their needs, their hopes, their aspirations or their sorrows. Such was Dorothy Day, who came to the Shrine and spent a day of prayer searching for and finding her vocation.

By its majestic size and beauty, the Shrine has a voice of its own and tells its own story. It has a life of its own that will go on into the future. The Shrine is built as a sign of the permanence of the faith. It is built entirely of stone and brick and cement. It has no wood or steel. It is built for the centuries, like the old cathedrals of Europe that have lasted for centuries and are still young.

The Shrine is a symbol of God's justice. There is now in the Shrine an African American Chapel. Who would have thought of such a possibility in the 1920s and 1930s when the Shrine was beginning?

The Shrine is a symbol of unity. There is a Byzantine Catholic Chapel in the Shrine. There are multiple chapels that represent the devotion of various nationalities to Our Blessed Mother. A Polish Chapel of Our Lady of Czestochowa looks across the nave aisle to the Lithuanian Chapel of Our Lady of Siluva. There is a chapel in honor of Our Lady of Guadalupe, which comes into particular significance at this time when the Hispanic population of the United States is constantly growing and when the Pope has recently reconfirmed Mary as the Queen of the Americas, and where Mary is being more and more honored as the comforter of the poor and the oppressed.

The Shrine is the symbol of the endurance of devotion of Our Lady. In the late 1950s and early 1960s, the religious brothers of a nearby religious community used to consider it a privilege to come to the Shrine for Mass. They had to ask for permission and wait their turn. During the summer months, perhaps a thousand nuns used to come to three morning Masses at the crypt and later to Masses celebrated in the Upper Church.

About 1965, there came a dramatic change. The religious brothers no longer wanted to come to the Shrine. In fact, they looked upon the Shrine as something old-fashioned and out of style. Hardly more than one hundred nuns would come to the Shrine for Mass. The others would seek out various religious houses to experiment with the new liturgies of one kind or another. There was a sudden decline in public devotion to Our Lady; nevertheless, there were hundreds of thousands and sometimes a million or more pilgrims visiting the Shrine each year.

Now, in the last decade of the 20th century, there has been a revival of interest in Our Lady. Numerous books are being published about Our Lady, her significance in the life of the Church and in the life of each Christian. Through all the ups and downs of popular sentiment, the Shrine has stood as a solid manifestation of enduring devotion to Mary.

As the 21st century approaches, the south wall of the Shrine has recently been covered with a massive marble-relief sculpture interpreting the "Universal Call to Holiness." It is a magnificent piece of art. At the same time, it is a reminder of the heart of the message of the Second Vatican Council. The message of the

Shrine is a growing phenomenon. It has the vitality of something that continues to grow to walk into the future.

At this time in the history of the world and of the Church, we are becoming more and more conscious of the diversity of cultures and the need for unity among them. The Church and much of the world had what might be called the European attitude, as if the whole center and focus of all life was in Europe or from its descendants. Now we are becoming more and more conscious that we live in one world and that all the different countries and cultures must be considered as part of that world. We must somehow come to live in peace and harmony and cooperation. The Shrine stands as a symbol of what that unity should be. It has chapels dedicated to the memory of various national saints, national devotions. It has accommodated many Byzantine ceremonies. It represents the diversity of many religious communities that have united in the funding and the erection of the Shrine. In the west transept, John Bosco speaks across the aisle to Our Lady of Mount Carmel. At the north end of the Shrine, the Dominican Chapel, Our Lady of the Rosary, faces the Vincentian Chapel of Our Lady of the Miraculous Medal. Filipino Catholics are represented by a chapel to Our Lady of Antipolo. Asian Indians are represented by a Shrine to Our Lady of Good Health, Vailankanni.

The meaning of the Shrine is not something that one grasps in a minute. It takes a good while to walk around the whole Shrine, see all the chapels, and to understand their meaning. It takes prayer and reflection to understand that the Shrine is much more than a tourist attraction.

In order to see the full beauty of the Shrine as an architectural piece, it is necessary to see it covered with snow and then in the springtime, surrounded by azaleas and dogwood tress; to see it in the rain and in the bright sunshine; to see it when, rarely enough, there are few visitors around, and to experience it when the great organs are thundering and the choir is singing so beautifully.

In the summer months, as the evening light begins to fade into dusk, the bells in the bell tower begin to speak forth. The sound drifts over the Soldiers' Home, the hospitals, the campus of The Catholic University of America, the traffic on Harewood and Michigan and Fourth Street. The sweet sound of the bells puts into melody America's hymn in stone. They say, "Hail, Mary, full of grace, the Lord is with thee."

BISHOP THOMAS J. GRADY

On this site will be erected
the National Shrine of the
Immaculate Conception

Endowment Membership 1000   Foundation Membership 500
Memorial Membership 250   Life Membership
Family Membership 50
(1/1 Monthly)   Charter Me
Make Application for membership
Rev. Bernard A. McKenna
Foundation Stone Laid Sept 23, 1920.

AMERICA'S CHURCH

A NEED DEFINED

∞

A CAUSE DIVINED

1895 – 1922

"A magnificent Catholic church is to be built at Washington, something after the style of the cathedrals of the Old World. It is intended by the Catholics to appeal for aid in this great undertaking to every congregation of their denomination in the United States" (*Lowell Courier Journal*, Jan. 29, 1846).

One hundred fifty-three years after the above announcement appeared in the pages of the Lowell, Mass., newspaper, a magnificent Catholic church, known to all of Washington, D.C., as "the National Shrine," is now a splendid reality — one of the monumental landmarks that define the distinctive skyline of the capital city. Its formal name, the Basilica of the National Shrine of the Immaculate Conception, is altogether befitting the largest Catholic church ever built in the Western Hemisphere and the eighth-largest religious edifice in the world. True to that brief newspaper account, the unique architectural features of this pre-eminent basilica of the 20th century are, indeed, "something after the style of the cathedrals of the Old World," revived and reinterpreted by a master architect

Bishop John J. Keane, first rector of The Catholic University of America.

who was born in the Old World but trained in the New. And, as the Lowell journalist reported more than a century in advance, the "great undertaking" was ultimately crowned with success because millions of Catholic faithful in every parish across the United States responded to appeals for aid and made possible the most resplendent Shrine to Mary Immaculate that now graces a prominent hill in America's capital city.

The announcement printed by the

Lowell Courier Journal turned out to be more an amazing bit of prophecy than anything else. Although the article seems to chronicle aspirations expressed during the Sixth Provincial Council of Baltimore in 1846, there appears to be no record of the source of that ambitious proclamation or of any plans for proceeding with the construction of a major Catholic church in Washington.

In Baltimore that year, the attending bishops discussed an appropriate way to memorialize their declaration that the United States would henceforth be under the watchful care of Mary Immaculate, Patroness of America. This declaration was significant for two reasons. First, it codified the relationship that the fledgling continent's earliest explorers, beginning with Christopher Columbus, had sought to advance. Second, it anticipated Pope Pius IX's dogmatic declaration of the Immaculate Conception by eight years. Nearly half a century would pass before the vision for establishing a "magnificent Catholic church" would again emerge.

∞
BISHOP KEANE'S DILEMMA

The adage "great minds think alike" proved especially true in the years immediately preceding the formal movement to establish a national shrine.

On July 22, 1895, Bishop John J. Keane, the first rector of The Catholic University of America, petitioned faculty members for suggestions on how to solve the enviable dilemma of a young university in the throes of severe growing pains:

"In moments of leisure, reflect on a problem which I will need the counsel of you all to help in solving. That is, what religious influences should be brought to bear on our lay students. Even the 'non-sectarian' universities see the importance of these influences, and do what they can to supply them. It would be a serious reproach, and a great delinquency if we left this all important element in the lives of young men entirely to the good sense and the good will of the young men themselves. And yet, just what to do, especially while we have no chapel meant for them and of easy access to them is a puzzle. Think it out, talk it over with the others, and give me your views." **(Catholic University of America Archives)**

The Catholic University of America was fast becoming a center of Catholic interests not only for the ecclesiastical and Catholic population of greater Washington, but for the nation. The establishment of a great university church would be regarded as clear evidence that the young pontifical university was firmly established and, in its own right, on its way to becoming a significant force in the intellectual and spiritual life of the Church in the United States. In 1904, the student population of the university numbered a mere 110. In the span of just 12 years, that figure grew to 554, with 154 identified as "ecclesiastical students." These figures did not include the students of affiliated colleges such as Trinity College or the Catholic Sisters' College, nor the several hundred students enrolled in summer-school sessions. The surrounding neighborhood, known as Brookland, was beginning to emerge in relation to the expanding university population. At this same time, a number of religious communities contributed to the identity of this area of northeast Washington, affectionately known as the "Catholic ghetto." A decidedly Catholic influence was asserting itself in turn-of-the-century Washington. The university was beginning to realize its potential for becoming a major center of Catholic discourse and learning in the United States.

∞

THE FOUNDER
— 'A NEW CATHOLIC OXFORD' —

A certain professor of Church history, Father Thomas J. Shahan, took to heart Bishop Keane's dilemma of providing for the spiritual needs of the burgeoning student population. He advanced the notion that establishing a suitable university church was a minimal requirement for maintaining the dignity of a

THE
SHRINE'S
FOUNDER

Thomas Joseph Shahan was born on either Sept. 10 or 11, 1857, in Manchester, N.H. (His birth date is recorded in the Founder's Chapel of the National Shrine as Sept. 11, while the archives of his home diocese of Hartford and passport list Sept. 10.) He was a first-generation Irish American, the grandson of Dr. Peter Shahan, who had practiced medicine in Killarney, County Kerry, Ireland. Along with thousands of their Gaelic countrymen, the Shahan family fled Ireland during the Great Famine of 1849 for new and more hopeful prospects in America.

In 1854, at the age of 24, Thomas Shahan's father, Maurice Peter Shahan, entered the Sulpician seminary at St. Charles College in Ellicott City, Md. Ironically, he became a classmate there of another ambitious young seminarian — the future Cardinal James Gibbons, archbishop of Baltimore, who in 1920 would bless the foundation stone of the National Shrine. After two years of intense classical training, Maurice determined that the priesthood was not his vocation, and he departed with the highest admiration for the Sulpician priests who administered the seminary.

Not long after he ended his seminary studies, he met, and eventually married, Mary Carmody from Salem, Mass. They settled in Manchester, where their son, Thomas Joseph, was born a year later. The Shahan family soon moved to Millbury, Mass., where Tom's sister, Hannah, was born. The family would later move again and resettle in Connecticut.

Young Thomas Shahan grew up in an enveloping atmosphere of Irish Catholicism that was nurtured amid the pressure of Calvinist prejudice in turn-of-the-century New England. Because his mother suffered from mental illness, he was raised by his pious grandmother, whose fervent piety had greatly influenced his father before him. According to Speer Strahan, who published an article on his life in Commonweal in 1932, Grandmother Shahan's intense Catholic devotion would have a lasting influence on Tom, defining his own faith and piety until his dying day:

"A cruel misfortune that early made of his mother a hopeless invalid . . . prepared the boy to become a man of exquisite tenderness. . . . Yet a world of similar tenderness came to him in the person of his father's mother and the memory of her dark eyes and such liturgies as the great cross waved with precision and faith over his head to protect him from night fears, and the four smaller crosses at the bed's four posts, signed and mingled with Gaelic prayers, lingered in the ears of the man seventy years afterward."

As his father before him, Thomas Shahan entered a Sulpician seminary — at Montreal College in Canada — at the impressionable age of 15 in 1872. In his six years in Canada, Shahan developed an enduring love of the classics that would anchor and guide him throughout his scholarly life.

In 1878, the young seminarian's plans to study in Rome were delayed when his local ordinary, Bishop Thomas Galberry of Hartford, Conn., upon hearing of Shahan's mother's mental illness, required proof that her condition was not a consistent trait within the Shahan lineage. Shahan's maternal aunt and uncle interceded, attesting under oath that there was no history of insanity in the Carmody family. Rather, they stated, Mrs. Shahan's affliction was of a "hysterical character" that did not similarly affect her children. Bishop Galberry accepted their testimony and dispatched Shahan for further study in Rome.

Thomas Shahan arrived at the Pontifical North American College on Oct. 12, 1878. He joined a class of 17 other newcomers that more than doubled the size of the college. Shahan reveled in his new surroundings. The friendships and acquaintances acquired in Rome enhanced not only the enjoyment of his studies but his prospects for becoming a prominent American churchman in his own right.

His close friendship with Giovanni Battista De Rossi, the official copyist of the Vatican Archives, greatly affected his appreciation for the venerable tradition of Christian art and iconography. According to Father Blase Dixon, T.O.R., who authored *The Catholic University of America, 1909-1928*, the young seminarian "was always attracted to Christian art, especially from the earliest period of Christian antiquity. His student days in Rome and the inspiration of De Rossi increased his love of this art and early Church history day by day, until the love of these two subjects became part and parcel of his way of thinking."

After receiving his Doctorate of Divinity in 1882, Thomas Shahan was ordained to the priesthood by Cardinal Raffaele Monaca La Valletta, vicar general to Pope Leo XIII, on June 3, 1882, at the Basilica of St. John Lateran in Rome. Upon his return to the Diocese of Hartford, he took up his new assignment as a curate of St. John's Parish in New Haven.

That assignment, however, would be short-lived. Less than a year after his ordination, Father Shahan was tapped by Bishop Lawrence S. McMahon to serve as secretary and chancellor of the diocese. It was at the cathedral of Hartford that Father Shahan first learned about The Catholic University of America. According to Speer Strahan, Father Shahan relished the prospect of furthering his academic studies:

"One winter morning at breakfast he opened the Hartford Courant and read of the founding of a national Catholic University at Washington, and that [Bishop John J.] Keane had been appointed its first rector. As he himself said many years later, 'When I read that notice, I closed the paper, and said in the slang of the day, "Me for that University!" ' It was not many weeks before Dr. Keane appeared in Hartford to ask the release of young Doctor Shahan for the ambitious project."

After Bishop McMahon consented to Bishop Keane's request, Father Shahan resigned as chancellor in November 1888 and departed for Rome to continue his studies. Bishop Keane was grooming Father Shahan for the university's chair of canon law.

Father Shahan received his licentiate in both civil and ecclesiastical law within the course of just one year. At Bishop Keane's suggestion, he then went on to Germany in order to pursue his greatest academic love, Church history, at the University of Berlin. He later studied at the Catholic Institute and the New Sorbonne in Paris.

Father Shahan's passionate devotion to his academic pursuits, however, was not at the expense of his equally great interest in and love of people. Strahan chronicles how, during his studies in Berlin, Father Shahan "went every Sunday by tram to a distant workmen's quarter to say Mass for some nuns so poor they could not afford a chaplain."

In Paris, Father Shahan adopted the approach that would endear him among both his fellow scholars and the countless people who came to admire him throughout his life. For him, what was required of a professor was "not the critical flame that consumed, but the gentle warmth that encouraged."

Upon returning to Washington in the fall of 1891, Father Shahan took up his new assignment as professor of Church history at Catholic University. From the outset, he emerged as a beloved figure within the university community. He was extremely popular among students and equally respected by colleagues. It quickly became apparent that Father Shahan's future and that of the fledgling university were inextricably bound together. ∽

pontifical university.

In October 1903, Father Shahan published an article in the *Catholic University Bulletin* titled, "Who Will Build the University Church?" In it, he evidenced his own developing concept for a "beautiful and commodius church on the grounds of the university" where "the multitude of our Catholic visitors would always find at hand the occasion to spend a few minutes of prayer and thanksgiving to the Almighty in the presence of the Blessed Sacrament. . . ." Father Shahan noted the advancing physical proportions of the university, but he reminded his readers that the most basic requirement of a pontifical university was still lacking: "Large buildings of every character are multiplying on its great campus, and in the immediate vicinity. Libraries, laboratories, and classrooms are not wanting. But we all miss the noble architectural pile that ought to rise heavenward amid this busy scene of intellectual labor, and consecrate visibly the whole work to the service of Almighty God."

Father Shahan recognized the potential of the university to impact the intellectual and spiritual development of not only the student population but of all American Catholics. He was aware of the great reputations enjoyed by other prominent Catholic learning institutions throughout the world, such as The Catholic University of Louvain, Belgium, the Sorbonne in Paris, and the University of Salamanca, Spain. For centuries, these institutions influenced the intellectual life of the Church and shaped Catholic piety through the education of seminarians and priests. Father Shahan no doubt longed for the day when Catholic University, as the only pontifical university in America, would assume its rightful place among the world's great institutions of Catholic learning and influence.

Washington was fast becoming the destination for civic, religious and special-interest assemblies. Not to be outdone by other religious denominations that designated the capital city as the location for any number of high-profile gatherings, Father Shahan was eager to see Catholic University become *the* assembly place for the nation's bishops and the increasingly great number of Catholic fraternal organizations:

"Religious bodies tend more than ever to meet here as at a national center. Only this year the Episcopalians celebrated in this city a kind of General Council that obtained for their body a universal attention and recognition. It is only natural that in the future similar meetings of Catholic dignitaries should take place within the limits of the National

Capital. For such occasions a worthy architectural edifice is a primary need" (ibid.).

Just four short years after Father Shahan's observation, the Episcopalians laid the foundation stone for their noble gothic cathedral in another part of Washington. Construction on the Cathedral Church of St. Peter and St. Paul — or Washington National Cathedral, as it is commonly known — on Mount St. Alban's commenced Sept. 29, 1907, in the presence of President Theodore Roosevelt and a throng of over 10,000 citizens.

According to his own account, Father Shahan harbored a vision of establishing a basilica to the Blessed Virgin as early as 1891. In an interview after the national drive to build the Shrine was well underway, he described how, when he first arrived that fall from the Diocese of Hartford, Conn., for his new assignment at Catholic University, he "looked out upon the lonely and desolate surroundings of that day," and there came to him a vision of a splendid basilica to the Blessed Virgin "around which would one day center the great edifices of a new Catholic Oxford."

That Father Shahan possessed the vision and determination to implement plans for this great national church was further evidenced in a July 28, 1910, correspondence to Michael Jenkins, a member of the university's Board of Trustees:

"Little by little it would become a museum of the finest statuary, of all the loveliest art in Church plate, vestments, etc., etc. In a word, no one would think he had truly seen the capital of the nation unless he had paid a visit to this Church. Inside and outside it would be a monument of artistic truth and sincerity, and thus a mirror of all the beauties of our venerable and holy religion."

∞

RECTOR SHAHAN

In 1908, Father Shahan, by then esteemed editor of the *Catholic University Bulletin* and Church historian for more than 20 years, was not initially regarded as the most likely candidate to lead the growing university. But Cardinal James Gibbons' failure to follow established Vatican procedures in nominating a new rector for the pontifical university set off a chain of events that would eventually lead to Father Shahan's selection as the university's fourth rector.

The third rector, Bishop Denis J. O'Connell, had let it be known that year that he did not desire a second term. The university's Board of Trustees, in deference to the rector's wishes, obliged his decision and submitted the name of Bishop John P. Carroll of Helena, Mont., to the appropriate Vatican congregation as was required of a pontifical university.

By sending Bishop Carroll's name as the sole nominee, Cardinal Gibbons, chancellor of the university and archbishop of Baltimore, had curiously ignored the requirement of the Vatican's Congregation of Seminaries and Universities to submit three nominations (see John Tracy Ellis, *The Life of James Cardinal Gibbons, Archbishop of Baltimore*).

Pope Pius X was not amenable to releasing Bishop Carroll from his episcopal responsibilities in Helena without a more thorough consideration of other qualified candidates. Neither the Pope nor the Congregation of Seminaries and Universities were predisposed to merely rubber-stamping the cardinal's recommendation. In all matters that fell under the Vatican's jurisdiction, the Pope alone maintained the final authority to veto a congregation's selection and designate a candidate of his own choosing.

It fell to the apostolic delegate of the United States, Archbishop Diomede Falconio, to announce the Vatican's decision as relayed in a cablegram from Cardinal Merry del Val, papal secretary of state:

"Your Excellency will inform the Cardinal Archbishop of Baltimore, that the Holy Father does not deem it opportune to transfer Msgr. Carroll from the diocese of Helena to office, Rectorship, Catholic University and that he commissions Rev. Professor Shahan to act provisionally as acting Rector until candidates shall be presented" **(Catholic University of America Archives).**

Father Shahan's growing reputation as a national authority on Church history and his popularity among faculty and students at the university may well have influenced Rome to disregard the university's recommendation in favor of his interim appointment. His adeptness in developing lasting associations with influential churchmen also proved invaluable in the circumstances that opened the door for his appointment as rector. He maintained strong connections to Vatican officials from his days as a doctoral student in Rome and was well-known and respected both among University officials and those in a position to advance him.

Cardinal Gibbons informed Father Shahan that he would be inaugurated as rector pro-tem on Feb. 25, 1909. During the meeting of the university's Board of Trustees later that year to nominate qualified candidates for rector, Father Shahan received the highest number of votes on the first ballot. Cardinal Gibbons likewise expressed his preference for Father Shahan and sent a new list of nominees to Rome. On May 27, 1909, Gibbons received the Vatican's approval of Father Shahan's selection as rector for a full term. On Dec. 16, 1909, he was appointed a domestic prelate, which gave him the honorary title of monsignor.

In later years, Msgr. Bernard A. McKenna, secretary to Msgr. Shahan and the Shrine's first director, recounted a conversation he had with Cardinal Gibbons following a visit to the impressive university campus. The cardinal, recalled Msgr. McKenna, was captured in a moment of wonder at how the university had prospered under Msgr. Shahan's guidance, even while betraying his early misgivings about a Shahan rectorship:

> *"After the cardinal had gotten in the car, he looked about at the buildings on the campus of C.U.A. and broke out into a reverie saying, 'The ways of God are strange. Who would have thought that Dr. Shahan could have erected so many buildings on the campus. My choice as new rector of C.U.A. was Bishop Carroll of Helena, Mont., as I considered Dr. Shahan a visionary, a poet, an historian and scholar but not a practical builder and yet he has surpassed everyone else as a real university man of the highest type. Yes, really the ways of God are strange!'"* (**National Shrine archives**).

A 'UNIVERSITY CHAPEL'

In 1911, the still-unresolved need to accommodate the university's increasing number of faculty and students with a suitable place of worship compelled Msgr. Shahan to devise a blueprint for the eventual National Shrine of the Immaculate Conception. In time, the New Chapel Fund Association was established as an organizing body of the university to attract nationwide support for the "University Chapel." Msgr. Shahan put forth his case in a special appeal brochure:

> *"The urgent need of a New Chapel for the Catholic University has long been evident. The actual small chapel of Divinity Hall, opened in 1889, was originally intended only for the forty or more young priests and the eight or ten professors resident in that building. No provision was made for lay students, the departments of the university intended for them not being ready at that time. Since then, however, the lay departments have been opened from year to year, with the result that the students have increased to about three hundred and fifty, and the professors to about fifty, with the certainty of a corresponding growth every year. A new chapel, therefore, much larger and in various ways more suitable, is very badly needed, to hold about seven hundred persons, i.e., the actual body of professors and students, and a reasonable number of visitors."*

Exactly when Msgr. Shahan expanded the "New Chapel" drive to conform to his more ambitious vision of establishing a "splendid basilica to the Blessed Virgin" is not clear. Word of his efforts reached Basilian Father J.J. Aboulin of Detroit,

APOSTOLIC LETTER OF POPE PIUS X

≈

To Our Beloved Son, James Cardinal Gibbons, of the Title of Santa Maria in Trastevere, Archbishop of Baltimore.

Beloved Son: Health and Apostolic Benediction.

Many pious Catholic women have by their intelligent zeal added another remarkable proof to the numerous evidences of active charity which we so frequently receive from the United States. We have been informed that they have created an association for the collection of funds to build on the grounds of the Catholic University of America a church which shall foster the piety of the youthful students and meet the spiritual needs of the vicinity. How highly We esteem this project We need not say, since nothing could be more useful to the Church or further more helpfully the welfare of the Republic. Both Church and State are, indeed, deeply indebted to those who guide the youthful mind at an early age to the places where it may be more fully and efficaciously imbued with that holy fear of God which is the beginning of wisdom.

It is most desirable, therefore, that all Catholics should promptly and generously contribute toward the happy completion of this Church, which so many praiseworthy Catholic women have undertaken. In this way will arise a masterpiece of religious architecture which will lift heavenward the minds of every student who enters it, make him thirst for wisdom from above, fill his heart with the same, and preserve it religiously while he lives.

May these holy prayers be heard through the Immaculate Mother of God, in whose honor it has been decided to build this Church, and may her motherly eyes watch day and night over the Catholic University at Washington.

Meanwhile as a pledge of divine favor and of our benevolence, We give you, Beloved Son, the Association of ladies above mentioned, your clergy and faithful, with all Our heart, the Apostolic benediction.

Give at Rome at St. Peter's, the eighth day of July, 1914, the eleventh year of Our Pontificate. — **Pope Pius X**

Mich., who proposed that the newly conceived university chapel serve not only the faculty and student population but the entire nation as a monument to Catholic piety and devotion to the Blessed Mother. Father Aboulin relayed his hopes to Msgr. F.J. Van Antwerp, vicar general of the Diocese of Detroit, who agreed to petition Cardinal Gibbons. Msgr. Antwerp reinforced his sentiments and those of Father Aboulin by enclosing with his letter to Cardinal Gibbons an impressive contribution of $1,000.

America's most prominent churchman was well aware of the interest among the members of the American hierarchy to build a cathedral-like shrine to Mary. In two previous gatherings of the nation's bishops at Baltimore, the prospect of erecting a national church had been a topic of discussion. Now, however, circumstances at the university and the collaboration of key American churchmen had brought the matter to the forefront.

Cardinal Gibbons facilitated what proved to be a defining moment in the history of the Shrine's early beginnings. During a private audience with Pope Pius X on the feast of the Assumption, 1913, he presented Msgr. Shahan, who outlined preliminary plans for building the National Shrine. The rector further discussed his intention to involve the Catholic women of the United States to raise funds for the ambitious project. His presentation won the Holy Father's immediate approval as well as the promise of an apostolic letter of support to American Catholics. Pope Pius was further moved to contribute financially to the cause. Reaching into his desk drawer, he retrieved in Italian lire what amounted to a $400 down payment on the Shrine's construction.

Returning from his favorable encounter with the Pontiff, Msgr. Shahan wasted little time. Having already appealed for their assistance in raising funds for the more modest "University Chapel" in 1911, he regarded U.S. Catholic women as his natural allies in the formidable endeavor now before him.

SALVE REGINA

"To All Lovers of Mary Immaculate. This is the first number of Salve Regina, a little magazine, if we may dignify it by that title, by which we hope to make known every quarter the progress we are making in collecting a fund for the erection of a National Shrine of the Blessed Virgin."

With this introduction, Msgr. Shahan inaugurated the "little magazine" of *Salve Regina* in January 1914 as the vehicle for spreading the good news that the National Shrine was no longer a matter of fanciful hopes. By gaining subscriptions to the journal, Msgr. Shahan planned to build national support for the Shrine's construction. He further used the pages of *Salve Regina* to record the Shrine's fund-raising progress and to expound on the spiritual rewards of Marian-centered piety and devotion.

In this first recorded account of the National Shrine's birth as a national symbol of Catholic prominence in the United States, Msgr. Shahan defined his vision for erecting the Shrine and the means by which its success would be ensured:

"By the National Shrine of the Immaculate Conception is meant a large and beautiful church in honor of Our Blessed Mother's most admirable title, to be built by a nation-wide cooperation on the grounds of the Catholic University at Washington, at the heart of the nation, as a great thank-offering for countless benefits received and a perpetual monument to the Immaculate Queen of Heaven raised by her countless clients in the United States and elsewhere."

Fortified with the resolve and dedication of American Catholic women, Msgr. Shahan was confident that enthusiasm for realizing his grand vision would spread swiftly among the Catholic population as a whole. What Catholic of even modest means would not seize the opportunity to be associated with the creation of a national memorial to his or her faith? Msgr. Shahan sought to compel contributors in early appeal literature by contrasting what he considered to be America's wasteful material consumption with the more virtuous expenditure on a lasting spiritual memorial:

"How much money is daily wasted, or spent on frivolous or useless objects, that would go far toward the creation of a most lovely church, whose noble proportions and interior beauty would appeal forever to the thousands of visitors to our National Capital!"

∞

A TRIBUTE TO WOMANHOOD

It was only natural that Msgr. Shahan should turn to the Catholic women of the United States to enlist their cooperation in building a Shrine to the Blessed Virgin Mary, who was considered the very ideal of womanhood, whom William Wordsworth called "our tainted nature's solitary boast." Women had long constituted the devotional stability of the Church and ensured the practical realization of its mission in the United States and throughout the world. After all, it was women who formed parish sodalities, gave generously of their time and labors in support of many apostolates on the local church level and, by their very role as mothers, symbolized Mary's fulfillment of God's perfect will as the Mother of Christ.

At the turn of the century, American women were asserting a new prominence in politics, business and even religion. Marian devotion was on the rise, and no one stood to gain more by its propagation than women themselves. Though highly romanticized in the poetic language of the day, Marian-centered piety affirmed the unique role of women in salvation history. Catholic women, emboldened by their newfound identification with the only human being to be born without sin, Mary Immaculate, were eager to do their part to ensure that this modern-day Shrine to Mary — and, by association, to womanhood — succeeded.

One of the earliest indications that American Catholic women would be expected to take on the task of building the National Shrine is reflected in this letter, dated Dec. 26, 1913, from Cardinal Gibbons to Msgr. Shahan:

My Dear Monsignor Shahan:
I rejoice greatly to hear of the zeal and the devotion with which the Catholic women of the United States have taken up the task of building a noble church in honor of the Immaculate Queen of Heaven. It seems most fitting that such a temple of divine worship should arise on the grounds of the Catholic University, which is the possession of our entire people, and is so happily located at the very heart of the nation. Here this beautiful

church will be most accessible and will be to many a rich fountain of heavenly graces and blessings. It is to the Catholic women of our beloved country that we owe in very large measure the white vesture of churches with which the land is covered. I feel assured that they will not rest in their new task until they have, on the one hand, endowed the University youth with a proper home for the service and the influence of religion and on the other have raised in honor of the Immaculate Mother of God, the glory of their sex, a church which shall forever proclaim their affectionate and generous hearts, and their well-known readiness to make many sacrifices in furtherance of the great works of our holy religion.

Most faithfully yours in Christ,
James Cardinal Gibbons

In a Nov. 21, 1913, letter to Mrs. F. Burrall Hoffman, president of the New York Chapter of the National Organization of Catholic Women (NOCW), Msgr. Shahan expressed his delight in learning that she had sponsored a fund-raising reception at the Waldorf-Astoria to benefit the National Shrine. Mrs. Hoffman enjoyed a prominent position in New York society and was thus well-positioned to advance the Shrine cause within her social milieu. Msgr. Shahan, no doubt, relished the potential of his new association with Mrs. Hoffman and her contingent.

The potential benefits of their collaboration, however, were soon obscured by Mrs. Hoffman's personal agenda. She harbored great ambitions for her son, F. Burrall Hoffman Jr., an architect of some accomplishment, to be appointed the architect of the National Shrine. Msgr. Shahan entertained this possibility in correspondences with Mrs. Hoffman, even recounting that he brought the prospect of her son's professional involvement before the university's Board of Trustees with the added assurance that "[I] expressed my own sympathy with that desire, and my belief that he could build, in a satisfactory way, the church we contemplate."

The board, while equally delighted with Mrs. Hoffman's endeavors, was reluctant to commit the Shrine's still-tenuous future to this mother-son enterprise. Msgr. Shahan attempted to allay Mrs. Hoffman's fears that her son might not secure the coveted appointment. Fearing that the board's less-than-enthusiastic reception of Mr. Hoffman's role might short-circuit the support of Mrs. Hoffman and her NOCW associates, Msgr. Shahan offered that "while we may not announce that the architect has been appointed, there is nothing to prevent your son from presenting a sketch of the proposed building, to be ready for the next meeting of the board after Easter." Msgr. Shahan prudently qualified his invitation with the caveat that it "be done without any expense to the university." Msgr. Shahan's encouragement opened the door for the development of the first architectural concept for the National Shrine.

∞
THE FRENCH GOTHIC DESIGN

"The style of architecture is French Gothic of the late fourteenth century," announced *Salve Regina* in April 1915. "This style was selected as being best suited by its delicate tracery and lofty proportions to symbolize Our Lady of the Immaculate Conception."

Mr. Hoffman advanced his French

(below) The plaster model of F. Burrall Hoffman Jr.'s Gothic version of the National Shrine, which toured the country in 1915.

Gothic design for the National Shrine in the hope that, if widely circulated at an early stage, it would become the image which most interested Catholics would envision as the National Shrine. Hoffman proceeded with creating a plaster model of his design. As he had hoped, his model served as the first tangible image of the Shrine for thousands of Catholics across the nation.

The April 1915 *Salve Regina* announced plans for Hoffman's model to tour the country, appearing first in New York City and then at the Panama Exposition in San Francisco. In New York, "The exhibition took place on the lower floor of the Dreicer Building, corner of Fifth Avenue and Fifty-Third Street, nearly opposite St. Patrick's Cathedral. A beautiful plaster model of the proposed church attracted the attention of thousands of visitors, and the large exhibition space was frequently crowded during the day." On display in San Francisco, it was exhibited in "a suitable space, properly ornamented, and attracts daily an increased number of visitors. The installation of the lovely model was cared for by Mrs. F. Burrall Hoffman, President of the New York Chapter of the National Organization of Catholic Women."

Sadly, Mrs. Hoffman's persistence in

seeking to control both the fund-raising and design efforts of the National Shrine would result in great personal disappointment. No one could dispute the invaluable role she played in securing a sizable financial base for the Shrine's eventual construction. Yet it had become increasingly clear to Bishop Shahan (he had been consecrated titular bishop of Germanicopolis on Nov. 14, 1914) and the Board of Trustees that the time had come to return the National Shrine fund-raising campaign to university influence and control.

THE FIRST DIRECTOR

❧

SECRETARY AND FIRST DIRECTOR:

— Father Bernard A. McKenna —

Throughout the National Shrine's long and often turbulent history, few individuals were more diligent, enterprising or single-hearted in their desire and efforts to advance the Shrine's cause than Father Bernard Aloyisius McKenna.

Bernard A. McKenna was born in Philadelphia in 1875 to Daniel and Anna McKenna. In the summer prior to his graduation from LaSalle College in 1895, he visited Ireland, England, Scotland and Wales, where he gained a lifelong appreciation for art and architecture. He later entered the Seminary of St. Charles Borromeo and was ordained to the priesthood for the Archdiocese of

Father Bernard A. McKenna studied sacred theology at The Catholic University of America, receiving his bachelor's degree in 1904 and his licentiate degree the following year. But his plans to pursue headlong a doctorate in philosophy were sidetracked when his elderly cousin — Father Charles H. McKenna, a prominent Dominican orator — invited him to tour the Holy Land. Concluding that such an opportunity might not again present itself, the younger priest postponed his doctoral pursuits and embarked with his cousin for the Holy Land in March 1906.

For Father Bernard McKenna, the pilgrimage was the education of a lifetime. The two priests visited all the major religious sites of the Holy Land and then sailed for Rome, where they immersed themselves in the history, art and architecture of the major churches, the catacombs and the ancient Roman ruins. Father McKenna attributed this extended excursion with his learned and respected cousin as laying the foundation for his lifelong preoccupation with sacred art and architecture, as well as his passion for erecting the National Shrine.

Although he would not be appointed as the Shrine's first director until 1929, Father (later Msgr.) McKenna performed virtually the same function during his years as Bishop Shahan's secretary (1915-1929). ❧

Philadelphia in 1903. After a brief assignment as an assistant at the cathedral in Philadelphia, he was sent to The Catholic University of America to pursue studies in early Church and medieval history under Father Shahan. It was during his years as a student at the university that his close friendship with Father Shahan first blossomed. The two men maintained a regular correspondence even after Father McKenna returned to his diocese to serve as a parish priest.

By the spring of 1915, the Shrine drive had gained a life of its own. With Mrs. Hoffman now removed as the point person for the Shrine's promotion and fundraising campaign, Bishop Shahan was eager to re-establish control over the movement he had begun. The National Shrine was now widely considered to have passed from the realm of implausibility to one of inevitability. Donations were coming in steadily from all parts of the United States. Subscribers to *Salve Regina* were being added daily. The stakes for the Shrine's success were becoming increasingly higher. Bishop Shahan realized that it was now necessary to develop a tighter organizational structure in order to fulfill the primary objective of getting construction started.

Father McKenna was a faithful contributor to his alma mater, and his frequent correspondence with Bishop Shahan occasioned an ongoing discussion of the university's progress and the Shrine plans. In a letter of May 22, 1915, Bishop Shahan informed the priest that he had petitioned the Philadelphia archbishop to release Father McKenna for a three-year term, during which time he would serve as Bishop Shahan's secretary — with his primary function being to advance the Shrine's cause throughout the country. By June 5, the request was granted. The rector gained not only a secretary but a partner whose indomitable will and boundless energy would carry the Shrine forward during the next 17 years.

With Father McKenna at Bishop Shahan's side, a new framework for coordinating the Shrine's fund-raising and publicity efforts was established. The July issue of *Salve Regina* instructed donors to send their financial support to the attention of "Rev. Bernard A. McKenna, Catholic University." The era of Mrs. Hoffman had passed. Unfortunately, the cooperation of the New York Chapter of the National Organization of Catholic Women passed with it. The minutes of their June 11, 1915, meeting recorded: "The members of the New York Chapter of the National Organization of Catholic Women have sent in their resignations as they feel their efforts to help build this Shrine in Washington have not been properly appreciated." In the few short years of their activity, the NOCW chapter had raised the impressive sum of $30,689.44 for the Shrine's construction.

Father McKenna seized his new duties with abandon. Almost overnight, his name appeared on all appeal literature as the one to whom contributions and inquiries were to be directed. With approximately $22,000 on hand, Father McKenna cast the net far and wide. He opened new avenues of support for the Shrine previously unexplored by the NOCW. No longer would the construction of Mary's "temple" be the sole mission of America's Catholic women. All Catholics — male and female, young and old, wealthy and those of modest means, religious, priests and laity alike — would be called upon to join in this great undertaking.

Bishop Shahan and Father McKenna operated very much as a building committee of two during the next several years. William P. Kennedy, in his book *The National Shrine of the Immaculate Conception (1917-1927)*, characterized their close collaboration this way:

"In the hands of these two — Bishop Shahan and his able assistant — lie all the intricate threads of the vast undertaking. Asked why a

A *"building committee of two"
— Bishop Thomas J. Shahan
(seated) and Father Bernard A.
McKenna.*

larger organization is not maintained to relieve him and his assistant of some of the duties that press down on them, Bishop Shahan replies that the work is not yet far enough advanced to be distributed from the hands of these two. The idea is to keep the work centered, unified and harmonized in a few minds that it may preserve its symmetry."

JEWELS FOR MARY'S SHRINE

Since there was still nothing to report in terms of actual construction on the Shrine, *Salve Regina* during this time served very much as a devotional journal of Marian poems and reflections from well-known Catholic writers of the day.

Still, Father McKenna never missed an opportunity to remind his readers of the objective at hand and of the critical role they played in providing the means to achieve that objective. Recognizing that the Shrine would eventually have need for a great number of chalices, monstrances and altar-plates, he frequently encouraged readers to consider a gift of jewelry or other cherished personal effects to be used in the decoration of the Shrine's sacred vessels. Under the heading, "Gold, Silver, Jewels," Father McKenna explained the need for "personal decorations," to his readers:

> "Here is a most honorable and useful way of disposing in the Divine honor, and in that of Mary Immaculate, of unused ornaments, old gold and silver, precious stones and personal decorations no longer worn, but kept as heirlooms or mementos of those who have gone before. What holier or more pleasing use could be made of them than to devote them to the Divine service by having them worked over into the rich vessels and plate that the tremendous mysteries of our holy faith call for and honor?" (Salve Regina, January 1916)

A BLUEPRINT FOR SUCCESS

By the spring of 1918, the Building Committee of the National Shrine, established by the university's Board of Trustees to oversee all of the Shrine's affairs, discussed the need to begin achieving some level of tangible progress beyond collecting funds and adding to the subscription rolls of *Salve Regina.* Many were beginning to wonder if the actual building of the National Shrine was ever going to get underway. The Building Committee decided the time had arrived to obtain an architect.

The committee, comprising Bishop Dennis J. Dougherty of Buffalo, N.Y., (later cardinal archbishop of Philadelphia) as chairman, Bishop J.F. Regis Canevin of Pittsburgh, Bishop Shahan, Philadelphia attorney Walter George Smith, Sir James J. Ryan of Philadelphia and Father McKenna as secretary, outlined eight primary objectives to guide their deliberations.

This definitive plan of action, vested with the full consent of the university's governing body, would define the Shrine's architectural style and estimated budget. The committee reaffirmed the nation's responsibility for ensuring the Shrine's completion as a "Catholic monument" worthy of the contributions of every U.S. diocese. Its eight resolutions established a clear course for the Shrine at a time when such basic issues regarding the intended style and budget had yet to be resolved:

> "(1) That the Holy See be petitioned to approve the New Church as the National Basilica of Mary Immaculate.
>
> "(2) That the New Church be monumental in

character and capable of seating several thousand.

"(3) That the style of the Church be Romanesque, liberally interpreted.

"(4) That architects be invited to compete, the decision resting with University Trustees.

"(5) That the stone shell of the Church be calculated at about one million dollars.

"(6) That every diocese of the United States be privileged to share the honor of this great Catholic Monument — our first National tribute to the Mother of God. For this reason the Committee suggests that every one of the 110 dioceses be invited to contribute to the cost, on the basis of its Catholic population.

"7. That private donations, both large and small, be constantly encouraged.

"8. That the rapid completion of the Holy work be earnestly commended to the prayers of the Catholic faithful."

Until this time, no architectural concept had been suggested other than F. Burrall Hoffman's French Gothic version. Father McKenna now resisted any attempt to suggest what the Shrine might look like when constructed except for the brief and oft-repeated description of "a beautiful votive church in honor of the Immaculate Conception."

A number of factors influenced the abandonment of the French Gothic design in favor of the Byzantine Romanesque style that would eventually prevail. Charles D. Maginnis of the distinguished Boston architecture firm of

Cardinal Dennis J. Dougherty, chairman of the Building Committee of the National Shrine.

Maginnis and Walsh (and the Shrine's eventual architect) recounted years later that the choice of a Romanesque design was inevitable, given the predominance of Greek and Roman architectural styles that characterized so many of the capital city's official buildings.

The July 1922 edition of *Architectural Record* cited the reasoning of Maginnis and Walsh for preferring the Byzantine style:

"The obviousness of the dome of the National Capitol in the Washington scene was not regarded as any determent here; it was recognized that there was place for another dome of great scale, which would have its individuality heightened by a graceful campanile, a striking feature of the composition, related to

Christian architectural traditions. . . . It was a determining consideration that the Byzantine system has that integrity of structure possessed by no other historical style of architecture except Gothic."

There were more practical considerations that precluded a Gothic design. Construction on the National Cathedral in northwest Washington was well underway. Established by an act of Congress and begun in 1907, the Gothic cathedral was intended to contrast with the monuments and government buildings of Washington and evoke the style of many of the great churches of Europe. The first Episcopal bishop of Washington, Bishop Henry Yates Satterlee, explained that the Gothic style was chosen to "kindle the same religious, devotional feelings and historic associations which are awakened in the breasts of American travelers by the great Gothic cathedrals of Europe."

Maginnis considered it redundant to erect a Roman Catholic version of a great Gothic cathedral on the opposite side of the city. Furthermore, the Byzantine-Romanesque style was regarded as far more compatible with a construction schedule that had no determined completion date. The estimated $5 million required to build the National Shrine and adorn the interior would take years

to raise in spite of Father McKenna's aggressive fund-raising tactics. Unlike a Gothic structure, which would necessitate the completion of the interior and exterior simultaneously, a Byzantine system would permit the use of interior spaces that were not yet completed even as their ornamentation continued over the years as funds allowed.

According to the Shrine's fifth director, Bishop Thomas J. Grady of Orlando, Fla., "The aim of the architects was to achieve an original building which would be closely imitative neither of Hagia Sophia or St. Mark's, nor of St. Peter's or any other specific church. The building was to be sunk deep in tradition; yet it was not to be 'just like any other cathedral'; it was to be distinctive, American, the United States' own National Shrine to the Immaculate Conception."

A 'TEMPLE WORTHY'

The spring of 1919 marked yet another significant milestone in the Shrine's emerging identity as a truly national church. In a letter to the American bishops dated April 10, 1919, Pope Benedict XV welcomed the prospect of the Shrine with the same enthusiasm as his predecessor, Pope Pius X. Not only did the Pontiff "rejoice" in the hope that the

POPE BENEDICT XV TO AMERICAN BISHOPS

To James Gibbons, Cardinal of the Holy Roman Church, Archbishop of Baltimore, William O'Connell, Cardinal of the Holy Roman Church, Archbishop of Boston, and to the other Archbishops and Bishops of the United States of America.

Beloved Sons, Venerable Brethren, Health and Apostolic Benediction.

We made known to you also how deeply We rejoice to hear that popular devotion to Mary Immaculate has greatly increased in view of the proposal to build on the grounds of the University the National Shrine of the Immaculate Conception. This most holy purpose merited the approval and cordial praise of Our Predecessor of happy memory, Pius X. We, too, have always hoped that at the earliest possible date there would be built in the national Capital of the great Republic, a temple worthy of the Celestial Patroness of all America, and that all the sooner, because, under the special patronage of Mary Immaculate your University has already attained a high degree of prosperity. The University, We trust, will be the attractive center about which will gather all who love the teachings of Catholicism; similarly, We hope that to this great church as to their own special sanctuary will come in ever greater numbers, moved by religion and piety, not only the students of the University, actual and prospective, but also the Catholic people of the whole United States. O may the day soon dawn when you, Venerable Brethren, will rejoice at the completion of so grand an undertaking! Let the good work be pushed rapidly to completion, and for that purpose let everyone who glorifies in the name of Catholic contribute more abundantly than usual to the collections for this church, and not individuals alone, but also all your societies, those particularly which, by their rule, are bound to honor in a special way the Mother of God. Nor in this holy rivalry should your Catholic women be content with second place, since they are committed to the promotion of the glory of Mary Immaculate in proportion as it redounds to the glory of their own sex.

After thus exhorting you, it behooves Us now to set an example that will lead Our hearers to contribute with pious generosity to this great work of religion, and for this reason We have resolved to ornament the high altar of this Church with a gift of peculiar value. In due time, We shall send to Washington an image of the Immaculate Conception made by Our command in the Vatican Mosaic Workshop, which shall be at once a proof of Our devotion towards Mary Immaculate and Our good will toward the Catholic University. Our human society, indeed, has reached that stage in which it stands in most urgent need of the aid of Mary Immaculate, no less than of the joint endeavors of all mankind. It moves now along the narrow edge which separates security from ruin, unless it be firmly re-established on the basis of charity and justice.

In this respect, greater efforts are demanded of you than of all others, owing to the vast influence which you exercise among your people. Retaining, as they do, a most firm hold on the principles of reasonable liberty and of Christian civilization, they are destined to have the chief role in the restoration of peace and order, and in the reconstruction of human society on the basis of these same principles, when the violence of these tempestuous days shall have passed. Meantime, We very lovingly in the Lord impart the Apostolic benediction, intermediary of divine graces and pledge of Our paternal good-will, to you Our Beloved Sons, to Our Venerable Brethren and to the clergy and people of your flocks, but in a particular manner to all those who shall now or in the future contribute to the building of the National Shrine of the Immaculate Conception at Washington.

Given at St. Peter's, Rome, the tenth day of April, 1919, in the fifth year of Our Pontificate. — *Pope Benedict XV*

"temple worthy of the Celestial Patroness of all America" would be erected in a timely fashion, but he encouraged all Catholics in America to contribute generously to "this great work of religion." Further, he promised to send a personal gift to decorate the high altar of the Shrine from the Vatican's own mosaic workshop. The mosaic would depict Bartolomé Esteban Murillo's famous rendering of the Immaculate Conception exhibited in the Museo del Prado in Madrid.

Pope Benedict, evoking the scriptural admonition that "to whom much is given, much will be required" (see Lk 12:48), called on American Catholics to take up the Shrine cause with the same fervent spirit as America was exhibiting on the geopolitical stage. "In this respect, greater efforts are demanded of you than of all others, owing to the vast influence which you exercise among your people," the Pope said. "Retaining, as they do, a most firm hold on the principles of reasonable liberty and of Christian civilization, they are destined to have the chief role in the restoration of peace and order, and in the reconstruction of human society on the basis of these same principles, when the violence days shall have passed."

The Holy Father's words of support and encouragement would have the effect of "rallying the troops" among the American hierarchy and Catholics throughout the country. The mission to build the National Shrine now had but one basic requirement: to succeed.

∞

THE ARCHITECT

The June 15, 1919, issue of *Salve Regina* announced the long-awaited selection of the Shrine's architect under the heading "Great Architects Obtained":

"The Trustees of the Catholic University of America have appointed Maginnis and Walsh of Boston, as architects of the National Shrine of the Immaculate Conception, and the news has been received by the Catholic press of the country with the utmost respect and approval. Both Mr. Maginnis and Mr. Walsh are architects of the first class, and with them is associated Frederick V. Murphy, the Professor of Architecture at the Catholic University. . . . In the selection of Maginnis and Walsh the step has been taken which will assure the architectural character of the Shrine which must soon arise to be the center of the national devotion to Mary Immaculate."

The Board of Trustees of Catholic University outlined the parameters of the Shrine's design according to established ecclesiastical guidelines. Undertaking an intensive study of the major European cathedrals, Maginnis and Walsh eventually arrived at several designs by December 1919 that they sub-

The man most responsible for the design
of the National Shrine was Charles Donagh
Maginnis. Born in Londonderry, Ireland,
Charles Maginnis emigrated to Boston at the
age of 18. Some years later, he established
the architectural firm that bore his name.
Eventually he became a member of the
American Institute of Architects in 1901, a
fellow in 1906, vice-president in 1932 and
president from 1937 to 1939. He received the
institute's Gold Medal, its highest honor, in
1948.

Maginnis was indeed a man of many distinctions. Pope Pius XII named him a
Knight of Malta. He was awarded the Laetare
Medal by the University of Notre Dame, and
he received numerous honorary degrees
from such academic institutions as Boston
College, Holy Cross College, Tufts University
and Harvard University. In 1932, he served
as the first president of the Liturgical Arts
Society of America. There were few architects of the day who achieved the level of
accomplishment and respect within both
the architectural profession and the
Catholic Church as Charles Maginnis.

Maginnis approached the Shrine project
with the aim of designing a church that captured the essence of the American spirit. In
his letter of introduction to Bishop Shahan,
dated Nov. 26, 1918, he expressed enthusiasm for developing a design of the "proposed
National Shrine" in "Byzantine terms."
Elaborating on his preference for the
Byzantine-Romanesque approach, he wrote:
"It happens that we have done several works
in this style which, if not of magnitude,
illustrate at least our capacity to realize the
spirit of this style, and to deal with it sympa-
thetically. We need hardly say that in the
event of our selection, we should apply our-
selves with all earnestness to achieve a result
of which the University would be proud."

Maginnis clearly regarded the Byzantine-
Romanesque style as most conducive to
achieving a noble and classic expression of
transcendent themes through a contemporary, uniquely American interpretation. He
was not one to experiment in modernism,

which he generally disregarded as having
tenuous merit. Rather, his aim would be to
design a dignified structure that clearly
articulated the "divine presence," one that
bore witness to the aspirations of a "nation
under God." In *Charles Donagh Maginnis,
FAIA, 1867-1955: A Selection of his Essays
and Addresses,* Maginnis is recorded as
resisting the "aggressive modernist"
approach, which attempts to advance the
merits of human ingenuity beyond that
which is timeless and universal and ultimately deserving of homage: "I am completely disconcerted when I encounter the
aggressive modernist with the conscience of
a Puritan or a Trappist monk who refuses to
make a sinful compromise with beauty."

Maginnis, it should be noted, considered
himself a "healthy" modern whose aim was
to achieve "an architecture of sanity, of distinction, true to its time but with no disloy-
alty to its national individuality." ∞

THE
ARCHITECT
∞

(top, bottom) Preliminary study of east and south elevation, Maginnis and Walsh, architects, Frederick V. Murphy, associate architect, as featured in Architectural Record, July, 1922.

(middle) An early model of the National Shrine, circa 1930s. Note the east-side placement of the campanille.

mitted to the Shrine's Building Committee. Although varied in size and architectural details, each was depicted with a tall campanile (bell tower) standing independent from the main structure, a more or less typical cathedral dome and an immense portal. The early renderings received favorable review for their compatibility with Washington's architectural landscape. In December 1920, an editorial in the *Washington Evening Star* noted:

"The proposed memorial shrine to be erected at Catholic University . . . will be a striking addition to the monumental features of the capital. Washington's notable structures have during the last twenty years grown in number. The Lincoln memorial is one of these. It is not yet completed, but is fully outlined and the promise of its impressiveness is fully disclosed. The Episcopal Cathedral on the heights northwest of the city will, when finished, be a commanding feature of the local landscape. The Catholic University memorial, as designed, will present a novel type that will be conspicuous and will add materially to the attractiveness of the capital. . . . Washington is now developing as a world city, and is destined to possess a remarkable number of imposing architectural features. Plans are now in embryo for other constructions that if they are developed and executed will make this the most attractive city in the world."

The February 1920 issue of *Salve Regina* announced, perhaps somewhat prematurely, that the National Shrine of the Immaculate Conception had passed "into the domain of accomplished fact." For the first time, the architect's rendering of the Shrine as it appears substantially today was depicted on the front cover. The impressive design was featured prominently in the pages of *Salve Regina* and in all outgoing promotional materials as if it were already an "accomplished fact." For Bishop Shahan, Father McKenna and the increasing number of Shrine proponents, "seeing was believing."

∽

FIRST PUBLIC MASS FOR THE NATIONAL SHRINE

Prior to the celebrated laying of the foundation stone in September 1920, the event that occasioned the earliest nationwide news accounts of plans to erect the National Shrine was the Dec. 8, 1917, Mass offered for the success of the Shrine by Father McKenna and held in the parlor of Caldwell Hall of Catholic University. The altar used for this premier liturgical celebration of the Shrine had been built in 1774 and used by America's first Catholic prelate, Archbishop John Carroll of Baltimore. The Mass was attended by 165 supporters, representing various regions of the United States, who traveled to the university despite an approaching blizzard. "Hundreds of thousands of loving hearts beat in unison with the adorers at this first Mass, and wished that they could have been amongst the number actually present on this historic occasion, on which the gifts presented to the Shrine by the devout clients of Mary Immaculate were made use of," reported the Catholic news service. These gifts, donated to the Shrine by Bishop Shahan, were its first set of vestments and a family-heirloom chalice along with two other chalices, "one made from the gold and silver and diamonds sent to the shrine by the ardent lovers of Mary Immaculate. . . ."

A few months later, on May 1, 1918, Bishop Shahan turned the first shovel of sod for the future National Shrine. A small A-frame church, named the Salve Regina Chapel, was erected on the grounds of Catholic University directly behind Caldwell Hall. Daily Mass was offered there and votive candles were lit for the success of the Shrine, while Msgr. McKenna and the Shrine staff recited the Rosary every afternoon there. The modest wood chapel was donated by Mother M. Antoinette and a Sister Louise of the Sisters of St. Joseph in Salina, Kan. — who, instead of building their own chapel at the time, decided to donate their funds to the National Shrine.

∽

SALVE REGINA BUILDING

By 1920, circulation of *Salve Regina*

∽

The National Shrine of the Blessed Virgin Mary

Where the great Potomac flows;
Where the Nation's glories shine;
There the art of beauty chose,
Beauty of Cararra snows,
For our Blessed Lady's shrine,
There were Freedom's smiling face
Shrines upon the Western strand;
Love hath built a heavenly place;
For Our Lady, full of grace
In her own Columbian Land.
'Tis immaculately fair;
Monumental drift of snow
Near The Halls of Freedom, where
Flowers of Freedom scent the air,
Wafting fragrance to and fro;
Bright, its Holy Cross of God,
Near the starry Banner blest,
Waving o'er the sacred sod,
O'er the path, that Freedom trod,
In the Washingtonian West.

Heavenly Queen! To thee we pray,
At the Nation's Shrine of white,
Guard our Nation day by day,
Safely on its heavenly way
In the Eucharistic Light.
— *Josephus*

∽

(above) The Salve Regina Building and Chapel (small wooden structure on right).

(below) Early enthusiasts of the National Shrine gather on the intended site, May 16, 1920.

McKenna laid the cornerstone for a new three-story office building alongside the Salve Regina wooden chapel behind Caldwell Hall. It was here that the profitable Christmas- and Easter-card campaigns were carried out and where Father McKenna began the early quest for the Shrine's independence from university control.

Father McKenna was joined in the day-to-day administration of Shrine affairs by his sister Rose and brother John, who kept offices on the second floor of the Salve Regina building. With John overseeing construction and later the Christmas-card campaign, and Rose keeping the financial books, the Shrine was, for all practical purposes, a family-run business.

was fast approaching the 300,000 mark. Msgr. McKenna and his dutiful corps of *Salve Regina* workers had fast outgrown the cramped confines of the borrowed room in Caldwell Hall where wooden boxes once served as desks and chairs. And so on March 25, 1920, Father

(left) Archbishop John Bonzano, apostolic delegate to the United States, blesses the site of the future National Shrine on May 16, 1920.

(below) Bishop Shahan and his secretary, Father McKenna, contemplate the monumental task ahead during the blessing of the site.

∞
A BLESSING AND A BEGINNING

In the presence of over 6,000 devoted Catholics on Sunday, May 16, 1920, Archbishop John Bonzano, apostolic delegate to the United States, officially blessed the site where construction of the National Shrine would soon commence. The area designated for the National Shrine was outlined with rope to indicate the church's massive proportions. In his sermon, Bishop Shahan again expounded on the appropriateness of establishing a National Shrine to the Immaculate Conception. This time, however, he alluded to the positive influence the Shrine would have in counteracting the forces of evil and moral permissive-

THE FIRST OF MANY STONES

One of the most significant Catholic events ever to occur in the United States up to that time took place one week later. On Sept. 23, 1920, over 10,000 gathered on the southwest slope of Catholic University's campus to witness the blessing of the Shrine's foundation stone by Cardinal Gibbons. This would be the last official act of the cardinal's illustrious episcopacy. An impressive contingent of members of the hierarchy, government officials and diplomatic dignitaries were on hand as testament to the significance of the Church's growing influence in official Washington and the United States. A cablegram from Pope Benedict XV was read during the ceremony, as well as one from Cardinal

Francis Bourne of Westminster, England, who likened the Shrine to a "victory memorial" to the fallen American soldiers of World War I.

The journey of the foundation stone — a huge block of highly polished New Hampshire granite — to the massive hole awaiting it in the parcel of land adjacent to the university campus was itself a celebrated event. In many ways, the journey symbolized the long and arduous path that proponents of the Shrine would travel in the work to complete the largest Catholic church in the Western Hemisphere. A gift of granite supplier James Sexton of Stratford, Conn., the granite block was cheered, kissed and reverenced by thousands of Americans, Catholics and non-Catholics alike, on an elaborate pilgrimage procession from its quarry at Milford, N.H., to its final destination in northeast Washington.

In New York, it was adorned with American and papal flags as it passed slowly down Fifth Avenue amid a dense throng of several thousand spectators,

(opposite) Cardinal James Gibbons descends to the location of the crypt foundation stone on Sept. 23, 1920.

(left) Cardinal Gibbons invokes the blessing over the foundation stone.

(bottom) An immense throng of 10,000 gather to witness the placement of the first of many stones.

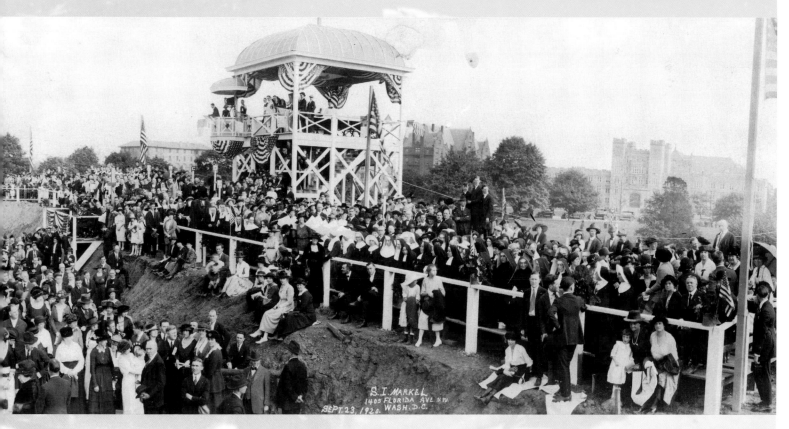

courtesy of a "bicycle squad of police." Pausing in front of St. Patrick's Cathedral, Archbishop Patrick J. Hayes and a contingent of bishops and clergy bestowed their blessing on the stone before sending it on its way.

The celebrated foundation stone arrived safely in Washington after a four-day journey in the late afternoon of Sept. 19, 1920 — appropriately, a Sunday.

The blessing ceremony was of singular importance not only because the work of building the National Shrine had finally begun, but also because it made clear that the Shrine was a noble cause in which every American Catholic could participate. This was to be their church, and they were to be its builders.

(right) Foundation-stone inscription with its erroneous date of Oct. 8, 1920: "This first stone of the Church of Blessed Mary, the Immaculate Virgin, was happily placed in position by Cardinal Gibbons, VIII Kal Octobris AN MCMXX, Benedict XV being Pope, Woodrow Wilson, President of the United States, and Bishop Shahan, Rector of the Catholic University, the stone being donated by DD James Joseph Sexton."

(below) The Shrine's foundation stone is lowered into place. The stone's donor, James Sexton, in a white tie, is at Cardinal Gibbon's right. Two of Sexton's sons are also present.

Bishop Shahan, in an article published in the June 1920 edition of *Salve Regina*, expounded on the democratic requirements of the faith that necessitated the active participation of every man, woman, and child, regardless of material means, in the "great task" of building the churches of Catholicism. He clearly recognized that the task of building the Shrine, and that of even a modest parish church, was not just the responsibility of the Church's administrators, but was the means by which lay men and women actively joined in the work of the Church with consecrated priests and religious:

"Rich and poor, old and young, men and women of every estate, have constantly upheld the hands of their pastors while they devoted themselves to this great task. And not only of their material wealth have they given in never-failing abundance, but with their contributions went holy prayers and warm affection and blessed hopes, and an unshaken confidence that those in charge of the sacred enterprise would never falter or weary in its execution . . ." ∞

ness unleashed in the modern world: "At the present time, when the modern world is given over to corruption and impurity of various kinds; when obscenity in thought, speech, action and dress are, more than ever before, eating away at the sources of national power and strength, the erection of a shrine to the Immaculate Conception will stand forever as a mighty symbol of Christian purity of life and uprightness of thought and speech."

A university choir of 487 voices provided the sacred music for the occasion. The same historic altar used during the first public Mass and belonging to Archbishop Carroll served as the table of sacrifice for the solemn "field Mass." Fifteen hundred Knights of Columbus and 600 members of the Daughters of Isabella from New York City traveled to attend the blessing. They were the first of many pilgrims who would journey to the Shrine in the years to follow.

∞

A 'WAR MEMORIAL'

Given the recent end to the war in Europe, the formal blessing of the foundation stone was regarded as a fitting tribute to American soldiers who had rendered the supreme sacrifice for their country. In one of the two cablegrams read by Bishop Shahan during his welcoming remarks at the blessing ceremony, Cardinal Francis Bourne of Westminster, England, pledged his prayers for the "blessing and success of the national shrine war memorial." The National Catholic News Service likewise referred to the Shrine as a "war memorial," as did many of the secular newspapers that chronicled the blessing ceremony. The other cablegram — from Pope Benedict XV and signed by Cardinal Pietro Gasparri, papal secretary of state — conveyed the Holy Father's apostolic blessing and personal satisfaction that the laying of the foundation stone of the National Shrine had finally come to pass.

The September 1920 issue of *Salve Regina* vividly detailed the high drama of the day:

"A platform on which stood the crimson-covered thrones of two cardinals and the apostolic delegate was placed to the north of the foundation stone, with steps leading downward. . . . A plentiful use of papal flags and floral decorations in the papal colors of white and gold, lent a striking background to the garb of the assemblage of Catholic hierarchy. . . . Walking between the Knights of Columbus, who were drawn up on either side of the steps with swords at salute, Cardinal Gibbons descended to the place where the foundation stone stood and read the blessing of the stone, while the choir from the University chanted a litany.

"As the cardinal pronounced the words of blessing over the stone, he touched each side

with a silver trowel. When the large granite block had been prepared for final placing on the concrete base, it was lowered by special apparatus."

Thus began the work of realizing what Bishop Shahan had long characterized as a great "hymn in stone." The foundation stone was actually the first and last stone put in place toward the Shrine's construction for the next two years. The work of building national support, however, proceeded with undiminished fervor.

∞

FUNDING WITH CAUTION

Exhilarated by the pageantry and excitement of the Shrine's cornerstone laying, the ever-resourceful Father McKenna moved swiftly to involve as many American Catholics as possible in the Shrine effort. The university's Board

of Trustees had established spending limits on the building of the Crypt Church on Dec. 9, 1919. Authorizing the sum of $280,000 for the crypt-level construction, the Shrine's governing body further stipulated on April 1, 1921, that construction could proceed only as long as funds were available. Nothing beyond the authorized amount could be spent or borrowed without the board's explicit consent.

In the January 1921 issue of *Salve Regina*, Father McKenna unveiled the earliest method for memorializing names of benefactors and their deceased loved ones at the National Shrine. He announced the "National Catholic Family Record," a forerunner of the Shrine's Memorial Hall, to serve as a national Catholic archives where the names of all American Catholics would be kept permanently on record. Father McKenna invited Catholic institutions and organizations — Blessed Virgin Sodalities, Children of Mary, Rosary societies, college institutions, community centers, guilds, fraternal societies, Catholic hospitals and religious orders — to be enrolled as "Confraternity Members of Our Blessed Mother's National Shrine." It was in this same issue of *Salve Regina* that the campaign to erect a memorial chapel to the Blessed Mother as a gift of all

Under the watchful eyes of Father Bernard McKenna, Salve Regina workers fill sacks with boxes of "exclusive [Christmas] cards beautifully colored, steel embossed and engraved." The shipment of 150 sacks was regarded "a fair day's work."

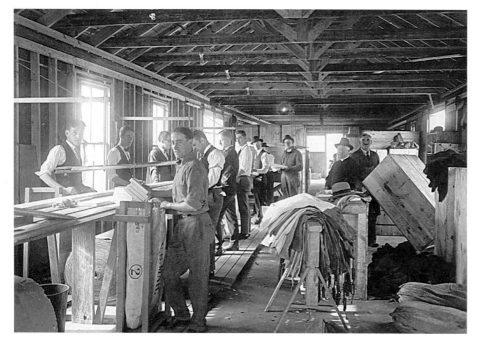

women throughout the country named Mary, or whose mothers were named Mary, was advanced as an initiative of the International Federation of Catholic Alumnae.

∞

DONOR NOTES

Father McKenna frequently printed letters of contributors that he received in the pages of *Salve Regina* to demonstrate the broad national support that the Shrine had gained among ordinary Catholics. Here is a sampling of "Thoughts and Devotion — From Far and Near":

"*Illinois — Enclosed find Sixteen Dollars ($16), as a contribution to National Shrine of the Immaculate Conception. Mrs. — gave Five Dollars ($5), Mrs. — one dollar ($1), and I, the writer, send you Ten Dollars ($10). Later on I think I can find some more who will subscribe towards this grand and glorious undertaking in honor of our Immaculate Mother, and well deserves our pious support.*"

"*Minnesota — I herewith send you $10 from my son, who has been blind in one eye for over ten years, and had to have an operation so as to save the sound eye; he was suffering terrible pain and was very despondent. I advised him to send one dollar for Vigil Lights in honor of the Virgin Mary, which I sent you on October 9. I also advised him to make a promise to pay, in honor of the Virgin Mary, a certain sum of money if he went through the operation successfully. The operation was more than successful, for now he can see from both eyes. . . . With best wishes in the under-*

taking of the great work of building this new church in honor of the Virgin Mary."

"*Maryland — Enclosed please find $5. Rev. Dear Father, I have to thank you for the great privilege of enrolling in the family record, but first of all I have to ask your permission of enrolling a real family of eight boys and four girls, wife and self, also of enrolling each of our own parents, I mean wife's parents and my own.*"

"*Iowa — It gives me great pleasure to go 'over the top' today in my humble drive for one hundred dollars for the National Shrine before Dec. 8th. Would that it were a thousand instead!*"

These are among the letters received from priests who responded to an appeal to construct the Shrine's eventual high altar:

"*Michigan — Please accept the humble offering I am making in behalf of the National Shrine to be erected in Washington, D.C. The little that I am offering can never repay in any way the great debt I owe to Our Blessed Mother for it was through her protection and through her intercession that I was spared on the battlefields of France. She it was that led me and guarded me while shot and shell fragments whirled dangerously close to me, yes she guided me through it all and brought me safely back home.*"

"*Pennsylvania — It is with my heart's love for and devotion to our Immaculate Mother that I contribute the sum requested for the High Altar of the National Shrine. It is certainly a pleasure for me to send you the enclosed and with it to express the hope that at least the*

Father McKenna and his "office force" prepare for the shipment of National Shrine Christmas cards to all parts of the United States and as far away as China from the Salve Regina building (circa 1922).

"Louisiana — I am sending enclosed my little contribution for the National Shrine of the Immaculate Conception. It is sent in the name of the new diocese of Lafayette which I have placed under the special protection of the Blessed Mother. . . . Enclosed please find check for $50, the very humble contribution of a very poor Bishop for the Shrine of Mary Immaculate. I hope to be able to do a little better later on."

great majority of the priests of our country will do likewise and I do not see why they should not."

"Wyoming — I am sending you $5 for the Shrine, and I shall send a little off and on for the same purpose. I can not say just how much, but I shall do my best. I sent you a little a few months ago. You thought I was a layman, but I am a parish priest in this little town."

"Kentucky — I am enclosing a $50 Victory Loan Bond which I presume you will accept as a $50 donation toward the High Altar of the National Shrine. I have not the ready cash on hand but presume that this would answer as well."

"Massachusetts — I am glad, yes delighted, to be able to send you $25 for the National Shrine. I need not tell a brother priest that 'the vineyard is large, but the laborers are few.' Since the war, it has been one demand after another. Whilst a few hold a deaf ear, the willing are almost overtaxed."

Father McKenna correctly gauged the intense appeal which the Shrine, as a truly national effort, would have among the Catholic faithful. In order to ensure that no one was excluded from the opportunity to contribute towards the Shrine's construction, he structured his fund-raising enterprise in a way that encouraged any level of support, great or small. His most ingenious and enduring program was the Christmas-card campaign, inaugurated in the September 1921 issue of *Salve Regina*. For the modest sum of $1 (plus 4 cents for postage), supporters would receive a box of 12 "exclusive cards, beautifully colored, steel embossed and engraved" to send to family and friends at Christmas.

Father McKenna and Bishop Shahan recognized Catholics' resentment over the increasingly secularized interpretation of the Christmas season. Commercialism was on the rise in the glamorous and freewheeling days of the "Roaring

'20s." Father McKenna seized the opportunity to reassert Christianity's claim over this most sacred of Christian feasts.

The Christmas-card campaign would prove a profitable undertaking in every respect. Not only did it result in an impressive income — over $40,000 by January 1922 — but it helped define a new role for the Shrine as an arbitrator of Catholic piety and orthodoxy. Even *The Washington Post* (Dec. 20, 1925) reported on Father McKenna's entry into the holiday greeting-card business:

"Up to this time, as we say, there had been an annual outcry in the press, more especially in the religious and Catholic press, that the beautiful custom of an exchange of Christmas cards was deteriorating into nothing more than an exchange of sentiments frequently stupid and usually pagan. . . . many felt it was part of a general attempt to discredit the historical associations that hung about the feast of Christmas. . . . In the summer of 1921, Dr. McKenna had become interested in the question, and the weeks prior to Christmas saw the first consignment of Christmas cards. . . . Twelve cards, each carrying a reproduction of one of the great madonnas, and with a few lines of well-phrased greeting and appropriate good wishes underneath. . . ."

In 1921, 50,000 Christmas cards were sent from the offices of *Salve Regina*. By 1925, Christmas cards were mailed to all parts of the United States, as well as to China, Japan, Canada, Korea, Hawaii, Puerto Rico and the Philippines. By 1927,

Cardinal James Gibbons

39 percent of the Shrine's contributions came from the sale of Christmas cards.

THE END OF AN ERA

On March 24, 1921, Cardinal Gibbons, the Shrine's most influential advocate, passed from this world. The Shrine could not have hoped for a more willing collaborator from among the members of the Church hierarchy than the cardinal archbishop of Baltimore. It was, after all, Cardinal Gibbons who made it possible for Bishop Shahan to gain papal approval for his plans to establish the Shrine at the audience with Pope Pius X in 1913. This began the long history of papal encouragement for the Shrine that continues in the present day. Cardinal Gibbons had suggested Charles Maginnis as the Shrine's architect. Further, it was the final act of Cardinal Gibbons' long and illustrious episcopacy to invoke the ancient and solemn blessing of the Church on the Shrine when he presided over the foundation-stone blessing in 1920. In the June 1921 edition of *Salve Regina*, Bishop Shahan recalled the significance of Cardinal Gibbons' association with the Shrine:

> *"It was his last act of a national character [the cornerstone blessing], and in his dying hours it was a great spiritual comfort to him that his name was inseparably connected with the great church in Mary's honor, even though he was not destined to see its mighty dome dominate the waters of the Potomac."*

With the great cardinal now dead, Bishop Shahan and Father McKenna were hopeful that his successor would demonstrate a similar level of commitment to the Shrine. The September 1921 issue of *Salve Regina* extended a warm welcome to Baltimore's new archbishop, Michael J. Curley. Father McKenna reprinted an earlier letter from Archbishop Curley, then bishop of St.

Augustine, Fla., in which he expressed to Bishop Shahan his overwhelming support for the Shrine and the promise to allocate diocesan funds toward its construction.

Father McKenna, in his memoirs, recounted how he and Bishop Shahan were buoyed by the news of the new archbishop's appointment. There was little reason to doubt that Archbishop Curley would prove a close collaborator in building the Shrine. Their hopes were validated early on when the new archbishop commended their work and assured them of his willingness to provide counsel and assistance.

∞
SEEDS OF DISCONTENT

Bishop Shahan's dual obligation as rector of the university and chief overseer of the Shrine would eventually place an untenable strain on his relationship with members of his faculty and, ultimately, with Archbishop Curley, who was also the university's chancellor. Unlike his predecessor, Archbishop Curley involved himself in many of the day-to-day considerations of the Shrine, especially those having to do with finances. To further complicate matters, the archbishop eventually adopted the view — shared by a select group of faculty members — that Bishop Shahan's intense involvement with the Shrine was inhibiting his ability to concentrate fully on his responsibilities at the university. In spite of the Shrine's much-noted progress, there were those who never fully expected the Shrine to succeed. Now that the efforts of Bishop Shahan and Father McKenna were demonstrating the likelihood of success, some feared that the Shrine would eventually eclipse the university as the nation's pre-eminent Catholic institution. Archbishop Curley's concern for safeguarding the high academic standards of the university and its continued growth prompted him to write to Bishop Shahan in April 1922 and urge his disengagement from the day-to-day affairs of the Shrine in order to devote himself more fully to his role as university rector.

This appears to be the first time that the work of the Shrine and the work of the university were characterized as conflicting endeavors. Eventually, Bishop Shahan would be forced to clarify another contentious issue, one regarding the appropriate separation of university and Shrine funds. The April 1923 *Salve Regina* made public the growing tension between the Shrine's financial administrators and officials charged with overseeing university funds. Bishop Shahan felt the need to set the record straight.

Under the heading, "Not a Cent of Catholic University's Funds Is Being Used in Work," Bishop Shahan defended Father McKenna and his associates at the offices of *Salve Regina* against unorthodox accounting practices:

> *"It has transpired that there is some misunderstanding as to the financial relations of the Catholic University and the National Shrine. The funds of each are kept strictly apart and so appear in annual reports. From the beginning the trustees of the University decided that no building contracts should be let on the Shrine for which the necessary funds were not available, and this rule is strictly adhered to as the holy work progresses."*

Bishop Shahan's attempts to mollify these concerns met with only temporary success. The issue of who should ultimately control the Shrine's funds, given that the Shrine was still a part of the university, would surface repeatedly in the next several years, culminating in a decisive confrontation in 1928.

A PUSH FOR INDEPENDENCE

Throughout 1922, the architects, in collaboration with the Building Committee, further defined the scope and detail of the Shrine. The committee, which continued to function in behalf of the university's full Board of Trustees, nevertheless asserted its independence in deciding all matters relative to the

APOSTOLIC LETTER OF POPE PIUS XI

To Our Beloved Sons William Cardinal O'Connell of the Title of St. Clement, Archbishop of Boston and Dennis Cardinal Dougherty of the Title of Sts. Nereus and Achilles, Archbishop of Philadelphia, and to our Other Venerable Brothers the Archbishops and Bishops of the United States of North America.

Beloved Sons and Venerable Brothers, Greetings and Apostolic Blessing.

Knowing full well how much can be done by Catholic Institutions for the right formation of heart and mind, We at the beginning of Our Pontificate, cannot but turn Our whole thought and care upon those noble seats of learning which, like your University, have been established in order to train up teachers of truth and to spread more abundantly throughout the world the light of knowledge and of Christian wisdom.

Accordingly, since We have ever loved that great work from the time it was founded, at the insistence of the American bishops, by Our Predecessor of happy memory, Leo XIII, also We have not failed, as occasion offered, to praise the zeal of those who strove by all manner of means to further it, in the firm conviction that the Church in America would derive the greatest benefit from a home of study wherein Catholic youth are more thoroughly trained in virtue and sacred science.

Now, among other reasons for founding the University which the Bishops presented in their letter to the Holy See after the Third Plenary Council of Baltimore, was "that condition of mind which can be protected against wide-spreading error and strengthened in faith by the deeper investigation of truth both revealed and natural on the part of the faithful and especially on the part of the clergy." Weighty as they then were, these reasons are of even greater weight at this time when all are striving to the best of their power for the restoration of order in human society. For it is plain that no such reconstruction will come about unless youth be rightly educated. Nor is any and every sort of education fitted for the attainment of the desired end, but only that in which instruction is based on religion and virtue as its sure foundation which the Church unceasingly has commended in every possible way.

But it is essential that youth while they study should be kindled with ardor for knowledge and piety alike, especially by devotion to the Great Mother of God who is the Seat of Wisdom and the Source of Piety, and therefore the American Bishops, Protectors of the University in Washington, have formed the excellent design of buildings on its grounds the National Shrine of the Immaculate Conception. For it is fitting that side by side with the temple of knowledge should stand the house of prayer, because "godliness is profitable to all things" and "knowledge without piety puffeth up." For this reason We, like our Predecessors of happy memory Pius X and Benedict XV, cherish with fatherly affection both the University and the newly planned Shrine; and We pray that this great work may soon be brought to completion so that from it as from the seat of her loving kindness, the Virgin Mother may bestow upon all America the heavenly gifts of wisdom and salvation.

Given at St. Peter's, Rome, on the twenty-fifth of April 1922, in the first year of Our Pontificate. — *Pope Pius XI*

ways and means of getting the Shrine built. This independent posture would prove both advantageous and problematic for the Shrine in the years ahead.

As early as 1919, it was suggested that the Board of Trustees should consider incorporating the Shrine as a separate institution. Sir James Ryan, a member of both the Board of Trustees and the Shrine Building Committee, was a principal advocate of separating the two entities and pressed the issue with Bishop Shahan and attorneys in Philadelphia and Washington. In December 1921, the Board of Trustees formally considered the proposal and referred the issue to the university's attorney. After a thorough review of the ramifications of such a move, it was deemed an unnecessary complication of the day-to-day management of the Shrine and university. Those who opposed the Shrine's separate incorporation feared that a formal separation would compromise the Shrine's proper maintenance and supervision — as was required of any other "university building." For the time being, the issue was put to rest.

POPE PIUS XI

In April, a third pope imparted his apostolic blessing and encouragement on the Shrine project. Addressing the American hierarchy, Pope Pius XI commended both the work of the university and the building of the Shrine. The Holy Father characterized the education of young people as equally important to fostering their spirituality. He further expressed his eagerness to see the Shrine completed — a sentiment that would serve to energize the national fund-raising campaign and instill a new sense of urgency among the American hierarchy.

"For it is fitting," wrote the Holy Father, "that side by side with the temple of knowledge should stand the house of prayer, because 'godliness is profitable to all things' and 'knowledge without piety puffeth up.' For this reason . . . We pray that this great work may soon be brought to completion so that from it as from the seat of her loving kindness, the Virgin Mother may bestow upon all America the heavenly gifts of wisdom and salvation."

NATIONAL SHRINE OF THE IMMACULATE CO
UNIVERSITY OF AMERICA WASHINGTON, D.

AMERICA'S CHURCH

FOUNDATIONS
⁓
FOR A GLORIOUS
⁓
FUTURE
1922 - 1933

The university's Board of Trustees received from Bishop Shahan the 10 bids submitted for construction of the crypt level, with quotes ranging from $385,000 to $535,000. In a move that would fortify the autonomy of the Building Committee, the board deferred action on the proposals in favor of allowing the Building Committee to choose the contractor, execute contracts and expend funds independent of the board's review. The committee awarded the contract to the low bidder, Charles J. Cassidy Company of Washington, D.C.

On May 31, 1922, the feast of Our Lady of the Sacred Heart, the work of building the northern section of the crypt was begun. The form of the Shrine was outlined, with three crosses strategically placed to convey the size of the planned structure. One cross was positioned at the back of the structure, one at the front, and the third where the main altar of the crypt would later stand. With the first and second crosses placed exactly 460 feet apart, one could begin to appreciate the Shrine's impressive dimensions that would distinguish it among the 10 largest churches in the world. Father McKenna's notes of Sept. 18, 1922, record that "Bishop Shahan, Bishop [Philip R.] McDevitt [of Harrisburg, Pa.] and Father McKenna, accompanied by many Sisters and laity, went to the site of the Shrine and, after prayers had been recited and while the litany was being said, each one present turned a spadeful of the soil on the spot where is now rising, in all beau-

CATHOLIC UNIVERSITY of AMERICA

construction was a constant preoccupation. Bishop Shahan and Father McKenna were eager to have the foundations for the entire Shrine poured, not just those of the crypt or "basement" level. Their seemingly hasty approach had practical implications. They recognized that if inadequate funding were to halt construction later, the Shrine's intended proportions would then be locked into place by the foundations, making it impossible to alter them without incurring exorbitant costs.

∽

THE CRYPT IN PROGRESS

The work of building the crypt began in earnest. By the end of March, according to Father McKenna's notes, more

Construction begins on the Shrine's foundations.

(bottom) Father McKenna (far right, in black) enjoys a panoramic view of the long-awaited construction of the National Shrine.

ty, symbolism, and majesty, the most beautiful church in all America."

With the monumental work underway, the question of how to maintain the momentum of both fund raising and

CRYPT OF NATIONAL SHRINE OF THE IMMACULATE CONCEPTION
CATHOLIC UNIVERSITY OF AMERICA, WASHINGTON D.C. OCT. 13. 1923.
#53.

(above) The north apse of the Crypt Church awaits a covering, Oct. 13, 1923.

(below) Sisters pray beneath scaffolding in the Crypt Church, June 1924.

than 8,085 bags of cement, 2,057 tons of sand and gravel and 188,000 bricks had already been used to establish the northern foundations. In the meantime, architects Maginnis and Walsh began to con-

sider what the Shrine might actually look like inside. From the outset, the architects stipulated that the Shrine was to be constructed using the finest materials available. Only the most accomplished artisans and craftsmen were considered for the work of creating the Shrine's architectural and artistc details.

The massive architectural scope of the Shrine was, by this time, beginning to attract critical attention. The July 1922 issue of *Architectural Record* featured the National Shrine in a favorable article accompanied by the early renderings and floor plans as designed by Maginnis and Walsh. The author situated the Shrine in the historical context of the great

Crypt of Nation Shrine of the Immaculate Conception. *[handwritten]*

A makeshift altar in the Crypt Church, 1924.

churches and shrines of Europe. Cited as important precedents were Santa Maria Maggiore in Rome, Santa Maria del Fiore in Florence, the shrines at Lourdes and Fourviere, the great Benedictine abbey shrine at Einsiedeln, Switzerland, and the New World shrine of Our Lady of Guadalupe, Mexico. Such acclaim from a highly regarded secular journal was a welcome validation of the envisioned design and scope of the project.

Once completed, the northeast entrance to the crypt was sectioned off to facilitate Masses and devotional services. On Easter Sunday, April 23, 1924, with only the northern apse nearing completion and a dense assembly of scaffolding hovering above, invited diplomatic, Church and government officials gathered with over 1,000 worshipers to attend the first Mass within the National Shrine. In the presence of the British ambassador, Sir Esme Howard, the French ambassador, Jules J. Jusserand, and the Spanish ambassador, Don Juan Riano y Gayangos, diplomatic, military and naval dignitaries knelt on the rough, unfinished concrete floor of the cavernous crypt — evoking an earlier and more precarious age when Christians gathered in the damp, dimly lit confines of the Roman catacombs — while Father McKenna intoned the ancient prayers of the Gregorian High Mass. Bishop Shahan was unable to attend this milestone as he was away on university business.

THE IDEAL OF WOMANHOOD

(above) Mary Chase Stratton, Frederick V. Murphy (associate architect and founder of Catholic University's School of Architecture), Father McKenna and Shrine architect Charles Maginnis, 1925.

(below and opposite) Details of Stratton's pewabic tiles for the Crypt Church.

With the basic structure of the crypt fast taking shape, arrangements were made to commence with the ornamentations that would eventually distinguish the crypt as a space of unparalleled artistry and beauty.

Mary Chase (Perry) Stratton, a Detroit-based ceramic artist, figured prominently at this stage. In 1925, Stratton was contracted to complete the interior ornamentations of the Shrine's Crypt Church. She would design and fabricate the ceramic tiles that would eventually adorn the massive Guastavino-vaulted ceiling of the crypt. Stratton was considered the best-qualified artist to create an iconographic scheme reminiscent of the early Christian iconography of the ancient Roman Catacombs. To that end, she made a pilgrimage to the Catacombs, where she began a painstaking study of Christianity's earliest recorded artwork. Later, she was also commissioned to produce 14 ceramic panels depicting the Stations of the Cross.

The Guastavino ceiling would comprise four great arches, each 54 feet long, and designed to withstand the weight of 1 million pounds. *The Detroit News* of

April 19, 1925, detailed the concept and process involved in Stratton's design:

"The extraordinary color, design and symbolism of these Guastavino tiles — which cost $100,000 to make and install — attract immediate attention. At the intersection of each apse are large medallions depicting the Virgin or one of her prototypes, together with inscriptional panels. The great expanse of the ceiling or background is of neutral-tone tiles and into this great dome are inserted panels depicting the Prophets and scenes from the Old Testament. Instead of the use of many tiny teserae, as in mosaic, Mrs. Stratton indicated her design for the figures by deeply incised lines. The color was applied in the form of a glaze, the whole medallion outlined in a leaflike pattern in gold."

Father McKenna attributed the inspiration of Stratton's design to Bishop Shahan who, as university professor, had lectured on the Christian symbols of the Roman catacombs in a series titled "The Blessed Virgin in the Catacombs." Characterized by Bishop Shahan as a "strange witchery of emotion and sympathy," Stratton's highly stylized method of combining claybodies, glaze formulae and intense firing techniques resulted in a brilliant artistic conception for the Crypt Church of the National Shrine.

THE GUASTAVINO CEILING

Rafael Guastavino (1842-1908) was an architect and builder who emigrated in 1881 to the United States from Barcelona, Spain, where he had previously designed factories and elaborate homes for wealthy industrialists of the Catalan region. He has been credited with having revived the ancient tile-and-mortar building system widely employed throughout the Catalonia region and other parts of Spain for centuries. It is a method that requires imbedding several layers of thin tile in mortar to create a curved horizontal surface. By 1900, Guastavino had successfully transferred his patented tile-building method to the United States and was frequently called upon by the leading architects of his time. Among the buildings where his work is in evidence are President Grant's Tomb, the Great Hall at Ellis Island, New York's Grand Central Station and Carnegie Hall, and the chapel at the U.S. Military Academy at West Point. The Guastavino system held great appeal for Maginnis and Walsh because of its inherent integrity and proven capacity to support massive loads. The combined

Workers on scaffolding install pewabic tiles over main altar area of Crypt Church, 1925.

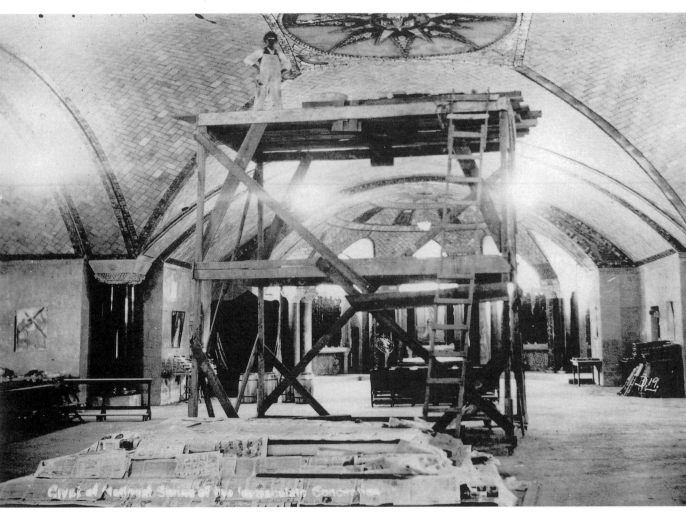

AMERICA'S CHURCH

weights of the great groin arch of the crypt (including the floor construction), the 125-ton altar and the live-load capacity for public assembly approximates 1 million pounds.

OUR LADY OF LOURDES GROTTO

George Logan Duval, a Catholic philanthropist with a zealous devotion to the dogma of the Immaculate Conception, had been an ardent advocate for the National Shrine from its earliest days. In a letter to then-Msgr. Shahan dated March 18, 1914, Duval revealed his magnanimous desire to personally fund the Shrine's full construction. However, he decided to forgo the solitary privilege in order that "none should be deprived of the chance" to share the work.

In 1918, he established the Chair of

the Immaculate Conception at Catholic University with a gift of $50,000. This was the first chair established in the history of any Catholic university in the world.

Resisting Charles Maginnis' appeals for a much-needed crypt sacristy, Duval in 1925 settled on a gift of the Shrine's first chapel beyond the Crypt Church proper — the Chapel of Our Lady of Lourdes, in keeping with his great devotion to Mary's apparition at Lourdes, France.

Sadly, Duval would not live to witness the completion of the chapel. As workmen positioned the statue of Our Lady of Lourdes within the chapel on the morning of March 16, 1931, Duval succumbed to complications from pneumonia.

(above) The Grotto Chapel of Our Lady of Lourdes was a gift from George Logan Duval (left).

EARLY PILGRIMS

∞

While still in its early construction phase, the National Shrine was promoted frequently in the pages of *Salve Regina* as a place of pilgrimage worthy of the journey of religious pilgrims from across the nation and every walk of life. As news of the Shrine and its progress spread, many groups hoped to claim the privilege of being the first pilgrims to journey to the Shrine. The distinction eluded all but a group of children from the St. Vincent's Home for Orphans in Washington, D.C. Led by the Sisters of Charity, the children gathered in the small chapel within the Salve Regina building on the feast of the Sacred Heart in 1918. Bishop Shahan was moved by these "little ones" and frequently invited them to return to view the progress of the Shrine in the coming days, proclaiming them the Shrine's "first pilgrims."

As work progressed on the Crypt Church, Father McKenna and Bishop Shahan were eager to convey that the Shrine was fast becoming the pre-eminent sanctuary of prayer and pilgrimage in the country. They began encouraging the nation's bishops to organize and send pilgrims from their dioceses to the Shrine in the hope of spreading excitement and enhancing support. Father McKenna dutifully recorded each and every pilgrimage in *Salve Regina*. Pilgrims were typically provided a guided tour of the unfinished crypt, complete with an explanation of the artistic symbolism of the crypt and a group photograph with the crypt's exterior as a backdrop. ∞

Bishop Shahan and Father McKenna greet early pilgrims to the National Shrine, under construction in the background, 1923.

∞

MARY MEMORIAL ALTAR

When the International Federation of Catholic Alumnae (IFCA) took on the project of a nationwide collection for the Mary Memorial Altar in 1921, they joined a chorus of Catholic organizations eager to become permanently associated with the National Shrine. Occasionally, however, the enthusiasm displayed by an organization was greater than its ability to fulfill its pledge. The Ladies' Auxiliary of the Knights of St. John provides a case in point. Members of this esteemed organization were only able to collect half of the needed $10,000 to build the St. Ann's Altar within the crypt. The

Shrine's regular contributors made up the shortfall.

IFCA co-founder Clara D. Sheeran was the driving force behind a plan to solicit 10,000 "Marys of America" to contribute toward the Mary Memorial Altar. Sheeran, however, was not the first to suggest a Mary Memorial in the National Shrine. A Terre Haute, Ind., schoolgirl named Mary Downs first wrote to Bishop Shahan in 1913 to suggest erecting a statue of the Blessed Mother as a contribution from all the Marys of the nation.

The Mary Memorial Altar, costing $50,000, is carved of semi-transparent golden onyx from Algiers, Algeria. The base consists of white Travertine marble.

The *mensa*, or table top, is a solid block weighing more than 5,000 pounds. The striking embellishments of the altar's support structure consists of 14 concave designs in brilliant but soft golden mosaics that accommodate depictions of Christ, the Twelve Apostles and St. Paul. The edge of the altar table is decorated with alternating leaf and cross designs covered in gold mosaics. The Mary Memorial Altar was formally presented on Nov. 19-20, 1927, by Sheeran and IFCA president Mary B. Finan along with many of the drive's organizers.

∞

FINISHING THE FOUNDATIONS

As early as 1922, the Shrine Building Committee agreed to authorize the completion of the entire foundations of the crypt — the reinforced concrete footings for the superstructure as well as the basement. In a meeting on Nov. 29, 1922, the committee resolved:

The bronze tablet commemorating the Mary Memorial Altar. Mary Finan, IFCA president; Bishop Shahan; Clara Sheeran, project originator; Mrs. Alfred Whitton, campaign chairman; and Father McKenna, Dec. 8, 1928.

AMERICA'S CHURCH

CRYPT ALTARS

∞

The Crypt Church of the National Shrine has often been characterized as a veritable reliquary of Christian art. Throughout the crypt, in nearly every nook and around every corner, is a priceless array of mosaic artwork and architectural detail that would easily rival the most splendid Churches of Christendom.

Among the gems of the crypt are the 15 chapels located within the west, north and east apses. The chapels are divided into three groups, dedicated respectively to the Father, the Son and the Holy Spirit. Each chapel is illuminated by lunette windows that depict the corresponding themes of Prophecy, Promise and Fulfillment.

The five chapels of the west apse, commemorating martyrs of both the Old and New Testament, are dedicated to God the Father. Included here are the chapels of St. Agnes, St. Agatha, St. Cecilia, Sts. Perpetua and Felicitas, and St. Anastasia. The north apse, dedicated to God the Son, include the chapels of St. Elizabeth, St. Joseph, the Blessed Sacrament, St. John the Evangelist and St. Anne. The final group of chapels in the east apse are dedicated to God the Holy Spirit and includes the chapels of St. Lucy, St. Susanna of Rome, St. Catherine of Alexandria, St. Margaret of Antioch and St. Brigid of Ireland.

The central chapel of the north apse is that of the Good Shepherd and is where the

Blessed Sacrament has been reserved continuously since 1926. Costing more than $20,000, the Good Shepherd Chapel was the first to be completed in the National Shrine. It was the gift of Sir James Ryan of Philadelphia, a trustee of the Catholic University who also served on the first Shrine oversight committee.

The mosaic depicting Christ as the Good Shepherd, like the other 14 crypt side-altar mosaics, was designed by the renowned mosaic artist Bancel La Farge. Prior to commencing work on the mosaics for the chapels, La Farge engaged in a five-year study of Christian art in Europe. Besides the exquisite mosaic depiction of a youthful, beardless Christ as the Good Shepherd and the golden Algerian onyx altar, the most prominent feature of this central chapel is the tabernacle. Designed by the Shrine's architects Maginnis and Walsh, the tabernacle is made of bronze-gilt and is studded with precious gems. It was created by the Tiffany Company of New York.

The first organization to donate a chapel to the crypt was the Daughters of Isabella,

An early view of the Crypt Church, 1924.

and it was determined to claim the distinction at an early stage. In a July 24, 1924, correspondence to Father McKenna (some time after the idea of having the Daughters donate a chapel had already been suggested by both Father McKenna and Bishop Shahan), national regent Mary E. Booth requested additional information about the Shrine and the anticipated cost of the chapel. She closed her letter with a pointed question: "Have the Catholic Daughters of America donated $10,000 for one as yet? I trust the Daughters of Isabella will be first." The race was on. One month later, Booth wrote again to inform Father McKenna that the Daughters of Isabella had, in fact, agreed to donate $10,000 for a chapel in honor of their heroin, Queen Isabella.

Eventually, the Catholic Daughters of America decided against donating an altar for the crypt. Their generosity would be reserved for another period of construction when the need was equally great — during completion of the of the Great Upper Church. The only other organization to contribute an altar to the crypt during this period was the Ladies of the Ancient Order of Hibernians, who gave the St. Brigid's altar in September 1925 as a tribute to Bishop Shahan. The other chapels of the west, north, and east apses were gifts of individuals, 10 of whom were women.

It is perhaps worth noting that even a non-Catholic stepped forward to assist in this early cause. Susanna Fay donated the Chapel of St. Susanna of Rome in memory of her son, Msgr. Sigourney Fay, a convert who was a member of the Catholic University faculty. Incidentally, it was Msgr. Fay who suggested to Bishop Shahan the title of the "little magazine" inaugurated "to make known [to] every quarter the progress we are making in collecting a fund for the erection of a National Shrine of the Blessed Virgin" — *Salve Regina*.

(left) North apse of Crypt Church with five side altars of St. Elizabeth, St. Joseph, Christ the Good Shepherd, St. John the Evangelist and St. Anne.

(below) The Good Shepherd Chapel, where the Blessed Sacrament has been reserved continuously since 1926 within the tabernacle created by the Tiffany Company.

The east "main entrance" of the National Shrine featuring neon signs.

"That (1) the plans be drawn by the architect for the remainder of the foundation walls of the entire structure of the Shrine; (2) that the whole of the basement be excavated; (3) and that the rest of the foundation walls be built up to the granite base; with the expressed provision that no debt be contracted and that there be no suspension of the present work on the crypt."

One of the principal reasons for completing the entire foundation as soon as possible was to ensure that it be of the same date and strength throughout. This was in addition to the concern shared by Bishop Shahan and Father McKenna that if the foundations for the entire length of the Shrine were not completed in a timely fashion, the few but vocal opponents might succeed in altering the dimensions of the Shrine to that of a more modest university chapel.

So on Oct. 19, 1925, while work continued inside the Crypt Church, a new phase of construction began on the crypt's middle section. It was announced that this new section, now known as the Hall of American Saints, would be referred to as the House of Nazareth. In this area, Maginnis designated the construction of Duval's Grotto Chapel of Our Lady of Lourdes. This section was deemed crucial for the superstructure in that it would form the foundations for the massive dome.

By March 1926, *Salve Regina* reported that "remarkable progress" had been made and the Shrine's length had increased by 100 feet.

Today, these rooms constitute the Executive Conference Room, the Center for Liturgy and Music, the Visitors' Center, the Lourdes Chapel and the Archives. This area served as the primary entrance to the Crypt Church for many years. The rather inglorious experience of entering through the east entrance, after negotiating precariously along a wooden platform, constituted pilgrims' first impression of the "magnificent" church they had hoped might more closely resemble the impressive artistic rendering frequently depicted in the pages of *Salve Regina*. Further compromising the experience was an unimaginative sign — which simply read "National Shrine" — affixed above the east entrance.

A GIFT OF THE FORESTERS

On April 27, 1927, during the semi-annual meeting of the American bishops at Catholic University, members of the Board of Trustees were interrupted from their deliberations for an unusual presentation by Thomas H. Cannon, the distinguished high chief ranger of the Catholic Order of Foresters. Accompanied by 14 other members of the Foresters' high court, Cannon presented Cardinal Dougherty with a check in the amount of $50,000. Five years earlier, the Foresters had passed a resolution committing their membership to collecting 50 cents per member "as a great expression of our gratitude to our patroness, the Virgin Queen of Heaven, for the many favors bestowed upon the American people through her intercession, and as a memorial in honor of the Foresters who died in the service of their country and of those who served our country. . . ."

The substantial gift provided for the payment toward the eight massive columns located within the crypt, which provide structural support to the main altar of the Upper Church, and the four smaller columns located at the entrance to the crypt, which had been installed earlier. A bronze memorial tablet in

Thomas H. Cannon, high chief ranger of the Catholic Order of Foresters, presents a check for $50,000 to Cardinal Dougherty.

honor of the Foresters who perished during World War I was placed in the crypt in July 1928.

A second memorial, honoring the deceased of World War II, is carved in one of the columns in Memorial Hall and was dedicated in 1951 by the Shrine's fourth director, Msgr. Patrick "P.J." O'Connor.

AN UNCERTAIN FUTURE

The year 1928 marked yet another turning point in the Shrine's growing independence from the university. For years, Father McKenna had to contend with mounting pressure from the university's principal financial authority, J. Harvey Cain, to adhere to the university's accounting methods.

Father McKenna resisted efforts to place the operations of his *Salve Regina*

Bishop Thomas J. Shahan

that the Shrine had struggled to achieve, at least in its financial operations and in asserting its national identity, was formalized in a resolution passed by the Board of Trustees at its meeting of April 18, 1928. The Shrine Building Committee was vested with the sole responsibility of collecting and expending funds to complete the Shrine's construction with the clear stipulation that "no money shall be borrowed for the Shrine unless authorized by the Board of Trustees or the Executive Committee."

The resolution further called for the appointment of a director and an assistant director "to whom the details of the work may be committed." This opened the way for Father McKenna's eventual appointment as the Shrine's first director in 1929. While this development seemed to continue a trend toward the Shrine's increasing autonomy from the university's governing body, in actuality, the Shrine and its custodians continued to be accountable to the university's board. Board members were reluctant to relinquish complete control over the affairs of the Shrine in the wake of a fateful meeting of Sept. 13, 1927, during which Bishop Shahan announced that he would step down as rector at the end of the next academic year. He was now 70 years old and almost entirely deaf.

office under anyone but himself and Bishop Shahan. Owing to Bishop Shahan's exhalted reputation with members of the Board of Trustees, Cain's efforts to gain control over the Shrine's finances were of little consequence for the first 12 years. Finally, the autonomy

Bishop Shahan had let it be known that he hoped to enjoy a few quiet years in rest and reflection after a life of service and remarkable productivity.

Not surprisingly, however, Bishop Shahan expressed his desire to remain active in the affairs of the Shrine in "retirement." He petitioned the board for a few accommodations: the title of rector emeritus, a modest pension and, most significantly, complete charge of the ongoing efforts to erect the Shrine. The board was unanimous in its approval of the bishop's requests.

Heaped with accolades and expressions of gratitude by academic and ecclesiastical colleagues, Bishop Shahan could now leave his beloved university with the assurance that his tireless work as scholar, university rector and churchman had made a lasting impression on the intellectual, spiritual and academic life of the Church in the United States. The university he had so zealously served and led as its fourth rector had assumed a significant place among the world's esteemed ecclesiastical institutions of higher learning. Although Catholic University had yet to ascend to the level of an "American Oxford" as was his hope early on, Bishop Shahan could take great pride in having steered the university on

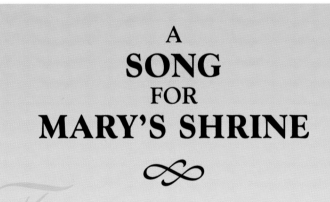

A SONG FOR MARY'S SHRINE

The cover of the January, 1928, edition of *Salve Regina* implored readers to "Pray for the Success of the John McCormack Concert — January 23, 1928." McCormack offered to perform a special Shrine fund-raising concert at the Washington Auditorium as a tribute to his fellow Irishman, Bishop Shahan, who was now in the final year of his tenure at the university. It was hoped that the announcement would inspire interest among Catholics of Irish descent to contribute to the Shrine, if for no other reason than to make possible the concert by the leading Irish tenor of the day:

"As the National Shrine is not only the work of the people of Washington and as there are many people, especially more of Irish descent, all over the country who will like to join this movement the *Salve Regina* will gladly receive any contributions for the 'Concert Fund,' and as a token of appreciation will send a copy of the McCormack concert program with the autographs of Bishop Shahan and Rev. Dr. McKenna to all those interested in the movement."

McCormack, who was known to millions throughout the country due to his widely circulated Victor recordings, received an enthusiastically positive review in the following morning's *Washington Post* despite a persistent cold:

"Triumphing over a heavy cold, which abridged his program somewhat and made his singing at all a marvel of vocal art, John McCormack, incomparable Irish tenor, held a capacity audience at the Auditorium last night enthralled by the magic of his interpretations of Irish folk songs, old English ballads, a weird Chinese dirge and several classical selections. The event was a benefit concert for the Shrine of the Immaculate Conception and high dignitaries of the Roman Catholic Church were present in the boxes and a goodly representation of diocesan clergy were noted here and there in the audience." ∞

Aerial view of Washington's "Catholic Ghetto" amidst the surrounding Brookland neighborhood at a time when the National Shrine's promising Byzantine form was still unfulfilled.

Additionally, Bishop Shahan was one of the founders of Trinity College, the Sisters' College and a primary figure in the creation of Basselin College.

Throughout this period of remarkable progress, Bishop Shahan prodded, cajoled, pleaded and ultimately prevailed in his personal campaign to gain support for the creation of the National Shrine among the nation's bishops and two popes. Now, with his academic tenure drawing to a close, he desired nothing more than to spend his remaining days advancing the work of the Shrine. That he would not live to see his beloved Shrine progress substantially beyond its modest crypt proportions likely never occurred to him.

By now, however, there was a growing sentiment that the Shrine was a faltering enterprise. Contributions were dwindling, while the actual cost of constructing the Shrine was rising. The modest contributions of $1, $5 and $10 from the subscribers of *Salve Regina* and ordinary Catholics were not enough to keep pace with increasing costs. It seemed that Father McKenna and the workers at the offices of *Salve Regina* had "hit a wall." The nation's bishops had yet to assume responsibility for raising funds on a massive scale within their own dioceses. As a result, seeds of doubt that the Shrine

a sure and steady course toward future growth.

His accomplishments were staggering. During his administration, the university's property was enlarged from 70 to 270 acres, consisting of roughly 30 buildings; various colleges run by religious orders and centering around the university increased in number from 2 to 24; four of the large university halls — Gibbons, Graduate, St. John's and the Engineering Hall — were erected, along with the Malone Chemical Laboratory, the Mullen Library, the gymnasium and stadium. Through his efforts, the university library was enlarged from 50,000 volumes to more than 300,000.

would ever be completed were beginning to sprout. Father McKenna, as the Shrine's clerk-of-the-works, chief fund raiser, primary administrator and publisher of *Salve Regina*, was increasingly powerless to achieve significant progress beyond partially completing the Crypt.

Msgr. James Hugh Ryan, fifth rector of The Catholic University of America.

BISHOP SHAHAN'S SUCCESSOR

Upon the retirement of Bishop Shahan, the Board of Trustees selected Msgr. James Hugh Ryan as the university's fifth rector. He was installed on Nov. 14, 1928, and, as a matter of course, was appointed to the Shrine Building Committee. Msgr. Ryan's first priority was to relieve the university of the debt that Bishop Shahan had accrued through his aggressive campus building campaign. The new rector was eager to put the university's financial house in order and expressed his concern that the National Shrine presented "a real problem to the university" in his ability to do so.

Given Bishop Shahan's continued oversight of the Shrine and all fund-raising activities, Msgr. Ryan was rendered powerless to assert what he perceived as his rightful prerogative with respect to determining the Shrine's future course. He predicted that the Shrine and its mounting debt would be assumed by the university after Bishop Shahan's death

and resigned himself to that eventual outcome out of deference to his esteemed predecessor. He concluded that "all we can do is to wait and to pray that when the burden is transferred to the shoulders of the university, it will not be too heavy to carry."

The Shrine, Msgr. Ryan felt, had inexplicably been transformed from a university church to a national enterprise, much to the detriment of the university he was now charged with overseeing.

PAPAL PROMISE FULFILLED

More than 10 years had passed since Pope Benedict XV first promised to send to the National Shrine a beautiful mosaic from the Vatican mosaic studios as evidence of his encouragement for the Shrine's completion. Father McKenna and Bishop Shahan now prepared for the long-awaited arrival of the papal gift at a time when publicity about the ongoing work of the Shrine could not have been more useful.

The papal mosaic held great significance. It actually represented the gift of two popes. Pope Benedict had decided that the mosaic should depict the Immaculate Conception but died before any real progress on it was realized. Not until 1923 did Benedict's successor, Pope Pius XI, personally select one of two depictions of the Immaculate Conception by Bartolomé Esteban Murillo as the subject for the Vatican mosaicists. The Murillo painting chosen by Pope Pius XI was titled "La Purissima Bionda" for the light color of the Virgin Mary's hair.

In his book *The National Shrine of the Immaculate Conception (1917-1927)*, William P. Kennedy records that "the Pope, having chosen this picture, told Count Muccioli [the director of the Vatican's mosaic studios] to go to Madrid to take an exact copy. He also instructed the artist to take every care so that the work would be a worthy testimony of the Pope's affection for the United States, and especially for the Catholic University of Washington."

Word of the mosaic's completion and

pending departure from the Vatican's studios was reported as an international event, even appearing in the Feb. 4, 1930, edition of *The London Times*:

"There is now ready for shipment from the Vatican to Washington a copy in mosaics of the Immaculate Conception by Murillo which is one of the principal glories of the Prado. The reproduction is worthy of the setting which it will find in the National Shrine of the Immaculate Conception, Catholic University of Washington . . ."

The hopeful news rejuvenated Father McKenna and those who toiled daily in the never-ending work of soliciting financial support for the Shrine. By now, the nation was in the grip of the Great Depression. Catholics, like most Americans, feared for the country's economic survival — and their own. To many, this was no time to be testing the good will of the Catholic populace in order to build a grand and opulent church in a corner of northeast Washington, the final cost of which eluded anyone's best guess. Despite a fairly steady stream of modest contributions, funds were not sufficient to sustain the enormous costs of materials and construction or the daily operating expenses of the fund-raising operation itself. It was hoped that the arrival of the mosaic and the ample publicity regarding the prestigious source of the gift might somehow renew the momentum slowed by the current national crisis.

At high noon on June 17, 1930, the long-awaited papal gift arrived on the campus of the university. In addition to Bishop Shahan and Msgr. McKenna — who had been named a monsignor on May 20 of that year, with Bishop Shahan conferring the honors during a ceremony in the Shrine crypt — the reception party included the apostolic delegate, Archbishop Pietro Fumasoni-Biondi, whose interest in the progress of the Shrine was genuine and enthusiastic. Due to its massive dimensions (10 feet 6 inches in height and 8 feet wide) and enormous weight of more than three

The Immaculate Conception mosaic is prepared for its departure from the Vatican mosaic studios, February 1930.

tons, it was necessary to have a large contingent of workmen with appropriate hoisting equipment to transport the priceless work of art into the Shrine. Bishop Shahan and Msgr. McKenna characterized the mosaic as the "heart of the National Shrine of the Immaculate Conception" and "the most important single gift from an independent sovereign ever to arrive in this country from Europe."

A special shrine at the entrance to the crypt was promptly established to accommodate the large mosaic and to allow for its reverence by all visitors. The exquisite mosaic, now displayed in the chancel area of the Great Upper Church to the left of the main sacristy entrance, represents a marvelous artistic achievement. Three of the Vatican's finest artists, under the direction of Count Muccioli, director of the Vatican Studio of Mosaics, labored nearly four years to piece together the approximately 800,000 bits of colored glass of more than 25,000 variations in color to reproduce Murillo's masterpiece. The artists included Ludovico Lucietto, dean of the Vatican's mosaic school,

and his colleagues named Chiaserotti and Sellini.

The mosaic was formally blessed in an elaborate ceremony during Catholic University's annual trustees' meeting. Cardinal Dennis Dougherty of Philadelphia, chairman of the Shrine committee, presided in the presence of two other cardinals, 10 archbishops, seven bishops, the full Board of Trustees, a large contingent of priests, the Italian ambassador, other distinguished visitors and hundreds of lay men and women.

Cardinal Dougherty cabled Pope Pius XI to inform him that the blessing had been accomplished and to express the gratitude of all associated with the Shrine. A brief one-sentence response was received that same day from the Vatican: "Holy Father grateful for message and pleased that Mosaic gives happiness, and bestows Apostolic Benediction on your Eminence (Dougherty). Signed, Cardinal Pacelli." This exchange of cablegrams between Cardinal Pacelli and the Shrine was particularly notable in that Cardinal Eugenio Pacelli would become the first future pope to personally tour the Shrine during his highly publicized visit to the United States and The Catholic University of America in 1936. ∞

(above) The "welcoming committee" for the Murillo mosaic.

(below) An invitation to the blessing of the mosaic (inset) and the Immaculate Conception mosaic depicting Murillo's "La Purissima Bionda."

Pope Pius XI (with hat) prepares for inauguration of the Vatican radio station and first worldwide radio broadcast of a papal address, Feb. 12, 1931.

FIRST PAPAL BROADCAST

An epochal event in the days leading to the halt in the Shrine's construction was the first worldwide radio broadcast by a reigning pontiff. On Feb. 12, 1931, the historic radio address of Pope Pius XI, inaugurating the Vatican City radio station, was heard in the Crypt Church by the apostolic delegate to the United States, Archbishop Pietro Fumasoni-Biondi, and a capacity crowd that consisted of the heads of Catholic and Georgetown universities, Italian Ambassador Nobile Giacomo de Martino, as well as ambassadors and rep-

resentatives of numerous other foreign embassies, members of Congress, and a large contingent of Church officials. Dressed in the splendor of their ecclesiastical robes, Msgr. McKenna and Msgr. McCormick, vice rector of the university, flanked the apostolic delegate during the papal address. Preceded by a "long and colorful procession of ecclesiastical dignitaries" into the crypt, the premier papal radio broadcast was made possible by the National Broadcasting Company. Originating from Vatican City's HVJ radio station, the broadcast was picked up at a receiving point on Long Island and transmitted by an overland wire directly into the Shrine. Amplifiers positioned near the altar boomed the Holy Father's voice throughout the cavernous crypt. The NCWC News Service noted:

"As the words of His Holiness came to the congregation every one listened with the most marked attention. Prelates, priests, nuns, diplomats, high officials, teachers, students and humble workers sat motionless, listening closely to every syllable of the Pontiff's message."

Following the address, Mass was offered, and the apostolic delegate received the diplomats in attendance.

∞

A 'MEMORIAL CHAPEL'

By 1930, a major effort was underway to complete the southern portion of the crypt level known today as Memorial Hall. The Oct. 30, 1930, meeting of the Building Committee produced a set of bold initiatives. It was decided that by Nov. 10 of that year, the Shrine would completely pay off its outstanding debt of $24,500. Further, it was decided that the committee would petition the university's board for the unprecedented accommodation of borrowing $200,000 to construct the Shrine's southern foundations. Cardinal Dougherty also suggested a new nationwide campaign to obtain the money to ensure the Shrine's completion.

At the Nov. 11, 1930, board meeting, Bishop Shahan emphasized the fact that the Shrine was completely free of debt. He reviewed the great progress that had been accomplished in the crypt, mentioning the new Vatican mosaic, and reminded the trustees of the upcoming bicentennial observance of the birthday of George Washington in 1932. Bishop Shahan deemed it critical for the Shrine to be in an acceptable condition to receive the thousands of tourists and potential benefactors who were expected to travel to Washington in honor of America's first president.

Bishop Shahan concluded with a motion to grant the Building Committee authority to secure a $200,000 loan from the university to finish the foundations and basement of the National Shrine. Bishop Shahan's motion was adopted unanimously.

Although the move to borrow construction funds marked a new and decidedly unorthodox approach, the board could hardly refuse Bishop Shahan when the opportunity for attracting new supporters was so great. It was a risk the board was willing to take.

On Dec. 8, 1930, the feast of the Immaculate Conception, the contract was awarded for the completion of the southern foundations. On Feb. 2, 1931,

A Shrine docent explains the memorial tablets to a group of visiting women in the 1940s.

Shrine shops. The first hint of the future use for the southern portion of the crypt level appeared in the November 1931 *Salve Regina*: "This southern section of the Crypt or Memorial Chapel is so-called because in due time it will contain the memorials for distinguished people, both clerical and lay, and benefactors of the National Shrine."

It was decided that the major columns of this area of the crypt would be finished in Roman Travertine marble. For a minimum sum of $100, the names of family members and loved ones would be inscribed on a "memorial tablet." The first of these tablets was claimed on Dec. 18, 1931, for Cardinal John McCloskey, the late archbishop of New York and America's first cardinal. Other historical figures connected with the early Church in the United States would also be memorialized in this way — Archbishop John F. Keane, founder of Catholic University; Archbishop John Carroll, first bishop of the United States; Father Demetrius Gallitzin, first priest ordained in the United States; and Mother Elizabeth Ann Seton, founder of the Sisters of Charity in the United States. Eventually, nonecclesiastical figures such as George Herman "Babe" Ruth and Knute Rockne would be added to the walls of the Memorial Chapel (present-day Memorial Hall). The

work was begun; by late September, the foundations for the entire crypt level were complete, with the exception of the present-day office area, cafeteria and

larger, more prominent positions of each column could be reserved for the sum of $15,000. Other desirable locations would be allotted for $1,250, $1,000, $750, $500, $250 and $100 for a small single unit. An altar of black-and-white marble was eventually erected in the center of Memorial Chapel. Daily Masses were offered for all who were represented by a memorial tablet.

By October 1931, the Shrine's intended length was beginning to take shape. During the Board of Trustees meeting of Nov. 10, 1931, Bishop Shahan announced the completion of the entire crypt of the National Shrine. In what would be his final report to the board, Bishop Shahan chronicled the Shrine's progress over the previous 15 years — not only in terms of physical construction, but as an important spiritual center for the nation.

Bishop Shahan did not anticipate the next course of construction beyond the completion of the Shrine's foundations. Owing to the dire economic circumstances gripping the country in 1932, contributions had slowed to a trickle. As a result, no plans were envisioned for beginning work on the superstructure. What new money was collected went instead toward sustaining the Shrine's daily operations.

Msgr. McKenna's efforts to generate new sources of revenue now met with drastically diminished returns. For the Shrine, the effects of the Depression were most notable in the significantly reduced number of Christmas cards sent to benefactors. Keeping in mind that Christmas-card receipts accounted for almost 40 percent of the Shrine's income, the stark drop marked an ominous trend: From a peak of 338,549 cards sent nationwide in 1926, the number had dwindled to a mere 109,482 by 1932.

Adding to the sense of general anxiety over the Shrine's future, Archbishop Curley and university officials began to make known their resistance to devoting further effort toward the Shrine's construction at a time when the university faced similarly dire financial conditions. By 1932, Bishop Shahan's failing health was beginning to undermine his ability to keep the Shrine cause alive. Msgr. McKenna was successfully proposed for membership to Catholic University's Board of Trustees by Cardinal Dougherty and Bishop Shahan. In adding Msgr. McKenna to the board, they had hoped to bolster essential support for the Shrine among its governing body. Inevitably, the pressing concerns of the university rendered Msgr. McKenna's presence and influence of little consequence.

DEATH OF THE FOUNDER

Bishop Shahan's death came swiftly in the early morning hours of March 9, 1932, at his residence at Holy Cross, not far from the university. After being aroused from sleep by chest pains, he awakened his colleague, Father John O'Grady, for assistance. Father O'Grady did his best to comfort the bishop and then appropriately administered the Sacrament of Anointing. Stricken with a heart attack a short time later, Bishop Shahan struggled for a final breath and died.

Four days later, the bishop's body, dressed in episcopal robes and with a chalice placed firmly between his folded hands, was brought to the Shrine for viewing in the Crypt Church. A cabled message of condolence from Pope Pius XI was received by the apostolic delegate. The Holy Father, through his secretary of state, relayed "his paternal sorrow" on receiving word of Bishop Shahan's death.

It came as no surprise that Bishop Shahan's final resting place would be in the crypt he inaugurated nearly 20 years before with the blessing and encouragement of Pope Pius X. Ironically, just four months prior to his death, Bishop Shahan and Msgr. McKenna had petitioned the commissioners of the District of Columbia to allow for burials in the crypt. The required permit was granted on Dec. 18, 1931, less than three months before the bishop's death. He had personally designated the place in the crypt where he wished to be buried. What was then known as the Ave Maria Chapel would later be renamed the Founder's Chapel by the Shrine's fourth director,

Father Patrick "P.J." O'Connor. It has been suggested that Bishop Shahan chose this location as his final resting place — the one closest to the south entrance and most recently completed at the time — to prevent any future attempt to alter the Shrine's intended length.

Msgr. McKenna waged an all-out campaign in the pages of *Salve Regina* to appropriately adorn the Ave Maria Chapel as a lasting tribute to his beloved mentor. Bishop Shahan's photograph appeared frequently in *Salve Regina* with a full-page appeal to raise $25,000 "to complete an appropriate chapel in memory of the Founder of America's first National Monument to the Mother of God." The appeal was joined with the promise that the names of all donors would be placed in the crypt of the Shrine. Besides the addition of Irish iconography within the chapel as a tribute to Bishop Shahan's ancestry, a marble sarcophagus was commissioned that depicted Bishop Shahan in death, attired in ecclesiastical robes. A Celtic crucifix was eventually placed above the altar, and on each side of the crucifix Irish saints were depicted in bas-relief: Sts. Comgal, Iarlath, Finnian, Ciaran, Patraic, Aedan, Columcille, Colman, Gall and Brendan. On the north wall are traditional symbols of Christ — a pelican

feeding her young with her own blood, representing Christ nourishing His followers with His sacrificial blood; and a phoenix rising from ashes, recalling Christ's resurrection.

∞

OBSTACLES TOO GREAT

With the death of the Shrine's founder, it became increasingly difficult to maintain a compelling case for continuing construction during the dire circumstances of the Great Depression. What had previously been unthinkable — and most definitely unmentionable — just a few short years before had now become inevitable. In early 1933, the Board of Trustees indefinitely postponed further work toward the Shrine's completion. With more than $3 million expended on the crypt's construction and a recently acquired debt of nearly $200,000, the eminently practical Archbishop Curley concluded that the Shrine had become a luxury which neither the university nor the Catholic populace could afford under the prevailing circumstances.

Then, at the April 26, 1933, meeting of the Board of Trustees, the newly elected Msgr. McKenna read a one-sentence letter that would seal the Shrine's fate for the next 20 years:

> *"To the Board of Trustees of the Catholic University, Washington, D.C.: The undersigned hereby resigns his membership in the Building Committee of the Immaculate Conception Shrine, Catholic University, Washington, D.C. — Cardinal Dennis Dougherty, Archbishop of Philadelphia."*

With the resignation of the Building Committee's prominent chairman, Msgr. McKenna became, for all practical purposes, the lone voice crying in the

BIRTH OF THE CATHOLIC WORKER MOVEMENT

∞

Seeking a moment of solitude while covering socialist demonstrations in Washington as a reporter in 1930, Dorothy Day made her way to the Crypt Church of the National Shrine to contemplate the future course of her life. A convert to Catholicism, Day recounted how she "offered up a special prayer, a prayer which came with tears and with anguish that some way would open up for me to use what talents I possessed for my fellow workers, for the poor." It was during this spontaneous visit to the Shrine — coincidentally, on the Dec. 8 feast of the Immaculate Conception — that she resolved to devote herself to changing society's prevailing attitudes toward the poor and dispossessed.

The Catholic Worker movement, which Day organized in 1933, inaugurated a new era of lay activism in the revitalization of the Church's social and spiritual ministry to the poor. ∞

wilderness. It took less than a month for him to come to grips with his diminished ability to advance the Shrine's cause. On May 2, 1933, Msgr. McKenna penned his own resignation letter to Archbishop Curley, in which he revealed his quiet heartache over his fate and that of his beloved Shrine.

The June 1933 issue of *Salve Regina* carried the news of Msgr. McKenna's resignation to the Shrine's supporters nationwide under the simple heading, "Our Friends":

"Dear Salve Regina Readers: I take this opportunity — now that I have severed my connections with the National Shrine of the Immaculate Conception — to thank all those who have so loyally supported me in my efforts to bring the Shrine up to its present proportions, as it has only been through your kind assistance that the Crypt of the Shrine has been completed. I shall always remember with sincere appreciation your hearty cooperation and ask God to bless and reward you for the honor you have done to His Immaculate Mother. One word more. May I ask you to remember me in your prayers that my efforts in the new work I am about to begin at the Church of the Holy Angels . . . may be successful. I remain, Sincerely and gratefully yours, Rt. Rev. Msgr. Bernard A. McKenna."

Msgr. McKenna returned to the

CRYPT OF NATIONAL SHRINE OF THE IMMACULATE CONCEPTION CATHOLIC UNIVERSITY OF AMERICA WASHINGTON, DC

Following the death of Bishop Shahan, Msgr. McKenna provided the "lone voice" for the Shrine cause. Here he contemplates the Shrine's prospects before a makeshift Marian shrine and confessional.

Archdiocese of Philadelphia, where he took up his new duties as pastor of Holy Angels Church. Characteristically, he threw himself into every aspect of this bustling parish community for the next 25 years. In 1941, Msgr. McKenna was elected president of the American Catholic Historical Society, a post he held for three years. Although his departure from the Shrine occasioned great personal disappointment and regret, his cherished hope of seeing the Shrine completed would not be frustrated. On Nov. 20, 1959, a special place of honor awaited Msgr. McKenna upon his return to the National Shrine on the occasion of the Shrine's solemn dedication.

DETERMINATION
AND DEVOTION

∞

DISAPPOINTMENT
AND DELAY
1933 - 1952

When the National Shrine's second director assumed his new duties, the prospects for the Shrine's future could not have seemed more hopeless. Although cash on hand totaled $9,705.95, the Shrine's indebtedness amounted to a staggering $232,797.23. The gains achieved in defining the Shrine as a separate entity from the university soon vanished in the face of such dismal conditions. It was promptly decided to place all matters pertaining to the Shrine once again under the direct authority of the Board of Trustees of Catholic University.

Msgr. David T. O'Dwyer was a priest of the Diocese of Denver, Colo., when he first began a regular correspondence with Archbishop Curley in 1925. He had achieved success in helping to manage the finances of the Denver diocese and, as a result, Archbishop Curley persuaded him to apply his keen financial skills on behalf of Catholic University. Msgr. O'Dwyer was released from his parish duties in January 1927 to become procurator of the university with primary responsibilities in the areas of financial management and fund raising.

At a meeting of the university's board on Nov. 14, 1933, Archbishop Curley announced that he had appointed Msgr. O'Dwyer to succeed Msgr. McKenna. The board approved the archbishop's choice.

During his first several months as Shrine director, Msgr. O'Dwyer worked tirelessly to restore some hope that the Shrine's dismal financial circumstances could be reversed. The following November, Archbishop Curley was able to report that the Shrine's income had improved considerably over the previous year's "lean" summer months under the new director's management. Yet while the archbishop persisted in championing Msgr. O'Dwyer's image as the Shrine's knight in shining armor, Msgr. O'Dwyer confessed to lacking the energetic spirit of his predecessor. He was acutely aware of Msgr. McKenna's enormous popularity among benefactors throughout the country. To reassure McKenna's faithful supporters that their beloved leader had not abandoned the Shrine, the following notation appeared in bold type in several subsequent editions of *Salve Regina*:

> "Msgr. McKenna has visited the National Shrine several times since his resignation as director. His zeal on its behalf is in no way lessened by reason of his severance of official connection with it. The Shrine owes a tremendous debt to the untiring effort with which he endeavored to build it, and it augurs well for its future that the riches of his experience and the inspiration of his zeal are still available for the cause."

Msgr. O'Dwyer, unlike his predecessor, was first and foremost a scholar, more at ease with theological and philosophical tomes than balance sheets and ledgers. His keen intellectual pursuits led him to transform *Salve Regina* into a scholarly journal of Mariological and theological reflection. Subsequent issues of *Salve Regina* featured lengthy treatises on popular Mariological themes: Mary's role in the New Testament, "Our Lady and the Oxford Movement," the Assumption and "Devotion to the Mother of God in Ireland." He also frequently included the familiar means that Msgr. McKenna used to achieve a steady flow of income to the Shrine: full-page appeals to encourage the purchase of memorial tablets, reminders to order Christmas cards, and invitations to pay tribute to the Shrine's revered founder by contributing to the ornamentation of Bishop Shahan's final resting chamber.

Msgr. O'Dwyer's pious reflections and appeals achieved little success in building widespread interest to contribute toward the Shrine's completion. A momentary flicker of hope, however, pierced the darkness of the prevailing circumstances at the Nov. 15, 1934, meeting of the bishops of the National Catholic Welfare Conference (NCWC), predecessor to the National Conference of Catholic Bishops. A motion was made to designate a Sunday in May for a special collection for the National Shrine of the Immaculate Conception.

Fearing that Catholics might confuse the Shrine collection with the annual collection for Catholic University taken on the first Sunday of Advent — and thus undermine this crucial income source for the university — more than one bishop voiced strong objection. The motion was quickly tabled. The National Shrine would not appear on the bishops' agenda for another 10 years.

DIMINISHING RETURNS

Msgr. O'Dwyer soon discovered that his heralded skills at financial management were powerless to reverse the trend of declining financial support. The Christmas-card appeal was a disappointing failure in 1934. A large number of boxed cards sent to formerly reliable subscribers resulted in a negligible return. Msgr. O'Dwyer was compelled to send out an appeal to emphasize the critical role that the Christmas cards played in staving off sure disaster for the Shrine's financial condition:

> "We realize that the Depression has made such a response difficult for many, and to those we say we shall be happy to accept for what we sent them any offering they choose to make. And if even a small offering is a hardship, let us know and we will cancel the debt. . . . Many are under the impression that the profits of Christmas cards are just a small addition to larger income from other sources. This is not so. From the beginning, the main support of the Shrine was furnished by the sale of Christmas cards."

THE SECOND DIRECTOR

For Archbishop Curley, who was eager to take hold of the Shrine's finances and future, Msgr. David T. O'Dwyer was an obvious choice as Msgr. Bernard McKenna's successor. Msgr. McKenna's was not a careful recordkeeper, and Msgr. O'Dwyer had achieved a commendable level of achievement and respect for his management of finances in the Diocese of Denver and as procurator at Catholic University.

But Msgr. O'Dwyer was never comfortable as a businessman. He preferred the life of a scholar to that of a fund-raiser and financial officer. Dorothy Dowd, who was his office manager at the Shrine, remembered him as extremely intelligent, very cultured and a "real Irish gentleman." It is worth noting that Msgr. O'Dwyer continued as procurator of the university along with his position as Shrine director until 1936, when he resigned as procurator to focus his energies exclusively on the Shrine. ∽

Msgr. O'Dwyer's efforts, unfortunately, had little effect. At the Board of Trustees meeting in 1935, Archbishop Curley was forced to report again that receipts failed to cover expenses, with a net loss of $10,979.16 in the Shrine's operating budget. Drastic cost-saving measures had to be taken. Curiously, Msgr. O'Dwyer elected to sacrifice the Shrine's primary lifeline to the nation. Publication of *Salve Regina*, begun in 1914 by Bishop Shahan to announce the Shrine and attract broad national support, was suspended at the end of 1935.

The future Pope Pius XII (third from left), Cardinal Eugenio Pacelli, papal secretary of state, visits the National Shrine in October 1936. Also pictured are (from left) Msgr. O'Dwyer, Archbishop Michael Curley, Archbishop Amleto Cicognani, apostolic delegate, and Catholic University vice rector Msgr. Patrick J. McCormick.

∽
'A MOST ILLUSTRIOUS VISITOR'

Arguably, the most significant event to occur at the National Shrine during the 1930s was the visit of Cardinal Eugenio Pacelli, then papal secretary of state, in October 1936. The only written account of Cardinal Pacelli's visit to Catholic University and the National Shrine appears to have been written by Msgr. O'Dwyer after the cardinal's election as Pope Pius XII. Immediately following a welcoming ceremony in the university's gymnasium (during which the distinguished visitor spoke extemporaneously for 35 minutes), Cardinal Pacelli arrived at the Shrine for a guided tour. Msgr. O'Dwyer and the secretary of state chatted amiably throughout the tour about the Shrine, and even discussed the peculiarities of the English language. Cardinal Pacelli seemed moved by the beauty of the Crypt Church and paused in prayer before the Blessed Sacrament. Msgr. O'Dwyer noted that "the kneeling figure had an intensity that made the material world seem millions of miles away."

∽
MODEST GAIN

Msgr. O'Dwyer continued to forge ahead in his attempts to gain greater control over Shrine finances. By 1936, his efforts were beginning to bear modest fruit as income nudged just barely ahead of expenses. But very little of what came in went toward reducing the sizable debt of $200,000 that had been incurred to complete the southern foundations.

Over the next two years, Msgr. O'Dwyer struggled under increasing pressure from Archbishop Curley and the Board of Trustees to secure additional funds. Eventually, he concluded that it had become necessary to again reach out to Catholics across the country, whose generosity had made the prospect of building a national patronal church possible in the first place. In 1938, Msgr. O'Dwyer prudently decided to revive the publication of *Salve Regina* on a quarterly basis. In this same year, the Shrine realized a net profit of $9,118.24, and $30,000 was reduced from the Shrine's $200,000 debt to the university.

By the fall of 1939, Msgr. O'Dwyer approached the end of his term as director. Faced with mounting pressure to consolidate the Shrine's finances with those of the university, Msgr. O'Dwyer concluded that he had achieved as much as he was likely to in the goal of stabilizing the Shrine's financial circumstances. In May 1940, Msgr. O'Dwyer returned to the Denver diocese and resumed life as a parish priest.

∞
THE THIRD DIRECTOR
— Father John J. Reilly —

The suggestion of Father John J. Reilly as the candidate to succeed Msgr. O'Dwyer came from the university's vice rector, Msgr. Patrick J. McCormick. The two priests, both from the Diocese of Hartford, Conn., had been friends and golfing partners for many years. Msgr. McCormick considered Father Reilly's easygoing temperament ideally suited to the pressures of directing the Shrine. By June 1940, Father Reilly had assumed his new duties as the Shrine's third director. Balancing the demands of the university's board with the objectives of advancing the Shrine would be no easy task. The fact that the two priests already enjoyed a close friendship was, at the very least, a step in the right direction.

∞
'MARY AND CONSCRIPTION'

By November 1940, the prospect of war was awakening a new spirituality among Americans. Unlike World War I, when the Shrine drive was slowed until victory was assured, the present threat served as an incentive for Catholics to regard the Shrine as a sanctuary of spiritual refuge and intercession.

Father Reilly enlarged the format of *Salve Regina* to accommodate lengthy

THE **THIRD DIRECTOR**

Born in New Haven, Conn., Father John J. Reilly attended St. Thomas Seminary in Hartford, Conn., and later continued his studies in philosophy at St. Mary's Seminary in Baltimore. He completed his theological studies at the Catholic University of Louvain, Belgium, where he was ordained by Cardinal Désiré J. Mercier on July 8. 1923.

Upon his return to the United States, Father Reilly served in several parishes within the Hartford diocese. He became well known throughout Connecticut as an orator and radio personality, resulting from his work in the office of Christian doctrine and as the diocesan director of the Holy Name Society of Hartford.

Father Reilly's writings in *Salve Regina* during the years immediately before the United States entered World War II tapped deep emotions among his readers. He presented the Shrine as a sanctuary of refuge for all who longed for peace and trusted in the power of Mary's intercession to diminish the likelihood of America's all-out engagement in the war.

Father Reilly became a popular representative of the Shrine, both on campus and in the Washington community. He was frequently heard on radio pleading the Shrine's cause and drawing stirring parallels between the concerns of the listener and those of the Shrine. ∞

articles of spiritual encouragement and theological perspective for Americans preoccupied with the fear of being dragged into a distant war. One of Father Reilly's early articles as the Shrine's director set the tone of the revamped *Salve Regina* for the years ahead. In "Mary and Conscription," he sought to reawaken among Catholic women an allegiance to the Shrine that, in turn, would provide them the spiritual resources needed to deal with the uncertainties of war and the precarious fate of their sons called into battle. Father Reilly asserted the Shrine's relevance in the lives of American Catholics:

> *"The machinery for drafting is being geared in Washington — the machinery that will take away your boy. But in another part of Washington an even greater force is being put in motion to bring him back to you untouched. More than a hundred student priests, most of them not much older than your boy, each day read Mass at the National Shrine under Mary's patronage. Your intention will be theirs as they commune with Mary, and we know what your intention is.... We of the Shrine are happy, at a time like this, that the Shrine can play such a role. . . [The Shrine] could serve its purpose in no better way than taking on itself and rendering assistance for the heartaches of the mothers of the world."*

Father Reilly produced stirring articles in *Salve Regina* to cultivate a new following for the Shrine. What better time to make a compelling case for the Shrine's necessity than in perilous times of war and Depression? American Catholics waited and watched the war from afar, not altogether convinced that their country could maintain a neutral posture indefinitely. In January 1941, Congress passed the Lend-Lease Act, authorizing the president to "sell, transfer, exchange, lease, lend" any defense articles "to the government of any country whose defense the President deems vital to the defense of the United States." The United States was strengthening its alliances and approaching the periphery of war. Now that America had staked out its position, Catholics were being asked to make clear their spiritual allegiance.

The Shrine was beginning to experience a rebirth. More and more people who desired to be united with its mission as a national sanctuary of prayer for peace were drawn to the Shrine.

In January 1941, the Shrine hosted the annual "Red Mass," which, even in the present day, takes place at the opening of Congress and the Supreme Court. Attended by Supreme Court Justices Harlan F. Stone, William O. Douglas and Frank Murphy, and Attorney General Robert H. Jackson, the Mass took on even greater significance with the threat of impending war. Father Reilly had suc-

Pearl Harbor under attack by Japanese forces, Dec. 7, 1941.

ceeded in asserting the Shrine's relevance to both spiritual and secular concerns. Politicians, government officials and foreign dignitaries alike congregated at the Shrine in prayerful anticipation of America's next move in the geopolitical chess game being played out ever nearer to home.

On Dec. 7, 1941, the United States was forced into decisive action. With the Japanese invasion of Pearl Harbor, the war in Europe had become America's war. Prayers for peace would now be coupled with prayers for victory.

The Red Mass of Jan. 18, 1942, was especially poignant given the tumultuous events of the preceding month. Among those who attended the solemn Mass in the crypt were Vice President Henry A. Wallace, Postmaster General

Msgr. Patrick A. McCormick, acting rector of The Catholic University of America, with Henry A. Wallace, vice president of the United States, Supreme Court Justice Frank Murphy and Sen. Pat McCarran (D-Nev.) following the Red Mass of Jan. 18, 1942, at the National Shrine.

America's preoccupation with the war, it was not to be. Instead, there arose a sense of increased urgency to get on with construction. Father Reilly successfully enticed thousands who had never thought seriously of the Shrine to become faithful supporters. In 1943 alone, the Shrine's debt was reduced by $100,000. The May 1943 *Salve Regina* proudly announced that:

> *"The first construction work done at the Shrine in a long time was inaugurated recently when fourteen of the massive columns in the Memorial Chapel were faced with beautiful Radio Black American marble. . . . On this marble will be inscribed the names of those who purchase Memorial Tablets, which will augment the thousands of names already in the Memorial Chapel, constituting a Catholic Hall of Fame in the National Shrine."*

Francis Biddle; Secretary of Labor Frances Perkins; and the Polish ambassador. Also in attendance were Supreme Court Justices Stone, Douglas, Murphy, Hugo L. Black, Stanley Reed and James M. Byrne. Several members of the Senate were in attendance, including the senior senator from Missouri, Harry S. Truman. Speaker Sam Rayburn (D-Texas) and Rep. John McCormack (D-Mass.) were among members of the House of Representatives present. This event marked the largest gathering of U.S. government officials at the National Shrine to date.

Prospects for the Shrine's future had improved so dramatically by 1943 that the Board of Trustees began to contemplate the cost of completion. Then Father Reilly's close friend, Msgr. McCormick, succeeded Bishop Joseph M. Corrigan (who had died on June 10, 1942) as the new rector of Catholic University. The tide seemed to be turning in the Shrine's favor.

∽ MOMENTUM REGAINED

While a compelling case could easily have been made to postpone further attempts to advance the Shrine due to

The Shrine, during the turbulent war years, played host to a number of notable individuals whose hopes for the swift defeat of Nazi aggression had great personal significance. Archduke Otto of Austria attended a special Mass on March 14, 1943, commemorating the fifth anniversary of the German occupation of his country. During the Mass offered for Austria's restoration, a noted Catholic orator, Dominican Father Ignatius Smith, delivered a terse sermon in which he railed against Nazi aggressors and the terror inflicted on the Austrian people.

BISHOP JOHN F. NOLL
— War Bonds for Mary —

Long before the National Shrine's first stone was quarried, it was suggested that the Shrine be built as a "Victory Memorial" to American servicemen who had paid the ultimate sacrifice for their country during World War I. Now, nearly 30 years later, a similar suggestion emerged in an editorial in the pages of *Our Sunday Visitor*, the prominent national Catholic weekly.

Bishop John F. Noll of Fort Wayne, Ind., the paper's founder and editor, had contributed to the first effort to raise funds for the building of the National Shrine as a young priest in 1916 and even attended the laying of the foundation stone in 1920. Bishop Noll's early interest in the Shrine while still in its "University Chapel" phase foreshadowed the prominent role he would play in ensuring the

Shrine's eventual completion as a national monument to Catholicism in America.

The October 1916 *Salve Regina* featured Father Noll's letter:

"Dear Bishop Shahan: Enclosed find two checks — for $100 each — to be applied to the fund for the Shrine to Mary Immaculate. One

Her clients hailed from many lands
That proved their loyalty
To Christ, His Church, nor ever failed,
Sweet Maid, to honor thee.
When raging billows lashed their bark
Upon the heaving main
"Star of the Sea!" they cried to thee,
nor did they cry in vain.

The grateful millions' glowing love
Would build a temple fair —
Sublime and stately structure —
A monument of prayer.
The diamonds' flash, the rubies' glow,
The sacred vessels grace
And speak the donors' silent love
In consecrated place.

'Mid war and strife didst shield our land
by they most potent prayer.
The mothers of the boys who fought
Invoked thee — everywhere.
The men who stood 'neath shell and fire
Oft whispered thy sweet name.
Now tens of thousands joyfully
Their gratitude proclaim.

Tens of thousands fain would see
This splendor — glorious scene!
When Nations' gift is offered thee,
Immaculate bright Queen.
While rays of golden sunlight
Through chancel windows fall:
Sweet Lady, pray they Son to bless
The donors — one and all!
— **Sister M.A.**

A
**NATION'S
GIFT
TO
CHRIST'S
STAINLESS
MOTHER**

resident of the U.S. Veterans' Hospital in Tucson, Ariz., which reinforced an earlier suggestion by Bishop Noll that a contribution from "every Catholic parent who had a boy in the Armed Forces" would help ensure the completion of the National Shrine as a "Victory Memorial to Her Who is the Patroness of our nation." It is difficult to overstate the impact that Mahoney's "hurriedly drawn" proposal would have in helping to revive the nationwide campaign to complete the Shrine:

> *"Some time ago Father Stoner, our chaplain, handed me a copy of Our Sunday Visitor, of which you are the editor, and I read in it a statement regarding the erection of a monument to Mary Immaculate, the Patroness of the United States, on the grounds of the Catholic University at Washington, D.C.*

> *"I am, and I believe most Catholics will be, heartily in favor of the suggestion, but since it is quite a problem to collect sufficient funds to complete the project of this kind at the present time, I submit for your consideration a plan, which I believe will be of considerable assistance to our nation in the present crisis, as well as supplying the necessary funds to complete the desired Memorial.*

> *"There are eight thousand Catholic schools in the United States. As our nation is at war, priorities would not be released at the present time, so my suggestion is, let us turn our war plans into the greatest Peace Memorial the world has ever known in the following manner: 8,000 schools multiplied by 8 grades equal 64,000 classes, each supervised by a sis-*

Bishop John F. Noll, founder of Our Sunday Visitor and chairman of the first episcopal committee for the National Shrine.

of these is from *Our Sunday Visitor* and the other from the writer. As you are probably aware, the surplus earnings of OSV are devoted to Home and Foreign Missionary Work, and we feel that the University Chapel could consistently be listed under the head of 'Home Missions.' Wishing your holy enterprise the most unbounded success, I am, Yours in Christ, J.F. Noll."

The March 14, 1943, issue of *Our Sunday Visitor* included a letter to the editor from a George Francis Mahoney, a

ter or a brother. Have each class fill one War Stamp book with $18.75 worth of stamps. The entire amount will equal $1,200,000 maturing in ten years at a value of $1,600,000.

"These books could be filled during the Lenten season and converted into War Bonds in May, Mary's Month. If sufficient funds are not collected in one collection, it may be repeated after school opens next September, and the entire amount converted and dedicated to the Immaculate Conception on December eighth.

"A miniature button, similar to the enclosed, may be presented to each child at the time of his making his donation to the teacher. All this could be very easily handled by the Sisters without any expense as the Government supplies the books and the stamps.

"I hope you will consider this rough plan, hurriedly drawn. Sincerely yours, George Francis Mahoney."

This was not the first time that war bonds were suggested as a means for contributing to the Shrine. In a small box in the August 1942 issue of *Salve Regina*, Father Reilly put forth the suggestion of joining patriotism and devotion with the heading, "Link Mary and America."

The response to the proposal reprinted in *Our Sunday Visitor* was overwhelming. Across the nation, countless schools took up the challenge to contribute to the building of the National Shrine through the purchase of war bonds. The first to accept Mahoney's

challenge was Our Lady Star of the Sea Academy in Solomons, Md. Divine Providence Sister Mary Hilda wrote:

"As our Academy is the youngest and the smallest in the Archdiocese [only fourteen students], we cannot do much, but we will do gladly whatever we do. Our Reverend Pastor, Father Alexander, desires me to send you today the price of one War Bond, $18.75. He advanced the money which we will collect as soon as possible from the children of the primary and intermediate grades. . . . Out of gratitude to Our Lady we would love to be the first, if the smallest, to gladly contribute to the completion of Her magnificent Shrine."

Bishop Noll ushered in a decisively new era of support for the National Shrine by appealing to Americans' sense of patriotism at a crucial hour. Americans united in the common effort to defeat any and all threats to God, nation and family. As armed forces persisted in defending America's democratic principles on the world stage, Catholics at home were eager to provide the spiritual reinforcements needed for success.

In the meantime, Father Reilly continued to diminish the Shrine's debt. On April 11, 1944, he paid $15,000 toward the balance due to Catholic University's endowment fund. Additionally, over $6,000 in bequests, $4,100 in "victory bonds" and nearly $32,000 in Christmas-card sales enhanced income. For the first time in 12 years, a serious review of the original architectural plans was underway along with a detailed cost estimate based on the early design. Father Reilly informed the university's board that the Maginnis and Walsh firm had only completed "preliminary" sketches of the superstructure some 13 years prior — not the detailed drawings that would be needed for a competitive construction-bid process. Charles Maginnis had recently informed Father Reilly that the 1929 cost for completing the Shrine's superstructure — not including the interior finishes — would approximate $2,950,000. The board could not reasonably anticipate the actual costs until working drawings were completed.

Father Reilly seized the occasion to suggest that a committee of bishops be formed to counsel him in devising the proper course of action. Father Reilly cleverly suggested that "some sort of national activity" be considered to appropriately mark the 100th anniversary of the proclamation of the dogma of the Immaculate Conception in 1954. He further reminded board members that bonds purchased in 1944 for the Shrine would reach their maturation in the same year as that important Church celebration.

Although no action was taken on Reilly's proposal at the time, the seed was surely planted. The progress realized during the preceding two years was beyond what anyone could have imagined. In many ways, Catholics had come to regard the completion of the Shrine as their spiritual safeguard against the terrible toll that the war had already required of a nation and its people. No longer was it a question of *would* the Shrine be finished, but *when.*

The November 1944 issue of *Salve Regina* announced that the Shrine was finally out of debt. That Father Reilly had succeeded in relieving the Shrine of its enormous debt to the university while reviving interest in resuming construction during World War II was a remarkable feat that opened the door for further discussion of the need to complete the Shrine.

Bishop Noll raised the issue with his fellow bishops during the U.S. bishops' meeting on Nov. 16, 1944. Not surprisingly, Archbishop Curley stressed that the Shrine should no longer be considered "a Washington project," but a truly national endeavor as a "Shrine to America's Immaculate Patroness." After further discussion, approval was given to Bishop Noll to form a special committee of bishops to study a plan for erecting the superstructure — reduced in size, but consistent with the architect's original design — to be reviewed at the bishops' next meeting.

The stipulation for a design of diminished proportions would be a problem to be addressed later. For the time being, the formation of the bishops' committee was a decisive step on the path to the eventual completion of the Shrine.

With the arrival of 1945, there was renewed hope that the end of the war was in sight. At the annual Red Mass on Feb. 4, newly elected Vice President Harry S. Truman was in attendance, along with Supreme Court justices, representatives of the District of Columbia, members of Congress and a large contingent of foreign diplomats. Less than three months later, Truman would be sworn in as the 33rd president of the United States.

∞

'A FRUSTRATED NOBLE EFFORT'

With the conclusion of World War II on Aug. 14, 1945, Father Reilly sought to instill among American Catholics a sense of gratitude for the peace that they had long awaited. Whereas his previous fund-raising appeals were carefully phrased so as not to convey frustration over the Shrine's partially completed state, Reilly felt the time had come to compel decisive action by laying bare the harsh reality. He characterized the

Vice President Harry S. Truman attends the Feb. 4, 1945, Red Mass in the Crypt Church. Directly behind Truman is Supreme Court Justice Frank Murphy.

Shrine's stunted proportions and deteriorating state as the result of sheer neglect.

The November 1945 edition of *Salve Regina* featured an article by a Father J. Peifer in which the Shrine was characterized as a "disappointment," the very picture of a "frustrated noble effort." Father Peifer continued: "There is no dome, no spire, very little, in fact, that would qualify it as a church at all. . . . The Crypt is the only part of the church that is more than lines on a blueprint." Previous attempts to inspire excitement that the Shrine was already "an accomplished fact" by featuring the architect's rendering on *Salve Regina*'s front cover, now gave way to stark descriptions of the Shrine's true condition: unfinished concrete walls, unsightly showcases in the Shrine's "Madonna Room" featuring odds and ends from missionary efforts, floors and walls of "cold and naked concrete," a "feeling of sadness for our Blessed Mother and Her seeming abandonment here in the hall of disappointment." The strategy was to shame a prosperous nation, giddy over the arrival of peace and their young men home from battle, and to remind Americans of their obligations to the One "from whom all blessings come."

It was not by chance that this new tactic of emphasizing the Shrine's failure coincided with the bishops' NCWC meeting that November. During this gathering, the newly organized Episcopal Committee for the Completion of the National Shrine held its first meeting. The committee comprised Bishop Noll as chairman, Archbishop Joseph F. Rummell of New Orleans, Archbishop John G. Murray of St. Paul and Minneapolis, Archbishop Richard Cushing of Boston and Bishop Peter L. Ireton of Richmond, Va., along with Msgr. McCormick and Father Reilly.

The committee rejected the earlier suggestion that the Shrine be reduced in size from its original concept. Architect Maginnis weighed in strongly on this point, emphasizing that the cost of establishing new foundations would consume whatever gains were to be realized from a renewed fund-raising initiative. Once again, the idea of promoting the Shrine as a "Victory Memorial" was advanced. This time, however, responsibility for its completion was placed squarely on the bishops' shoulders. Bishop Noll expressed his belief that sufficient funds could be raised over a five-year period through an annual collection to be taken in every U.S. parish on Mother's Day. He further proposed that the "sixty thousand school rooms in Catholic schools could each be asked to raise ten dollars a year for five years in honor of our Blessed Mother, Patroness of America." Archbishop Rummel continued that "if the hierarchy only speaks the word, the devotion of our people to the Blessed Mother of God and their sense of gratitude to her for peace in answer to their prayers, will inspire their generosity."

Following further discussion, the bishops' committee approved an amendment favoring completion of the Shrine and authorizing the committee to solicit the personal endorsement of each bishop in writing as evidence of broad support. Unfortunately, the 1946 Mother's Day collection never took place. Slightly more than half the bishops responded, and their consensus was for only one collection rather than for Bishop Noll's five-year plan.

At the following November meeting of the American bishops, the completion of the Shrine was again on the agenda. Bishop Noll reported that 52 bishops had expressed in writing their support for resuming construction, with only eight expressing opposition. Bishop Noll raised a number of relevant points in the hope of conveying a sense of urgency to the work. Even the advancing age of architect Maginnis was suggested as reason to expedite its completion. Bishop Noll reported the committee's unanimous recommendation that construction be resumed and that the bishops authorize a five-year national collection to raise the estimated $5 million construction cost beginning on Mother's Day of the following year. It was further suggested that the Shrine's completion be scheduled to coincide with the 1954 centennial anniversary of the declaration of the dogma of the Immaculate Conception.

America's most powerful churchman, Cardinal Francis J. Spellman of New York, objected strongly to the suggestion of imposing yet another fund-raising campaign on the bishops. He reminded the assembly that the War Emergency Relief Collection, with its goal of raising

Cardinal Francis J. Spellman

$5 million, was also underway. His opposition was further fueled by the failure of the bishops to fulfill their commitment to raise $2 million for the new North American College in Rome.

Surprisingly, when a motion was made to approve the committee's report, it was seconded by Cardinal Spellman. As if to call their bluff, Cardinal Spellman offered an amendment to authorize the committee to proceed with the Shrine's completion only after receiving from each bishop a pledge to accept a specific quota for each of the next five years. Ironically, Cardinal Spellman

Photo of the National Shrine used in the 1946 booklet, "Proposed National Shrine of the Immaculate Conception."

would later resist the imposition of a quota.

Cardinal Spellman was unsuccessful in slowing the Shrine's newly gained momentum for a fund-raising collection. The bishops approved the committee's report and authorized a Mother's Day collection for the following year, 1947. The five-year plan proposed raising a total of $5 million through a broad appeal to the 5 million members of the Rosary Societies and other organized Catholic groups. The appeal would even be extended within the 65,000 classrooms of the nation's Catholic schools.

Prior to the bishops' 1946 meeting, the Episcopal Committee cleverly devised and distributed a booklet titled "Proposed National Shrine of the Immaculate Conception." It had the look

of a professionally designed advertising brochure with all of the relevant information the bishops would need to make a compelling case for the Shrine's completion within their dioceses. Bishop Noll, as the Shrine's most impassioned proponent of the day, clearly had a hand in the booklet's design and content. In the attempt to dispel any hint of opposition on the part of Catholic University for resuming work, the first page featured a letter to Father Reilly from his friend, the university's rector, Msgr. McCormick, in which the earliest rationale for erecting the Shrine was again put forth:

> *"I believe it would be well to stress the point that the University has real need of a commodious church for the accommodation of its students and the religious of the affiliated houses of study. As you know, we are obliged to limit the attendance from these religious houses at the academic functions held in the Shrine which is much to be regretted. . . . Quite apart from our longing to see this monument to our Blessed Mother gloriously completed, we are prompted by University needs to urge your best efforts toward an early completion of the structure of the Shrine."*

The page that followed revealed a most unflattering photograph of the incomplete Shrine. Rather than the majestic Byzantine-Romanesque monument to the Mother of God envisioned by its founder, Bishop Shahan, and sanctioned by four popes, the Shrine looked more like an abandoned turn-of-the-century prison, complete with overgrown shrubbery and knee-high grass. The notation below the photograph read simply: "National Shrine at present. Approved by Pope Pius X in 1914."

The message was clear: American Catholics had cause for shame. Bishop Noll and the other members of the committee were determined not to repeat the mistakes of the past. This time, the Shrine, as if by necessity, would finally succeed.

On Mother's Day 1947, hundreds of thousands of Catholics across the country were invited at Sunday Mass to respond to the first nationally organized appeal to complete the National Shrine of the Immaculate Conception. Actually, less than half of all dioceses participated in the collection, resulting in a $300,000 shortfall of the $1 million goal set by Bishop Noll. In an October letter to the nation's bishops, Bishop Noll made clear his disappointment and again implored the bishops to provide the resources to complete the Shrine:

> "There is no greater authority behind any collection — with the exception of Peter's Pence and Mission collections — than there is behind the collection for the National Shrine. Nearly every nation in the world has a national shrine to Mary. Australia is now collecting for a national shrine to her, to be erect-

ed at Darwin, as a Victory Memorial. If single dioceses can raise $1,000,000, year after year, for Catholic Charities, surely the whole nation could raise that much, amounting to less than twenty cents per family, for a National Basilica, without feeling it."

As if to shame the bishops for failing to fully cooperate in this first appeal, Bishop Noll alluded to an earlier cause when Americans were called upon to erect the pedestal for the Statue of Liberty in 1882:

> "As to your National Shrine, we have the situation in reverse. The late Monsignor Shahan conceived the idea of erecting a national monument to Mary Immaculate, but never got beyond the 'pedestal' or the 'Crypt' stage. That pedestal has been clamoring for twenty-seven years for the monument which was to be erected thereon, slowly deteriorating throughout these years."

During the bishops' meeting of Nov. 13, 1947, Bishop Noll reported that the 58 participating dioceses in the first "Mother's Day Appeal" had resulted in a total of $1,091,803. He further reported that the Shrine's cash assets amounted to $1,150,000. The nation's Catholic priests had contributed $100,000. Bishop Noll spoke on behalf of the bishops' Shrine Committee and made two specific requests:

> "(1) that money to be collected or already collected should be sent to the financial committee of the Catholic University; and (2) that

the Committee on the Shrine should be authorized to engage an architect to draw up plans and specifications."

The first request was granted with little discussion. The second issue, however, raised the question of whether the bishops had the authority to engage an architect without the consent of the university's Board of Trustees since all of the buildings on campus belonged to the university. The concern was laid to rest when Bishop Peter L. Ireton of

Archbishop Michael J. Curley

Richmond, Va., rebutted that the board functioned primarily as a "creature" of the American hierarchy. Therefore, all that was needed to engage an architect was the bishops' assent.

Their concerns addressed, the bishops approved unanimously Bishop Noll's petitions.

DEATH OF ARCHBISHOP CURLEY

With the death of Archbishop Michael J. Curley in May 1947, the Shrine lost both a prominent skeptic and an ardent supporter. Archbishop Curley had been an early enthusiast for the Shrine prior to his appointment as archbishop of Baltimore in 1921. Soon after his installation as Cardinal Gibbons' successor, Archbishop Curley acquired a keen interest in all aspects of the Shrine — much to the chagrin of Msgr. McKenna and Bishop Shahan, who preferred to keep the day-to-day functions of fund raising and planning mostly to themselves.

It was Archbishop Curley's intense involvement in the financial affairs of the university and Shrine that led to his eventual decision to halt further construction. At the height of the Depression, he feared that Catholics across the country could not afford to contribute to both the university and

Shrine and, under the circumstances, the university had much more to lose. Having earlier requested Bishop Shahan to focus primarily on his work at the university, leaving the concerns of the Shrine to Msgr. McKenna, Archbishop Curley had clearly defined his priorities.

Archbishop Curley was an early advocate of requiring the American bishops to assume responsibility for the Shrine's construction. With the new era of cooperation among the hierarchy in the Shrine project during the late 1940s, Archbishop Curley once again joined the ranks of those committed to finishing the "great work" that had been initiated 35 years earlier. One of the archbishop's last official acts was to instruct pastors within the Archdiocese of Washington (Washington had been established as a separate archdiocese in 1939, but remained under the Baltimore archbishop until 1947) to participate in the Mother's Day collection for the Shrine in 1947.

In hindsight, Archbishop Curley's earlier decision to halt construction until broader support was established was a prudent course of action. It eventually forced the bishops to confront their responsibility, involving the majority of American Catholics in a work that they could justifiably claim as their own.

ARCHBISHOP PATRICK A. O'BOYLE

Patrick Aloysius O'Boyle was born on July 18, 1896, in Scranton, Pa. His father, Michael O'Boyle, an immigrant steelworker, died in 1907. Patrick, as the only surviving child, and his mother, Mary Mary (Muldoon) O'Boyle, were left to make their way in difficult times. As a boy, Patrick worked two paper routes, took jobs as a farm hand and in textile mills, and even spent a year as an office boy for $3 a week to supplement his mother's meager income as a rectory housekeeper.

In 1917, he earned his undergraduate degree from St. Thomas College (now Scranton University) and then pursued theological studies at St. Joseph's Seminary in Yonkers, N.Y., graduating in 1921. He was ordained a priest of the Archdiocese of New York at St. Patrick's Cathedral on May 21 of the same year.

Early in his priesthood, Father O'Boyle exhibited a strong interest in social work. His first assignment was at St. Columba's Church in the Chelsea section of New York City. He became executive director of the Catholic Guardian Society after completing five years at St. Columba. In 1931, Father O'Boyle obtained a graduate degree from the New York School of Social Work. During the 1930s, he taught at Fordham's School of Social Services while working as the assistant director of the child-care department for Catholic Charities of New York and as the executive director of the Immaculate Virgin Mission on Staten Island.

Archbishop Edward Mooney of Detroit appointed Father O'Boyle director of War Relief Services for the National Catholic Welfare Conference on Aug. 18, 1943, and in a little less than four years, he was named executive director of Catholic Charities for New York by Cardinal Spellman. He quickly gained a reputation as an adept fund raiser and competent administrator on behalf of the Church's many apostolates. His talents in the area of financial management, combined with his strong devotion to the Blessed Mother, distinguished him as the right man to complete of the superstructure of the National Shrine. ∞

ARCHBISHOP PATRICK A. O'BOYLE

On Jan. 21, 1948, Archbishop Patrick A. O'Boyle was installed as Washington's first resident archbishop by the apostolic delegate, Archbishop Amleto Giovanni Cicognani, in an elaborate ceremony in the Cathedral of St. Matthew the Apostle. The February 1948 edition of *Salve Regina* made special note of the new archbishop's well-known devotion to the Blessed Mother and alluded to the hope that he would take an active role in promoting the Shrine — which, after all, occupied a prominent space within his archdiocese. As archbishop of Washington, Archbishop O'Boyle would necessarily also hold the position of chancellor of the university and thus maintain responsiblity for the National Shrine.

THE NATIONAL SHRINE OF THE IMMACULATE CONCEPTION, INC.

The separation of the Shrine from the university had long been considered advantageous for the Shrine's emerging identity as a distinctly national Catholic institution. Msgr. McKenna's independent approach to managing the affairs of the Shrine had resulted in numerous conflicts with the university's financial officers and led to his unhappy departure from the Shrine. Subsequent direc-

tors functioned mostly as caretakers of what was considered one among many buildings on the university campus, subject to the authority of the rector and the Board of Trustees. The Shrine's directors had little authority to make major decisions beyond administering the crypt's liturgical schedule, coordinating *Salve Regina*'s publication and devising ways to increase financial support.

By 1947, circumstances were considerably more hopeful. The Shrine's status as a national enterprise was beyond dispute. Funds were coming in steadily, and the nation's bishops were lining up to share in its completion. No longer was the Shrine merely the cherished hope of a select few. Rather, the U.S. bishops and American Catholics had finally claimed it as their own. Completing the Shrine was now their ambition, the measure of their resolve to establish a lasting testament to the lively devotion and accomplishments of the Catholic Church in America.

During a meeting of the university's Budget Committee early in 1948, treasurer William Galvin recommended that the committee formally propose the Shrine's separate incorporation from the university. Clearly, Galvin and the trustees were eager to relinquish the legal responsibilities concomitant with the oversight and allocation of Shrine funds. With the completion of architectural plans and bid documents, contracts would need to be signed, payment applications would have to be reviewed and approved, and coordination among contractors, subcontractors, artisans and laborers would become a day-to-day responsibility. Separate incorporation was now regarded as both practical and necessary.

In November 1948, the university's Board of Trustees approved the plan as presented. It was agreed, however, that while the university would continue as the Shrine's legally appointed oversight body, the land that the Shrine occupied should be surveyed and deeded to the Shrine by the university. Along with this, the Shrine's assets and liabilities would be transferred to the new corporation as well.

On Dec. 8, 1948, the feast of the Immaculate Conception, the Shrine was legally and perpetually incorporated as the National Shrine of the Immaculate Conception, Inc. While this new independent status did not have a discernible effect on Shrine operations initially — a separate board would not be established until 1968 — it underscored the Shrine's distinct national identity at a time when the country was rallying to

complete it as "a monument to the patroness of our nation."

❧

PRESSING AHEAD

Initially, it would have seemed that the Shrine's separate incorporation from the university would speed the Episcopal Committee's resolve to obtain an architect and prepare construction documents for the superstructure. The Shrine, however, was now subject to an even stricter deliberative body — the full membership of the American bishops — which resisted the only sure means of garnering the substantial funds necessary for completing the massive structure.

The issue of an imposed quota on each bishop and diocese of the country again surfaced at the November 1948 meeting of the National Catholic Welfare Conference. Bishop Noll recounted the Shrine's history for the bishops, as he had on numerous occasions before, and reminded them that the Shrine Committee had yet to retain an architect or establish a schedule for resuming construction. The bishops unanimously approved a motion to proceed with architectural plans and specifications but failed by one vote (27 to 26) to approve a mandatory quota. Bishop Noll and other supporters were beginning to

THE
FOURTH
DIRECTOR

On Feb. 15, 1950, Msgr. Reilly's resignation as the Shrine's third director became effective. Just days before, the Catholic University's rector, Msgr. McCormick, tapped a member of his faculty to take the reins of the Shrine, as was still his prerogative even with the recent separation arrangement.

The Shrine's fourth director was highly regarded as a preacher and professor of eloquence in the university's School of Sacred Theology. Father Patrick "P.J." O'Connor assumed his new post in much the same manner as he had previous assignments throughout his university career: dutifully and with the formality that distinguished him as a gentleman scholar.

Father O'Connor was born in Savannah, Ga., on Jan. 23, 1902. His father, a prominent and successful lawyer, established the Chair of Gaelic Studies at Catholic University with a personal contribution of $50,000 to Bishop Shahan. Father O'Connor, as an undergraduate at the university, attended the Shrine cornerstone-laying ceremony in 1920 and eventually developed a keen respect and admiration for Bishop Shahan and a lasting friendship with the Shrine's first director, Msgr. McKenna.

Ordained for the Diocese of Savannah in 1933 and appointed to the faculty of Catholic University in 1936, Father O'Connor was well acquainted with the Shrine's early beginnings and uncertain progress over the years. Although the directorship of the Shrine was widely considered a difficult assignment, Father O'Connor did not shrink from the new challenge imposed on him. ∞

gain ground in getting the bishops to accept the inevitable. The quota issue would return to confront the bishops another day.

Bishop Noll was undaunted in his efforts to build nationwide support for the Shrine both in the pages of *Our Sunday Visitor* and in his private correspondences with fellow bishops. Again, in 1949, he urged the bishops to take up collections within their respective dioceses, cautioning that "the people" were beginning to doubt that the Shrine would ever be completed. Once again, the bishops resisted approving a quota, and merely accepted the bishop's report with perfunctory expressions of gratitude. With the passing of yet another year, the cost estimate for completing the superstructure would rise 25 percent in keeping with the postwar inflation rate.

∞
1950 — A DECADE OF ACTION

In the 10 years since Father Reilly became director in 1940, the prospect of completing the Shrine had been transformed from a fanciful dream to what an increasing number of Catholics and bishops now considered a foregone conclusion. Only the timing remained to be worked out. During his term as director, Msgr. Reilly succeeded in relieving the Shrine of its considerable debt while building a sizable construction fund of over $2 million. The Shrine's support base, which previously consisted mainly of *Salve Regina* subscribers, now included two-thirds of the 120 dioceses throughout the country. Msgr. Reilly, with the persistent aid of Bishop Noll, had managed to revive what was arguably the most ambitious undertaking ever pursued by American Catholics at a time when the prospects for its realization had never seemed more implausible.

As the decade of the 1940s neared its end, Msgr. Reilly prepared for his departure from the Shrine. The Episcopal Committee, under Bishop Noll and Archbishop O'Boyle (who joined the Shrine's Episcopal Committee in 1948), were chiefly responsible for determining the Shrine's future course. It was now clear to the nation's bishops what they needed to do in order to complete the Shrine, and no director, however enterprising or persuasive, could accomplish the task that was theirs alone to fulfill. If the National Shrine was to be truly "America's Catholic Church," then the Catholic populace, at the urging of their bishops, would have to provide the funds to build it.

Msgr. Reilly returned to his former parish of St. Patrick's in Norwich, Conn.,

Pope Pius XII

and later was named chancellor of the diocese. When the Shrine was dedicated in 1959, he took his honored place among two of the Shrine's previous directors to celebrate the proud fruit of his dedicated labors.

THE DOGMA OF THE ASSUMPTION

If the events of the decade begun in 1940 served to rescue the Shrine and establish a more promising outlook, circumstances in 1950 and events in the decade to follow provided the momentum to ensure its completion. The Shrine's prospects were considerably bolstered when Pope Pius XII designated 1950 a Holy Year. Later that year, on the feast of All Saints, the Pope proclaimed the dogma of the Assumption, only the second Marian dogma proclaimed by any pope in 100 years. In this same year, the university's rector, Msgr. McCormick, was consecrated a bishop at the Shrine, and Father O'Connor was made a monsignor.

The timing of Pope Pius' proclamation could not have been more propitious for the Shrine. Catholics in America were keenly interested in completing the National Shrine, having participated in several Mother's Day collections. With the proclamation of the dogma of the Assumption, Catholics had a new impetus to establish a national monument to Mary's role as protectress and intercessor. Once again, a reigning pope would help make the difference in inspiring widespread support for the National Shrine.

During a visit to the apostolic delegation in Washington in 1950, Msgr. O'Connor secured the promise of a second mosaic from the Vatican: a reproduction of Titian's painting of the Assumption. (The exquisite mosaic, created by Vatican mosaicists, eventually arrived at the Shrine during the pontificate of Pope John XXIII.)

The August 1951 edition of *Salve Regina* recorded a significant event that served to further validate efforts to complete the Shrine. Pope Pius X was beatified by Pope Pius XII, the first step toward

Mosaic of Titian's "Assumption," gift of Popes Pius XII and John XXIII.

his eventual canonization in 1954. Honoring the saintly Pontiff's enthusiastic endorsement of the National Shrine, the work of completing the church was now regarded as the mandate not only of the American bishops, but of a future saint. It was, after all, Pope Pius X who, in his 1914 apostolic letter, declared that "nothing could be more useful to the Church or further more helpfully the welfare of the Republic" than the establishment of the National Shrine.

In the early part of 1951, Archbishop O'Boyle expedited plans to resume construction by authorizing the architects to draft the first set of architectural proposals in nearly 30 years. In the 1920s and 1930s, the Shrine's architects had been preoccupied with completing as much of the crypt level as possible before dwindling funds necessitated an indefinite halt to construction. As a result, Maginnis and Walsh had not ventured to produce detailed architectural drawings of the Shrine's Great Upper Church. Archbishop O'Boyle expressed the urgent need to produce the drawings of what, until now, had existed only conceptually as a "magnificent Catholic church" with "cathedral-like proportions." The Shrine Committee had conceded in 1950 that the Shrine could not be completed by 1954.

Washington's new archbishop was in a prime position to speed things along. In anticipation of the bishops' meeting of November 1952, Archbishop O'Boyle commissioned Eugene F. Kennedy Jr., an architect with Maginnis and Walsh, to draw up three separate proposals — each one of differing physical proportion and detail — to present to the bishops for a vote. The proposal selected would establish the parameters that the architect would need to produce actual plans and specifications. Archbishop O'Boyle was intent on forcing the nation's bishops to proceed. He shrewdly calculated the advantage of presenting three different plans, thus enabling the bishops to claim responsibility for deciding both the scope and, ultimately, the amount to be

(from left) **Cardinal Edward Mooney of Detroit, Cardinal Samuel Stritch of Chicago, Cardinal Francis J. Spellman of New York and Cardinal James F. McIntyre of Los Angeles review a archectectural rendering of the "proposed" Shrine, November 1953.**

"It was not, Mother of the Incarnate, (Sweet Rose of Sharon and God's spotless maid)
Designed that one conceived Immaculate
And nowise by the breath of sin dismayed
Should know the dust and darkness of the grave."
— Daniel E. Doran

expended on the Shrine's construction.

Meanwhile, Bishop Noll continued to point out the inevitable financial consequences of delayed construction. In a letter to the nation's bishops in the summer of 1952, He noted that since 1946, the cost estimate for the superstructure had nearly doubled, from $4,168,000 to an estimated $7,382,500. He further chastised the bishops for not encouraging schoolchildren of their dioceses to do their part and suggested that "their teachers are probably the most interested of all in the completion of this Shrine to the Heavenly Mother, whose name each one of them bears. They could easily induce the children to give a nickel or dime a year during a period of five years." Bishop Noll was determined to gain the necessary funds in every way imaginable. Each and every Catholic, regardless of

An architectural model of the proposed National Shrine of the Immaculate Conception, circa 1930s.

In 1951, prospects for completing the National Shrine had never seemed more promising. The nation's bishops, at the promptings of the Episcopal Committee and Bishop Noll in particular, were showing signs that they had begun to accept the inevitable. Still, Bishop Noll was more insistent than ever that the Episcopal Committee contract an architect — any architect — to complete working drawings for the Shrine's superstructure. The advancing age of Charles Maginnis caused more than a few members of the Episcopal Committee, most notably Archbishop O'Boyle, to question the wisdom of contracting him to produce the drawings necessary for gaining competitive construction bids. Even Archbishop Richard Cushing of Boston was dragged into the debate over Maginnis' competency. Noting that Maginnis and Walsh had recently produced a set of superbly drawn plans for a $5 million hospital intended for his archdiocese, Archbishop Cushing suggested that the 40-member firm could easily produce working drawings within a year.

A contract with Maginnis and Walsh was signed on Dec. 8, 1952, a month after the bishops' approval for the national appeal at their November meeting.

Anxiety over the ability of the Maginnis and Walsh firm to fulfill the ambitious task

of completing detailed architectural drawings, however, was not easily dispelled.

Prior to signing the contract with Maginnis and Walsh, the Board of Trustees required that Maginnis' son, Charles Jr., be added as a full partner to ensure the firm's "legal perpetuity" in the event of the elder Maginnis' death. Soon thereafter, unfortunately, the younger Maginnis was diagnosed with cancer, requiring further assurance of the firm's legal perpetuity beyond the debilitation or death of the firm's principals.

William L. Galvin, the university treasurer, proposed a solution: In the event of the younger Maginnis' death, either the firm would be made a corporation, or Eugene F. Kennedy Jr. — who was chief designer of the firm from 1926 to 1941 and whose previous projects included three cathedrals, several college buildings and a hospital — would be made a full partner.

The younger Maginnis died on Feb. 25, 1954. That same year, the firm became Maginnis, Walsh and Kennedy, and Kennedy became the primary architect of the National Shrine. He continued to work with Archbishop O'Boyle and a succession of directors to complete the Shrine interior until his death on Nov. 7, 1986. ∽

CONTRACTUAL INTRIGUE

(above) Msgr. Patrick "P.J." O'Connor speaks with Paul J. Hauck, of McShain Contracting Company, as plans to resume construction progress.

(left) Eugene F. Kennedy Jr.

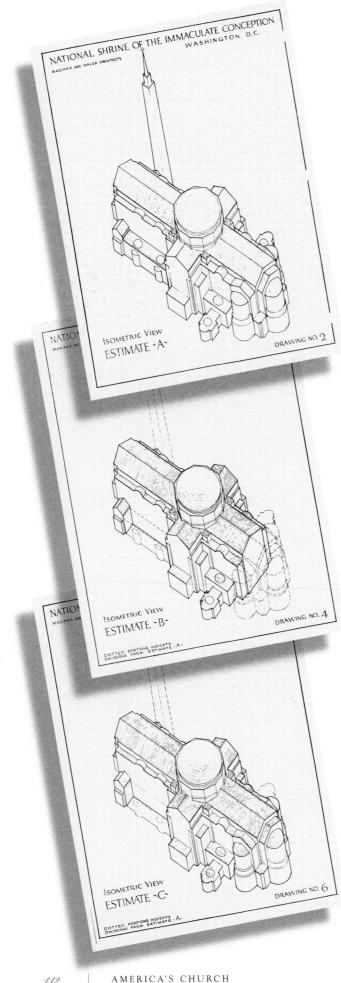

NATIONAL SHRINE OF THE IMMACULATE CONCEPTION
WASHINGTON D.C.

MAGINNIS AND WALSH - ARCHITECTS

ISOMETRIC VIEW
ESTIMATE ~A~

DRAWING NO. 2

ISOMETRIC VIEW
ESTIMATE ~B~

DRAWING NO. 4

DOTTED PORTIONS INDICATE
OMISSIONS FROM ESTIMATE ~A~

ISOMETRIC VIEW
ESTIMATE ~C~

DRAWING NO. 6

DOTTED PORTIONS INDICATE
OMISSIONS FROM ESTIMATE ~A~

age or means, would be called upon to do his or her part.

It should be noted that Bishop Noll was equally committed to ensuring that the nation's priests contribute as well. If even four-fifths of the nation's clergy contributed a mere $5 a year (or $25 during the five-year period), he reasoned, an additional $1 million could be raised. "But they have not been asked to do anything by their ordinaries," he admonished.

'A, B OR C?'

On April 3, 1952, in response to Archbishop O'Boyle's initiative, the university's Board of Trustees directed the Executive Committee of the Shrine to review the architect's proposals and vote on the version to recommend to the nation's bishops. On June 25, 1952, the committee reviewed the three distinct proposals and their respective cost estimates as presented by Charles Maginnis Jr. and Eugene Kennedy of the Maginnis and Walsh firm.

The first proposal, titled "Estimate A," included the exact proportions that had first been suggested 33 years prior. The "original" scheme was estimated to cost $18,932,879. The architects made clear that to reduce these intended proportions would substantially compromise the integrity of Maginnis' grand design and incur additional costs to modify the foundations.

The second proposal, "Estimate B," included many of the major elements of "Estimate A" but eliminated the campanile (Knights' Tower), the lateral nave chapels, the triple apse of the superstructure and the west sacristy (present-day Blessed Sacrament Chapel). This considerably scaled-down version was given a cost estimate of $14,761,125.

The third estimate, "Estimate C," likewise excluded the campanile, the lateral nave chapels, and the west sacristy, but maintained the triple northern apses of the superstructure.

The architects further suggested two supplementary proposals that allowed for compromises to the interior design in addition to the alterations already suggested for the exterior. "Estimate B-1" was essentially "Estimate B" with the exclusion of bronze doors, interior marble cladding and stained glass. This version came with a cost estimate of $11,155.456. "Estimate C-1" was patterned after "Estimate C" (including the triple northern apse) and called for the same interior exclusions as "Estimate B-1." This plan was estimated to cost $12,284,735.

The Executive Committee insisted that the architects adhere to the Shrine's

The Shrine's fourth director, Msgr. Patrick "P.J." O'Connor, and visiting students look wistfully upon the planned National Shrine, still in its model phase.

original plan ("Estimate A") with its inclusion of the campanile. The committee further requested that a total cost estimate for the entire interior completion be prepared, including architectural fees, as well as the potential costs that would result from postponing construction of various sections. London's Westminster Cathedral provided a precedent for building a great church without interior marble cladding. The committee proposed a careful study of a brick interior "until sufficient funds have been secured for the installation of marble veneer."

The committee's views, however, were not shared by the full Board of Trustees of the university. The trustees were unanimous in their decision only to consider "Estimate C-1." There would be no campanile, side lateral nave chapels or west sacristy; nor would there be bronze doors, marble walls or stained glass. Archbishop O'Boyle had no choice but to present the trustees' recommendation to the nation's bishops at their fall meeting.

∞

THE QUOTA

At the 1952 bishops' meeting, two key issues concerning the Shrine had yet to be resolved. The first was relatively simple compared with the more controversial issue of establishing a quota. Bishop Noll reiterated the inherent problems involved with scaling back the original proportions, given that the foundations were already in place. He emphasized that the architects, too, were opposed to diminishing Maginnis' original design even minimally. Still, the bishops could not ignore the fact that a reduction of the Shrine's height by a mere 10 feet would reduce the Shrine's cost by $500,000. The bishops agreed to the recommendation of the university's board to proceed with the signing of the contract for "Estimate C-1."

Clearing the way for the architects to proceed with actual drawings, the bishops now grappled with the more contentious issue of how to raise the necessary funds for construction. Archbishop O'Boyle stressed the need for the bishops to agree, once and for all, to accepting a minimum contribution quota before authorizing the architect to proceed with detailed drawings. He stipulated that no funds were to be borrowed for construction, encouraging instead an all-out campaign by the nation's bishops during 1953 and 1954 to raise the estimated $8 million needed to get the job done. Slightly over $4 million had already been collected by Oct. 31, 1952.

As in previous meetings, the proposed quota occasioned considerable discussion and disagreement. Some of the bishops expressed concern that a quota would actually limit some dioceses from contributing more than the quota amount. Others, principally Cardinal Spellman of New York, cautioned that the bishops would be committing themselves to an amount equaling 36 times their annual assessment to the National Catholic Welfare Conference. To mollify these concerns, Bishop Noll and Archbishop O'Boyle explained the formula for arriving at a diocese's particular quota: If each of the nation's 28 million Catholics were to donate a mere 25 cents (or $1 for a family of four) over the course of five years, the estimated $8 million for

construction would easily be raised.

After a protracted discussion, the issue finally came to a head. The bishops were assured that funds already committed by their dioceses would be deducted from their quota. It was further suggested that dioceses should not be limited in the amount they wished to contribute. The quota would serve only to establish a minimum requirement. Archbishop John F. O'Hara, C.S.C., of Philadelphia urged that the fund-raising drive begin on Dec. 8, 1953, and continue through 1954.

In the end, Bishop Noll and Archbishop O'Boyle prevailed. The nation's bishops had finally agreed to the quota — and, with it, accepted their formal responsibility for ensuring the completion of the nation's patronal church.

Msgr. O'Connor greets pilgrims of all ages during the Holy Year of 1950.

A MAGNIFICENT CATHOLIC CHURCH

A PROPHECY FULFILLED

1952 - 1959

The nationwide campaign to collect the nearly $9 million required to build the superstructure of the National Shrine was an unprecedented undertaking by America's Catholic bishops. No other effort had received greater notoriety or involved greater risk. When the earlier phase of building the crypt was halted by Archbishop Curley because of a lack of funds, it was not widely regarded as a failure on the part of the nation's bishops to lend adequate support, but as a result of forces beyond anyone's control — the Great Depression. Furthermore, because the Shrine had been begun by Bishop Shahan, first as a university chapel and only later as a national tribute to Mary, many considered the Shrine to be the personal project of Bishop

Shahan and his trusted assistant, Msgr. McKenna.

Now the stakes were higher. The generosity of America's Catholics was being tested. It was a cause that simply could not be permitted to fail. Bishop Noll obtained a letter, dated Dec. 11, 1951, and signed by Msgr. Giovanni Montini (the future Pope Paul VI), expressing the approval of Pope Pius XII that the bishops were collaborating in the work to raise funds to complete the Shrine. Bishop Noll sent the letter to Archbishop O'Boyle in order to further impress upon him the importance of their collaboration in sufficiently preparing for the 1953 appeal.

Archbishop O'Boyle devised a strategy to ensure that the high expectations for

the first nationwide appeal of 1953 would be fulfilled. He enlisted the help of three men whose expertise in the areas of finance, public relations and administration was tried and true. Edward M. Kinney, general manager of Institutional Commodity Services in New York, would provide valuable advice on the costs and logistics of a national appeal. Burke Walsh, assistant director of the National Catholic Welfare Conference News Service (now Catholic News Service), would coordinate publicity. Father John B. Roeder, vice chancellor of the Archdiocese of Washington and director of the Family Rosary Crusade of 1951 that brought more than 75,000 people together at the Washington Monument, would serve as the appeal's national director. These men, along with Catholic University treasurer William L. Galvin and assistant treasurer Msgr. James A. Magner, constituted the brain trust of the Shrine project.

Earlier in the century, the Shrine had successfully used radio broadcasts to build national support. In 1952, however, a new medium was available to spread the "good news" of the Shrine's impending completion and prepare Catholics for the upcoming national appeal. Fortunately, the host of one of America's most popular television programs of the day was also a prominent Catholic prelate who was only too willing to advance the Shrine's cause on the airwaves. Bishop Fulton J. Sheen provided the necessary "star power" needed to ensure success of the Shrine appeal.

At a meeting of the Executive Committee for the Shrine on May 27, 1953, it was decided that Sunday, Dec. 6, would be the national collection date. It was noted that the Shrine had a total of $3,600,142.68 in the bank; that the total cost of building the superstructure was estimated to be $12,284,735; that the amount needed to be collected was $8,684,592.32, a quota 37 times each diocese's annual assessment by the NCWC. The committee further agreed to request a definite commitment from each ordinary to accept a specified quota, with the stipulation that the bishops accept responsibility for any outstanding balance that fell short of their quota after the Dec. 6 appeal.

Archbishop O'Boyle was appointed general chairman of the appeal, and the National Shrine was designated as the official headquarters for coordinating appeal efforts.

The impressive publicity machine of the National Shrine was now prepared to shift into high gear. Under the able direction of public-relations director

Walsh, one of the most extensive publicity campaigns ever undertaken by the Catholic Church in the United States was launched. Between September and November 1953, Walsh sent out nine separate press releases to the Catholic and secular press describing the Shrine's early beginnings, the resounding support expressed by five popes and pending plans to resume construction. Diocesan directors were provided specific details of all aspects of the planned appeal. Newspaper fillers and sample letters to the editor were also suggested.

It was clear that the role of the diocesan directors would be invaluable. They would ultimately be responsible for disseminating the avalanche of information concerning the Shrine for the Catholic

(opposite) A solitary statue of "Mary, Mother of Mankind," within a partially completed Memorial Hall.

(above) A student nurse from Mercy Hospital observes the start of the Marian Year, Dec. 8, 1953.

Msgr. O'Connor greets the apostolic delegate, Archbishop Amleto Giovanni Cicognani, with filial respect upon his arrival at the Shrine to mark the beginning of the Marian Year, 1953.

ed an editorial that read in part:

"For the Catholic community the Shrine particularly honors Mary as patroness of America, but to other Christian groups it has attraction as a tremendous affirmation of the teachings of Her Son, the principal founder of civilization. It follows that all Americans, even those who profess no religious affiliation, should wish to share in bringing the work to completion. Every aspect of its progress will be an answer to the threat of materialism and specifically the challenge of communism."

and secular media. Directors were also provided "The Handbook for Teachers," which contained extensive information on the dogma of the Immaculate Conception, historical details of the Shrine and information about notable Marian shrines throughout the world. Directors also received professionally printed fact sheets, historical data, time schedules, collection envelopes, pictures for use in newspapers, as well as recommendations from appeal headquarters on how to further publicize the all-important mission of completing America's pre-eminent church.

Walsh's efforts achieved their intended effect. The secular media eventually took the bait and did their part to bolster publicity for the Shrine. On Oct. 20, 1953, Washington's *Evening Star* includ-

If there remained any doubt about the validity of the cause to complete the Shrine, the apostolic letter of Pope Pius XII, addressed to Archbishop O'Boyle and dated Oct. 2, 1953, provided the highest validation. It was Archbishop O'Boyle who petitioned the apostolic delegate, Archbishop Amleto Giovanni Cicognani, for a letter from the Pope, knowing the positive impact it would have on the bishops. The Pope's letter, which concluded with the assurance of an apostolic blessing for the "noble undertaking," represented unqualified support for the great undertaking now at hand.

In the Shrine's nearly 50-year history, never had all of the necessary components needed to ensure its success combined so smoothly as they had in 1953. The bishops of the United States had rallied to ensure that the Shrine's construc-

tion was truly a national enterprise. Catholics were eager to finish the project that their parents and grandparents had begun through modest contributions. The Catholic and secular media were generating a steady stream of publicity about the impending appeal and construction. And the Pope himself had provided added momentum by declaring the year of the appeal (1954) a Marian Year.

In his encyclical *Fulgens Corona Gloriae* ("Shining Crown of Glory"), pro-

mulgated on Sept. 8, 1953, the feast of the Nativity of Mary, Pope Pius XII urged Catholics throughout the world to observe 1954 as a Marian Year to commemorate the centenary of the proclamation of the dogma of the Immaculate Conception. In urging renewed devotion to Mary, the Holy Father stressed the benefits of public devotions and pilgrimages to Marian shrines in various parts of the world as a way to "furnish beautiful demonstrations of the love of

Attired in the splendor of his ecclesiastical robes, Archbishop Cicognani processes into the Crypt Church to celebrate the Holy Father's designation of 1954 as a Marian Year.

the faithful for the Heavenly Mother. . . . Since in all cities, towns and villages wherever the Christian religion thrives there is a sanctuary or at least an altar, in which the sacred image of the Blessed Virgin Mary is enshrined for the devotion of the Christian people."

∞

DAY OF RECKONING

By October, CBS-TV confirmed its intention to air an interview with Archbishop John O'Hara of Philadelphia regarding the approaching national collection during its Nov. 20 broadcast of *Lamp Unto My Feet;* the CBS Radio program *The Church of the Air* likewise planned to feature a talk by prominent Catholic historian Msgr. John Tracy Ellis on the same day; and a 15-minute radio broadcast was planned by the Mutual Broadcasting Company featuring Bishop Sheen speaking from the Crypt Church just prior to appeal Sunday.

Among the most important publicity events was a major address by Bishop Sheen, to be broadcast as a kinescope and carried nationally by NBC-TV affiliate stations. Bishop Sheen spoke from the crypt on Wednesday, Nov. 18, 1953, at 2 p.m. His address was telecast to New York, where it was filmed and edited.

With Bishop Sheen as the "celebrity" spokesman, it fell to the appointed diocesan directors to put eloquent words into discernible action. Each diocesan director was responsible for contacting his local NBC affiliate to request that it order the kinescope from New York and

From left, Archbishop Noll, Bishop Fulton J. Sheen, Archbishop O'Boyle and Msgr. O'Connor gather in the crypt for Bishop Sheen's nationwide-broadcast appeal, made available as a kinescope by NBC.

air it prior to the Dec. 6 national collection. In addition to the Bishop Sheen broadcast, 75,000 posters were distributed to parishes throughout the country. The posters featured a rendering of the Shrine with the words, "A Gift to Mary for a Shrine to Signify Catholic America's Devotion to the Mother of God. Pray to Mary — Give to Mary." Nine million collection envelopes, background leaflets, a strategy handbook for each diocesan director and a variety of publicity aids were provided.

By the end of November, 115 of 127 dioceses throughout the country were poised to take up the collection. The efforts of Burke Walsh, the campaign's publicity expert, had paid off. The secular media responded to his "pitches" and ultimately played an important part in enhancing the profile of the Shrine appeal.

On Nov. 29, on that same day CBS Radio and TV were publicizing the approaching appeal, Archbishop Noll's newspaper, *Our Sunday Visitor*, ran a large front-page article about the National Shrine appeal. On Nov. 30, novenas to Mary Immaculate were begun across the country. As planned, Bishop Sheen took to the radio and television airwaves three days before the Dec. 6 appeal to present a stirring justification

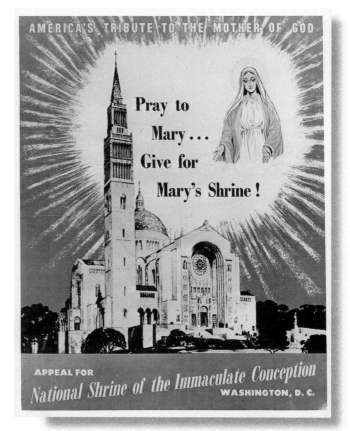

for the completion of the National Shrine for the millions listening and watching. The pre-eminent Catholic television personality implored the nation's Catholics to build the National Shrine as a "national act of worship to God" for the inalienable rights of life, liberty and the pursuit of happiness — rights evoked by the Founding Fathers but ultimately emanating from God. Bishop Sheen further urged Catholics to build the Shrine as a force for combating evil — and, more specifically, communism, "the mystical body of the antichrist."

Suggesting Marian devotion as the proper antidote to communism, Bishop Sheen railed against the ominous forces that threatened to undermine the dignity of the human race:

"Thirty-seven out of 100 people in the world today are beaten by that hammer and cut by that sickle. There is danger that we might be engulfed by these barbarians. . . . If there be this evil thing marching through the world, it is fitting that we make some sacrifice in order to affirm our love of God and to invoke the assistance of the woman whom God said would overcome the Red Serpent!"

In his characteristically dramatic style, Bishop Sheen concluded:

"Through these sacrifices we will pile under the architecture of divine love stone upon stone until it all cries out in praise to God and in truth that we love the woman whom God chose — His mother — and yours."

In the week following the national collection, the National Catholic News Service issued an early report of collection results and proclaimed the appeal a "triumphant success." Funds continued to trickle in as late as the spring and summer. But by October 1954, the final figures revealed that the collection had actually failed to reach the amount pledged by all the participating dioceses. The total amount collected came to $6,156,719.69, bringing the Shrine fund to a total of $9,756,862.37. The appeal had missed the quota target by nearly $4 million and was roughly $4.2 million less than the 1954 estimated construction cost. In the months and years ahead, Archbishop O'Boyle would successfully urge his fellow bishops to provide the remaining funds needed to complete the National Shrine.

THE BUILDER

In 1954, there were few contractors in the country more qualified to build a structure of the magnitude of the National Shrine than John McShain Jr. of Philadelphia.

A devout Catholic, McShain made a lasting imprint on the landscape of the nation's capital. His more notable accomplishments included the Jefferson Memorial, the Pentagon, the buildings of the State Department, the Department of Agriculture and the Bureau of Printing and Engraving, the Department of Housing and Urban Development, the National Institutes of Health in Bethesda, Md., the renovation of the White House during the Truman administration and the John F. Kennedy Center for the Performing Arts. Still, McShain regarded the opportunity to complete the superstructure of the National Shrine as the culmination of his life's work, the fulfillment of his "life's ambition." In later years, he characterized the National Shrine project as "the greatest project I have ever undertaken," and further recalled that "looking back over the 55 years I have spent in the building business, no single enterprise or undertaking

that offers the thrill or the satisfaction which I received from the assignment to erect the superstructure of the Shrine of the Immaculate Conception."

McShain was determined to win the contract to build the Shrine and even resorted to lobbying the general secretary of the National Catholic Welfare Conference, Msgr. Howard J. Carroll. At one point, he contemplated writing each bishop of the country to make known his intense interest in the Shrine project, as well as his impressive credentials. As it turned out, McShain's aggressive lobbying strategy proved unnecessary, since Eugene Kennedy of Maginnis and Walsh was intent on inviting McShain to bid on the Shrine job. Two other firms were also invited to bid: the George A. Fuller Company of New York and the McCarthy Brothers Construction Company of St. Louis.

Early in his career, McShain adopted the practice of submitting his bid for a particular job based on what he thought the job might actually cost — rather than inflating his bid to enhance his profit margin. This approach served McShain well over the years and ultimately resulted in his winning the contract to build the Great Upper Church. McShain's low bid of $12,197,000 (actually $87,000 less than the architects' 1953 estimate) secured for him the mantle of the Shrine's "builder." Inflation over the next five years, however, would render his figure, as well as the 1954 cost estimate of $11,104,800 developed by

(above) Archbishop O'Boyle presides over a blessing rite on Nov. 15, 1954.

(right) Assisted by the Shrine's first director, Msgr. Bernard A. McKenna (far left), Archbishop O'Boyle officially resumes construction on the National Shrine during a blessing ceremony on Nov. 17, 1954. Also on hand are (from right) Msgr. John Reilly, Msgr. O'Connor, Msgr. James Magner (partially hidden), Eugene Kennedy, John McShain, William Galvin, Bishop McEntegart and two unidentified clerics.

(inset) Ceremonial trowel used by Archbishop O'Boyle to resume construction, along with trowel and mallet (black handles) used by Cardinal Gibbons to bless the foundation stone on Sept. 23, 1920.

NO TURNING BACK

Described as "the major Marian Year project of the Church in the United States," the National Shrine actually represented the most significant single project ever undertaken by the Church in the United States. To inaugurate the resumption of the building project, Archbishop O'Boyle presided over a blessing rite on Nov. 15, 1954, in the presence of 100 bishops, the apostolic delegate and four American cardinals at the conclusion of a Marian convocation hosted by Catholic University. The large assembly of distinguished churchmen, laity, and government and diplomatic officials gathered for this official Church event was unprecedented. No one could have felt greater pride and personal satisfaction on the occasion than the elderly monsignor assigned to assist Archbishop O'Boyle during the ceremony, Msgr. McKenna. The Shrine's first director traveled from his parish in Philadelphia to the place where he had toiled for 17 years alongside his friend, collaborator and mentor, Bishop Shahan, to ensure that the Shrine would one day become a reality.

With construction at last underway, the Shrine had entered a new era as a distinctly national enterprise — no longer a local project aimed at just satisfying the liturgical needs of The Catholic University of America.

Edward Sharf, meaningless. *Salve Regina* announced McShain's selection in its November 1954 edition and, as if to remind the builder of his higher obligations, noted:

> "We know that this work of the McShain Company will be looked upon by its officers not only as a business venture of the highest merit, but as a venture of great spiritual achievement."

Facing the painful prospect of relinquishing his cherished teaching position, Msgr. O'Connor decides instead to depart the Shrine.

THE FIFTH DIRECTOR
— Msgr. Thomas J. Grady —

Faced with the impending construction of the largest church in the Western Hemisphere, Msgr. O'Connor felt the strain of balancing his cherished role as a university professor with the Shrine's increasingly complicated management. Eventually, he concluded that his talents could better be utilized at the university than at the Shrine. He submitted his resignation as director to the university's board on Oct. 10, 1955, in order to resume full-time teaching.

Archbishop O'Boyle was eager to have a director undivided in his attention to the affairs of the National Shrine. He approached Cardinal Samuel Stritch, archbishop of Chicago, to determine if he might have a priest available to "loan" to the Shrine. The Chicago prelate was well acquainted with Msgr. Thomas J. Grady's skills as an administrator; he was procurator of Mundelein Seminary on the outskirts of Chicago where, incidentally, the Cardinal maintained an auxiliary residence. Throughout the spring and summer of 1956, Cardinal Stritch spoke often to Msgr. Grady about the National Shrine and sought to gauge his feelings about a Shrine appointment. According to Msgr. Grady's own recollection, he expressed his willingness to go wherever the cardinal desired to send him, yet repeatedly assured his superior that he was content with his position at Chicago's prominent seminary.

Thomas J. Grady was born in Chicago on Oct. 9, 1914; the son of Michael J. Grady, a Chicago police captain and chief of detectives. He attended Quigley Preparatory Seminary in Chicago from 1927-32, and St. Mary of the Lake Seminary in Mundelein, Ill., from 1932-38. He was ordained at the seminary on April 23, 1938. Msgr. Grady continued his studies at Gregorian University in Rome from 1938-39, after which he returned to Chicago to take up duties as English professor and spiritual director at Quigley. In September 1945, he was appointed procurator at Mundelein; in 1953, he was elevated to the honorary rank of monsignor.

After his appointment to the Shrine in the summer of 1956, Msgr. Grady immersed himself in all aspects of his new position. He even contributed two lengthy articles on the Shrine's history and iconography for *American Ecclesiastical Review.* Among his first priorities was to gain a firm grasp on the financial situation; the bookkeeping and formal reports were still prepared by the staff of Catholic University. For his first

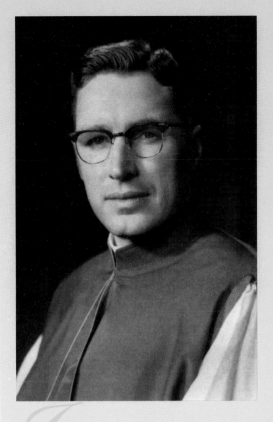

THE FIFTH DIRECTOR

In the summer of 1956, Cardinal Samuel Stritch of Chicago asked Msgr. Thomas J. Grady, then procurator at St. Mary of the Lake Seminary in Mundelein, Ill., to accompany Archbishop Patrick O'Boyle of Washington and others concerned with the Shrine to St. Joseph's Oratory in Montreal, Canada, to study food service. During the trip, Msgr. Grady and Archbishop O'Boyle intensely discussed the Shrine and the many aspects that would have to be considered after its completion. The archbishop saw in Msgr. Grady the keen reasoning ability and decisiveness that would serve the Shrine well. Shortly after his return to Chicago, Msgr. Grady received a perfunctory letter from Cardinal Stritch informing him of his appointment as director of the Shrine.

(above) Inspecting the highest reaches of "his" church, Msgr. Thomas J. Grady scales the "great forest" of scaffolding for a closer look, circa 1957.

This included overseeing the construction process, resolving the inevitable conflicts that surfaced among artisans, subcontractors and contractors, producing frequent progress reports for the Episcopal Committee, devising solicitations to send to the Shrine's benefactors, writing and editing the *Salve Regina* newsletter and administering the active liturgical schedule, which continued uninterrupted in the Shrine's crypt.

three years, Msgr. Grady single-handedly managed the whirl of activity at the Shrine as the sole "priest-in-residence."

The construction process moved ahead as anticipated, and the shell of the National Shrine gradually began to take form. With each new edition of *Salve Regina*, readers could begin to see the fruits of their generosity through dra-

matic photographs and detailed descriptions of the work underway. The wood scaffolding erected by construction crews created the appearance of what Archbishop O'Boyle described as a "great forest." Builder John McShain later recounted the most challenging aspect of the Shrine's construction:

"Perhaps the most trying part of the work involved the dome, and while the design was not too unusual, the installation of the form work, the laying of the tile and concrete work had to be done very carefully and with precision. Each piece of tile was marked and set in place according to a plan. We found it very difficult to find men with the necessary experience to do this work. The average age of these men was 50 years, and unless the applicant had a background of experience he would not be acceptable. The weather was also a problem and little progress was made on the dome during the second year of construction. No erection of materials was per-

missible unless the temperature was above 32 degrees [Fahrenheit], and there were periods when no work was done for a week or longer. Every day after the men installed the materials it was necessary to protect this work with tarpaulins. As the dome gradually was completed and the wood formwork was removed, the tile work looked perfect and received high praise from the architect. There was however a period of time while we were removing the supports that we had many anxious moments for we knew that the failure of any part of the shoring would mean a catastrophe. So once again our prayers were answered."

Archbishop John F. Noll

∞
'IF IT HAD NOT BEEN FOR HIM'

Just as the Shrine's long dormant stage was ending, the man most responsible for reviving strong national interest in the Shrine passed from this world. On July 31, 1956, Archbishop Noll died. (He had been named a titular archbishop in 1953.) The August edition of *Salve Regina* recorded Archbishop Noll's indispensable role in reviving efforts to resume the Shrine's construction with the heading, "If It Had Not Been for Him."

What Bishop Shahan was to the Shrine prior to the commencement of construction in 1922, Archbishop Noll was to the Shrine in the years leading to the resumption of construction in 1954. Few in the Shrine's history worked as tirelessly to build national support for the Shrine as Archbishop Noll. He was unabashedly stubborn in his resolve to gain the backing of the nation's bishops to complete the Shrine. To him, the method was simple: Every Catholic in the United States, from schoolchild to senior citizen, would be asked to join in the work of erecting a national monument of Catholic faith in America.

For Archbishop Noll, one's commitment to the work of completing the Shrine was a litmus test of allegiance to Catholic faith and devotion. His most difficult challenge and greatest accomplishment involved gaining the full support and cooperation of the nation's bishops in the effort. He cajoled, pleaded, and often badgered his fellow bishops into accepting a quota based on the number of Catholic households in their respective dioceses as the surest means of acquiring the funds necessary to resume and complete construction.

Beginning in 1943, and continuing into the early 1950s Archbishop Noll frequently employed the weekly *Our Sunday Visitor* to plead the Shrine's case among its vast readership. His determined efforts resulted in the formation in 1944 of the bishops' Episcopal Committee, which he chaired, to study the feasibility of completing the Shrine. By 1952, Archbishop Noll had succeeded in bringing the issue of a national fund-raising campaign to a decisive vote among the bishops. In the succeeding year, the national appeal was being prepared and an extensive publicity machine was churning out a regular supply of supporting information to the secular and religious media as well as to the nation's diocesan directors responsible for coordinating the appeal on the local level.

Although slowed by an initial stroke in 1951 that required him to relinquish his chairmanship of the Shrine's Episcopal Committee, Archbishop Noll continued to keep abreast of the fund-raising and building progress until his final day.

In 1953, Msgr. O'Connor, in the presence of Archbishop Noll, unveiled a testimonial tablet in Memorial Hall honoring the archbishop's unsurpassed efforts on behalf of the Shrine as the chairman of the Episcopal Committee for the Shrine. The tablet carries the heading, "Mary's beloved son." Prior to his death, Archbishop Noll took great satisfaction in the knowledge that his efforts had made the difference in advancing the Shrine's completion.

AN ANONYMOUS GIFT

In early January 1957, Msgr. Grady received a letter addressed simply, "To Whom It May Concern," in which the sender enclosed a check in the amount of $40,000. The generous writer indicated his desire "to make a gift toward the construction of the Shrine partly to discharge an obligation we all have toward building it and partly to make it available — a little sooner, perhaps — in its completed form to Catholics to worship."

As amazing as the unsolicited donation was to Msgr. Grady, the letter went on to explain that the $40,000 was only the first part of a much larger gift. Eventually, the remaining amount was transferred to the Shrine in the form of stocks and bonds, resulting in a total gift of $119,000. The generous benefactor closed his letter to Msgr. Grady with the expressed desire to remain anonymous. This represented the largest gift ever given by a single individual to date.

The question of who would give such a significant amount must surely have intrigued Msgr. Grady. Tracing the address listed on the donor's stocks and bonds, the director attempted to telephone the man, assuming that he must be an elderly, well-to-do, retired business executive. After eventually reaching the donor's brother, Msgr. Grady learned that his benefactor was not an aged philanthropist, but a young man only 25 years of age. It was decided that the young man's generosity would be designated to fund the majestic Pantocrator mosaic intended for the north apse.

On the Day of Dedication, a special seat was reserved for this devoted son of Mary's shrine.

∞

ICONOGRAPHY OF
THE NATIONAL SHRINE

What few saw amid the public campaign to resume construction of the National Shrine were the tedious deliberations involved with determining the iconography of the country's patronal church. As early as 1954, plans were underway to establish an iconography committee charged with selecting the appropriate theological themes to be translated on the Shrine's massive exterior by some of the world's foremost sculptors of the day.

Among the first to be retained as a consultant was John De Rosen, whose credentials in ecclesiastical art had been firmly established by his work in creating murals and stained-glass windows for the Armenian Catholic Cathedral in Lwow, Poland, in 1925-37, and his commission to decorate the private chapel of Pope Pius XI at Castel Gandolfo in 1933. Born in Warsaw, Poland, in 1891, De Rosen studied at the universities of Lausanne, Munich and Paris. After service in the French and Polish armies in World War I, he devoted his life to art. In 1937, De Rosen emigrated to the United States and became an American citizen. From 1939 to 1946, he lectured at The Catholic University of America while occupying a Chair of Liturgical Art.

Eugene Kennedy had advocated the formation of an iconography committee early on, knowing the delicate nature of suggesting proposals for the Shrine's iconography to the body of churchmen

THOU ART THE GLORY
OF JERUSALEM THE JOY OF ISRAEL
THE HONOUR OF OUR PEOPLE

IN THEE SHALL
ALL BE BLESSED

LET US SING
TO THE LORD

TO BRING THEE
GOOD TIDINGS

HAIL MARY FULL OF GRACE
THE LORD IS WITH THEE

MY EYES HAVE SEEN
THY SALVATION

OUR LEAST ACTION WHEN DONE FOR GOD IS PRECIOUS

responsible for overseeing the Shrine. De Rosen offered his services to Archbishop O'Boyle in June 1954. After a lengthy discussion on the necessity of finding a qualified person well-versed in sacred iconography to work with a committee of theologians from the university, Archbishop O'Boyle was convinced that De Rosen was the right individual for the complicated task ahead. After obtaining further assurances from Archbishop Karl J. Alter of Cincinnati, who had been delighted with De Rosen's work in completing the magnificent frescoes of his prior cathedral in Toledo, Ohio, Archbishop O'Boyle succeeded in having De Rosen appointed as an iconography consultant by the Executive Committee on Oct. 1, 1955. The committee consisted of Msgr. Joseph C. Fenton, Sulpician Father Edward P. Arbey and Paulist Father Theodore C. Peterson, all professors at the university.

The committee seized the monumental task before it with clear vision and purpose. Meeting on more than 40 separate occasions between 1954 and 1955, the committee made great progress in arriving at "a comprehensive and original iconographic scheme" to be carried out by the stone carvers on the exterior and by mosaic artists and sculptors on the interior. Statuary, mosaics and scrip-

ST. BRIGID OF IRELAND

tural and patristic texts were deliberated and selected, often in open disagreement with the recommendations of the architect.

One of the most significant decisions concerned the decoration of the north apse. The architects had projected a large vertical window for this area. De Rosen strongly objected to this design. He felt that a window would only "blind" the congregation during the daytime and

(opposite) South facade of the Great Upper Church with Ivan Mastrovic's "Mary Immaculate" supported by angels above. John Angel's "Annunciation" is located at the facade's center. Other bas-relief panels flanking center doors are by Lee Lawrie.

(inset) John Angel's bas-relief carving of "St. Elizabeth Ann Seton," located on the south wall of the west exterior porch.

(above) "St. Brigid of Ireland," by George Snowden, located on exterior facade of north apse.

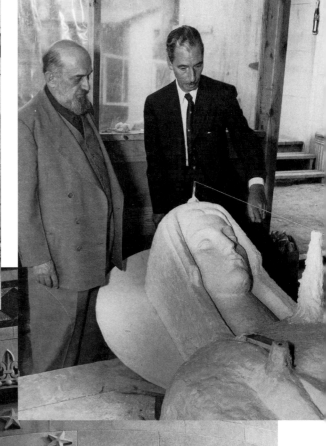

(above) Msgr. Grady inspects the full-size plaster model of "Mary, the Immaculate Queen of the Universe," by famed Croatian sculptor Ivan Mestrovic, upon its arrival at the Shrine.

(top right) Shrine architect Eugene Kennedy (right) and Ivan Mestrovic discuss progress on the master sculptor's relief of "Mary, the Immaculate Queen of the Universe."

(right) The completed bas-relief sculpture at the north exterior apse of the National Shrine.

create a disconcerting dead space during evening liturgical events. Rather, he proposed a great mosaic composition depicting the figure of Christ for this prominent space. It was not then, by chance, that De Rosen was selected to design the mosaic of the Pantocrator ("Christ in Majesty"), which now presides triumphantly over the Great Upper Church.

De Rosen maintained clear and uncompromising standards when it came to liturgical art. His determined yet collaborative approach kept the committee on course with an eye to the larger picture throughout its deliberations. He had no illusions that committee decisions and the completed iconography would be spared criticism. He maintained that "it is futile to anticipate the same degree of discrimination from everyone; neither can one nor should one expect from all, perfect good taste and knowledge which would temperate, unify or tune up those different opinions into one harmonious chord. There will always be a number of plausible and completely dissenting opinions. The solution of this problem is similar to any tactical operations: Retreat at one point and advance at another, so as to balance, as far as possible, the final results."

De Rosen was somewhat critical of

Joe Cox, supervisor of production for Maginnis, Walsh and Kennedy, reviews blueprints with Msgr. Grady.

With George Snowden's plaster model of St. John Kantius on site, a stone carver uses a caliper and chisel to replicate the design in stone within the north exterior facade of the east apse.

lem stemmed from the abstract nature of dogmas proclaiming Mary's role in the Church and salvation history. De Rosen insisted on a careful choice of Marian images "so as to voice in words of today the faith eternal and the prayers for the current needs and the dangers of gathering storms."

He felt it a mistake for the Shrine's iconography to attempt to express the whole of Marian theology. Rather, he advocated a careful selection of Marian images, familiar to the Christian populace but reproduced according to the highest possible standard of artistic form.

Additionally, De Rosen and the committee recommended, for the first time, the incorporation of ethnically diverse expressions of Marian devotion. The Executive Committee concluded that different ethnic groups in the United States "should be given the opportunity to offer chapels dedicated to images of Our Lady particularly revered in their country of origin."

The Iconography Committee was keenly aware of the potential conflicts resulting from "too many cooks in the kitchen" once the tedious process of stone carving and mosaic design commenced. De Rosen and the other members of the committee strongly recommended that the artists hired to repro-

Marian iconography produced during the previous century. He maintained that the first 1,800 years of Christianity had produced a "vast reservoir" of subjects and symbols of sacred art, while Marian art had not kept pace and instead had evolved into superficial and sentimental depictions. Part of the prob-

duce the religious iconography in mosaic and stone should be left to perform their art, unimpeded by the critiques and subtle suggestions of "lay people." The committee specified that "three or four indisputably great artists" be selected and provided with "a reasonable freedom of interpretation and form."

By Dec. 10, 1954, the Iconography Committee agreed that a statue of the Blessed Virgin of "heroic" proportions would be created for the south main entrance of the Shrine, as opposed to architect's recommendation of a statue of the Virgin atop a large column and placed on the front lawn; that the east porch accommodate a depiction of the early Church in America; and that the west porch convey the accomplishments of American Catholics in works of chari-

The stark interior of the Great Upper Church prior to the installation of John De Rosen's "Christ in Majesty" mosaic within the north apse, the completion of floors in marble and the addition of pews, early 1959.

THE PANTOCRATOR

∞

(above) The massive north apse awaits the installation of what was then the world's largest mosaic, "Christ in Majesty."

(opposite top) An early study of the Pantocrator ("Christ in Majesty") mosaic by John De Rosen.

(opposite right) The north apse as it appears today.

(opposite left) Artist and Iconography Committee chairman John De Rosen with a detail of the full-size cartoon of his Pantocrator, completed in St. Louis.

For the mosaic of the Pantocrator, or "Christ in Majesty," John De Rosen envisioned a version considerably more modern than those of the shrines at Monreale in Canada and Cefalu in Sicily. Yet he desired one that maintained the basic tenets of the image of Christ as Celestial Emperor, which first appeared in the East during the fifth century. De Rosen's Christ is depicted wearing the alb and the cloak, the folds of which are outlined with gold. He is stern and heavily bearded, powerful and conquering, a figure ideally suited to the Byzantine architecture. It was De Rosen's intention to develop a figure that was both traditional and new for this truly modern American shrine. Although the text is not among those inscribed on and around the enormous mosaic, De Rosen derived the inspiration for his Pantocrator from the prophet Isaiah: "Who is that that comes from Edom, with dyed garments from Bosra, this beautiful one in his robe, walking in the greatness of his strength? Why then is thy apparel red and thy garments like theirs that tread on the winepress?" (Is 63:1-4).

Commissioned on Sept. 23, 1957, "to design and provide all necessary cartoons for the large mosaic in the North Apse of the National Shrine of the Immaculate Conception," De Rosen required a full year to complete the set of full-size drawings for his "Christ in Majesty" mosaic. The process would require another year to execute the mosaic's construction and installation. De Rosen labored through numerous versions and discussions with committee members regarding the most suitable image for the Shrine: Should the figure of Christ be shown from the waist only, as was the traditional depiction? Or should the complete figure be represented sitting on a throne, the size of which would fill the entire surface of the north apse, as was more common in Western versions and evidenced most notably in the Cathedral of Santiago de Compostella in Spain? How could De Rosen's Pantocrator be true to the traditional, centuries-old artistic form while conveying originality and a fresh interpretation of ancient themes?

The choice of appropriate texts to accompany the image of the Pantocrator had to follow the same rules as the selection of texts for the exterior of the Shrine. Each fragment had to be limited to a certain number of words or letter-spaces. The most important text was designated for the arch above the great mosaic:

"Christ conquers, Christ reigns, Christ rules — Eternal Victor, Eternal King, Eternal Master." At a meeting on July 20, 1959, the Iconography Committee expanded the text to fill two lines as required by the architect's design of this area: "His power is the everlasting power that shall not be taken away" (Dn 7:14).

ration for the domes and vaults of the Great Upper Church. To the original committee were added Msgr. Grady and Carmelite Father Eamon R. Carroll.

Defining the interior iconography of the Shrine, even in general terms, proved a much more challenging task than deciding the exterior ornamentation. The original committee had the benefit of working in tandem with the architects and contractors during construction of the exterior. Every other month, the committee was required to submit suggestions to the Executive Committee; if approved, the suggestions were immediately entrusted to the team of sculptors and mosaicists. These artisans, in turn, would bring to life the committee's instructions. Theory quickly gave way to action under this arrangement. According to De Rosen, "Nothing could have been more rewarding."

This time, the conditions facing the Iconography Committee were considerably different. The committee's mission consisted of arriving at a general scheme that, because of its broadness, did not necessitate an immediate discussion by the architects. The committee was instructed to provide a basic theory and a general direction to be defined and carried out when funds for interior ornamentation became available. Once again,

ty. Additionally, the committee decided to depict prophets of the Old Testament, the apostles, and holy women associated with Mary on the south fascade. Remarkably, by November 1955, the general iconographic scheme for the exterior of the National Shrine had been decided.

INTERIOR ORNAMENTATION

In November 1957, Eugene Kennedy requested that the Iconography Committee begin defining an "outline" of deco-

budget realities were a looming concern.

Eugene Kennedy attempted to clarify the committee's mission by noting that "the interior design of the National Shrine is still very much in the embryonic stage. It would be a tremendous mistake to determine a detailed iconography at this time since to do so could effectively shackle the designer's future work. As we see the problem, the Committee on Iconography could, at this time, do no more valuable service than to determine the iconographic scheme in its most general terms."

The committee, having labored arduously to devise an exterior iconographic scheme that conveyed true theological harmony and artistic integrity, was not about to leave the Shrine's interior ornamentation open to broad interpretation. Unlike most architectural examples common among churches in the West, the Byzantine form dictated that the whole decorative design be placed high above the side walls of the nave, along the cornices and rims of the cupolas. The committee's deliberations involved deciding which texts, figures and symbols would accompany the Christ Pantocrator within the north apse; the iconography of the east and west apses; the chancel and sanctuary domes; the main vault over the choir gallery; the vault in the narthex; the small domes in the east and west stairwells of the narthex; the domes and vaults of the future Blessed Sacrament Chapel and the vaults of the main sacristy and the appropriate texts for the stained-glass windows.

While it was necessary for the committee to determine certain details, each subject had to be described in its broadest sense, so as to provide the architect and the artist with as much latitude as possible to interpret the subject. Four basic principles guided the committee's deliberations: Each subject had to be related to the general iconographic scheme; each had to be theologically sound; each would have to lend itself to being related through painting or mosaic, avoiding excessive symbolism or tepid allegories; and each subject had to be new and original.

∞
WEST APSE
WOMAN OF REVELATION

Although the west and east apses would not be completed until 1967, the creative process was begun a decade earlier when the Iconography Committee deliberated over the design and execution of the appropriate iconography for these areas of the Great Upper Church.

The figure of Mary had appeared in early renderings of the Pantocrator, but

The Woman of Revelation

"A great portent appeared in heaven: a woman clothed with the sun, with the moon under her feet, and on her head a crown of twelve stars. She was pregnant and was crying out in birthpangs, in the agony of giving birth.

"Then another portent appeared in heaven: a great red dragon, with seven heads and ten horns, and seven diadems on his heads.

"His tail swept down a third of the stars of heaven and threw them to the earth. Then the dragon stood before the woman who was about to bear a child, so that he might devour her child as soon as it was born.

"And she gave birth to a son, a male child, who is to rule all the nations with a rod of iron. But her child was snatched away and taken to God and to his throne" (Rv 12:1-5).

the Iconography Committee eventually decided that she should be given a special place in the decorative scheme of the Great Upper Church. Several members of the American hierarchy suggested that the remaining two apses be dedicated by the mothers of America to the Blessed Virgin and by the workers of America to St. Joseph.

Concurring with this suggestion, the committee designated the west apse for a prominent depiction of Mary and the east for a large mosaic of St. Joseph. After considering several options for Mary's depiction, it was finally decided that the apocalyptic Mary as the heroic "woman clothed with the sun" (Rv 12:1) would

best harmonize with the general apocalyptic theme already established by the Pantocrator in the north apse.

In choosing the apocryphal image of Mary from Revelation, the Iconography Committee endorsed the creation of only the second known mosaic representation of this ancient theme. (The other appears in the dome of the Presentation Chapel in St. Peter's Basilica at the Vatican.)

From earliest times, both the Virgin Mary and the "woman clothed with the sun" of the Book of Revelation have been understood as distinct symbols of the Church. The woman is depicted suffering the pangs of impending childbirth. The

dragon, symbolic of the ever-present evils that threaten the Church, prepares to devour the Child but is repelled by heavenly power even as the Child is borne away safely by angels to God in His heavenly throne.

∞

EAST APSE

ST. JOSEPH, PATRON OF WORKERS

Given the scarcity of early Christian art representing the husband of Mary, the committee struggled to arrive at an appropriate image of St. Joseph for the east apse. In the few examples available, most notably the sixth-century mosaic that adorns the triumphal arch of Santa Maria Maggiore in Rome, St. Joseph is depicted as a solitary and weary old man, with head bent and brow furrowed. Not until the 15th century was St. Joseph resurrected in Christian art. He maintained his patriarchal, dignified and traditional appearance until the 18th century, when he was sentimentalized, along with most prominent figures of Christianity, including Christ. St. Joseph, beginning in this period, was reduced to a saintly babysitter, credited with protecting Christ in infancy. Further compounding their deliberations, the Iconography Committee struggled to maintain the apocalyptic motif that had been clearly established in the west and north apses.

A GALLANT RESCUE BY OUR LADY'S KNIGHTS

∽

With construction on the superstructure steadily advancing, Archbishop O'Boyle, Msgr. Grady and others intimately involved with the construction process concluded that the Shrine could not be considered complete without the soaring campanile envisioned in all early renderings of the Shrine. Bishop Bryan McEntegart of Brooklyn, N.Y., suggested that Archbishop O'Boyle approach Luke Hart, supreme knight of the Knights of Columbus, for the necessary funds to

build the tower. Msgr. Grady later recalled the events leading to the campanile's completion:

"Archbishop O'Boyle was convinced that the Knights of Columbus would provide a million dollars for the construction of the tower. At the instigation of the Archbishop, I arranged to meet Luke Hart in New Haven on a certain day. When that day came, Archbishop O'Boyle and I boarded the train in Washington and went to New Haven. Archbishop O'Boyle did not like to fly. In mid-afternoon we met with Luke Hart. I was rather surprised that Luke Hart was alone. We presented the idea of having a Knights' Tower at the Shrine, showed him pictures of the architect's sketches. At the Shrine store we had some fairly large postcards which showed the Shrine as it would appear. I doctored one of these postcards so that the Tower was eliminated. Where the Tower would be was just a blue sky. In particular, this seemed to interest Luke Hart. He kept going back to the way the Shrine would look with the Tower and the way it would look without the Tower. At the very end of our interview he called in Joseph Lamb who was, I think, the treasurer of the Knights at the time. We had a brief discussion about the tower and left without any commitment, but just a general feeling that he was open to the request.

"Perhaps a month or so later, on a Sunday morning, I got a phone call from Luke Hart. He said that on that day he was going to dedicate a statue to Father [Michael J.] McGivney, the founder of the Knights of Columbus and at that dedication he was going to announce that the Knights were giving a million dollars for the construction of the Knights' Tower."

The Knights pledged one dollar for each of its 1 million members — ensuring that the tower would be completed by the time of the Shrine's formal dedication planned for Nov. 20, 1959. Remarkably, it wasn't until early 1958 that construction actually began on the tower. The southwest corner of the Shrine had actually been completed without the campanile — though its foundations had already been poured. Archbishop O'Boyle had likened a completed Shrine without the tower to that of "a man in full evening dress with no high hat." This fearful prospect, however, would not come to pass, and the soaring campanile would henceforth forever be known as the "Knights' Tower."

(opposite) Archbishop O'Boyle and Supreme Knight Luke Hart look upon a model of the Shrine's carillon tower, which would come to be known as the Knights' Tower.

(above) The colorful polychrome tiles of the great dome depicting the traditional symbols of Mary: Tower of Ivory; fleur de lys; intertwined A and M for Ave Maria; and Cedar of Lebanon.

(right) A worker caulks the joints of the south Rose Window frame.

The committee set out to reestablish the true character of St. Joseph through a careful study of scriptural and early Christian texts. It was decided that the husband of Mary and the surrogate father of Jesus would be depicted as St. Joseph the Worker and St. Joseph the Patron of the Universal Church. The three windows flanking the mosaic would serve to reinforce a fresh artistic representation of St. Joseph. The texts selected for these windows were:

(1) "The Queen of Heaven called you her master. He who created the sun was subject to you, — Mother and Son were beholden to the

∞

A 'HAPPY FULFILLMENT'

Early in 1958, John McShain laid out an aggressive schedule to ensure the Shrine's completion by December of the following year. Archbishop O'Boyle felt the need, however, to inform McShain that plans were underway for the Shrine's dedication and that all work would have to be completed by the fall of 1959. In the meantime, De Rosen worked diligently on his rendering of "Christ in Majesty."

By January 1959, the scaffolding was removed from the great dome, revealing the brilliantly colorful polychrome tiles

(left) The Shrine's narthex prior to its completion in marble and mosaic in the present day.

(below) Workers secure pews to the floor as the Great Upper Church is readied for dedication.

bearing the ancient iconographic symbols of Mary. With the Shrine's outer walls erected, the inner and outer roofs completed and the south, west and east porches and terraces nearing completion, the work of completing the exterior of the Shrine was nearly accomplished. The narthex, too, was complete, and clear glass (to be replaced with stained glass) was set in the 216 windows. Sixty-eight pieces of sculpture had been completed to date, and another 15 were still in the process of being carved. Ten mosaics were delivered for installation in the east and west porches.

All of the domes were finished in plaster, and the intricately detailed marble floor was installed. Work continued throughout 1959 on the public-address system, lighting, plumbing, heating, ventilation, pews and main altar.

Completing the Knights' Tower in time for the Shrine's dedication proved a heroic accomplishment. McShain later recalled that concern for workers' safety was the primary consideration: "One of the big problems with the tower was the scaffolding for 325 feet in the air. We were also delayed when the tower rose above 200 feet, as it was almost impossible for the men to work on the scaffolding due to the high winds. The winter, too, played havoc, since no men were allowed to work unless conditions were perfectly safe, and we estimated that 25 percent of the time it was impossible to do so."

The August 1959 edition of *Mary's Shrine* — newly renamed by Msgr. Grady and formerly known as *Salve Regina* — had much good news to report. Not only was the Knights' Tower nearly completed to its full height of 329 feet, but the majestic Pantocrator mosaic intended for the north apse had at last arrived. A brief description of what was hailed as the "largest single mosaic in the world" was provided:

> "In 24 huge wooden cases, weighing about 4 1/2 tons, what may be the largest single mosaic in the world was recently trucked from the Ravenna Mosaic Company in St. Louis to the National Shrine. When erected in the north apse, the mosaic, designed by artist John de Rosen, will depict Christ in majesty. It will cover 3,610 square feet.
>
> "Composed of countless thousands of tesserae, or pieces of marble, the great work of art is estimated to have between 3,000 and 4,000 shades of color, including more than 200 shades of gold and more than 300 shades of red."

In this same issue of *Mary's Shrine*, the long-awaited "Day of Dedication" was announced. Archbishop O'Boyle and Msgr. Grady selected Friday, Nov. 20, 1959, to ensure the participation of as many as possible of the nation's bishops, who would be in Washington for their annual meeting. The intention was to make the celebration a truly national event. The Episcopal Committee eventu-

Msgr. Grady and Archbishop O'Boyle share a moment of pride as the National Shrine's Day of Dedication approaches, 1959.

REMEMBERING
THE
DAY

∞

In a 1996 interview, Bishop Thomas J. Grady, the Shrine's fifth director, recalled the momentous Day of Dedication:

"On the Day of Dedication, I was stunned! When I came to the Shrine three years earlier, there was no Upper Church. Great slabs of limestone were piled up around the construction site. Wooden scaffolding was just beginning to creep up the walls, which were hardly above the lower roof level at that time. For three years, day after day, I had watched the walls rising, the building taking shape, the scaffolding growing more encompassing, then finally beginning to disappear, piece by piece, the building taking a final shape and form. I had been studying the Shrine, its history, the iconography of the Crypt, all of the details of the Upper Church, the new chapels and the mosaics and the sculptures, the various donors, the collections, the preparation for the Day of Dedication.

"The year 1959 had been a year of intensive activity. Until October, I was still the only priest at the Shrine. In October, we got an Oblate priest [Rev. Lawrence J. Frank, O.M.I.]. As the dedication approached, we got help from some priests of the Archdiocese of Washington through the good offices of Archbishop O'Boyle. We had been told that a pretty church is not news. There must be 'an event' before the media will take note. So we tried to make the dedication an event. We hired a public-relations man [Burke Walsh] from the NCWC. We arranged to have a movie made 15 minutes before the dedication, showing the history of the Shrine and the Crypt Church and what we could of the exterior of the Upper Church. We arranged to have another 15 minutes made during the actual ceremony of the dedication. We tried to get the first 15 minutes distributed around the country to be shown on TV and to work up interest in the Day of Dedication. We limited the seating to 3,000. There was a great clamor for tickets. I suddenly discovered that I had relatives I had never heard of before. We were fighting against time to get the work done before the Day of Dedication. We actually worked until 1 or 2 in the morning on the Day of Dedication. In the final year, we had trouble with the insurance. The insurance people suddenly realized that all the wooden scaffolding was like kindling around the Shrine. Many of the insurers canceled out. We were in danger of losing all our insurance. That all had to be straightened out. Great precautions were being taken to avoid fires. Machinery had to be put in the sand. No smoking was allowed. At any rate, it had all been very busy for three years and the last year was extraordinarily busy. The Shrine was a scene of construction, a hard hat place. We were trying to keep people out. All of a sudden, overnight, the Shrine became a church. People with tickets were freely walking in and out of the church. A choir was singing, the organ was blaring, the Shrine had come to life! It was like a resurrection."

ally drew up a three-day program to be carried out in every parish in the country to ensure that all of the approximately 39 million Catholics had the opportunity to participate in the Shrine's dedication celebration.

The enormous task of coordinating the Day of Dedication fell primarily on the shoulders of the Shrine's director, Msgr. Grady. It required not only a keen attention to detail, but an exacting knowledge of protocol in welcoming the vast number of Church hierarchy members, federal and local government officials, and foreign dignitaries expected to attend.

The formal dedication of the National Shrine was scheduled for 10:30 a.m. that Friday. Three additional liturgical celebrations were planned and presided over by various members of the Church hierarchy to accommodate the large number of groups expected for the historic occasion. Archbishop O'Boyle, in a smaller ceremony, performed the blessing of the Shrine and consecrated the main altar actually five days before the Day of Dedication. On the evening of Nov. 20, Cardinal Richard J. Cushing of Boston presided at a Pontifical Low Mass and delivered the sermon, with Bishop Bernard J. Flanagan of Worcester, Mass., as celebrant; on Saturday morning,

(above) First pilgrims to the Great Upper Church on the Day of Dedication, Nov. 20, 1959.

Cardinal James F. McIntyre of Los Angeles celebrated the Solemn Pontifical Mass for Religious, with Archbishop Karl J. Alter of Cincinnati as homilist; on Sunday afternoon, Cardinal John F. O'Hara of Philadelphia presided over the Solemn Pontifical Mass for the Laity, with Bishop Stanislaus V. Bona of Green Bay, Wis., as celebrant and Bishop Charles P. Greco of Alexandria, La., as homilist.

The most sought-after invitation, however, provided admission to the Solemn Pontifical Mass scheduled on Friday morning with Cardinal Spellman

(above) A film crew from Norwood Studios captures the elaborate ritual of the Church's ancient dedication rite.

(right) Pope John XXIII

Vagnozzi, climbed the main pulpit to read the definitive acknowledgment of the Shrine's importance for American Catholics, the nation and the Church Universal:

"It was an extremely gratifying and enduring joy that filled Our heart on the receipt of the news which you, Venerable Brother, took care to have announced to Us, namely that, in the coming month of November, in Washington, a Shrine is to be dedicated with solemn religious rites to the Immaculate Virgin Mother of God, thus bringing to Happy fulfillment after so many vicissitudes a purpose which the noble and renowned nation of the United States of America had undertaken. . . . There now rises up to heaven a Shrine, high and massive, wondrously bright within with metal and marble and pictures and with its dome and lofty tower dominating the scene far and wide, a clearly visible manifestation of your

of New York as celebrant. This was to be the formal Dedication Mass of the National Shrine. The enormous interest among the secular media was unprecedented. CBS provided a live nationwide broadcast of the ceremony, while NBC taped the Dedication Mass for later broadcast. Coverage by Voice of America, Mutual Public Radio and local network affiliates further created the sense that the Shrine's dedication was a significant event for the entire nation. Film of the Dedication Mass was shot by Telenews, Movietone, MGM, Norwood and Fox studios.

The assembled throng in the Great Upper Church hushed in silence as the apostolic delegate, Archbishop Egidio

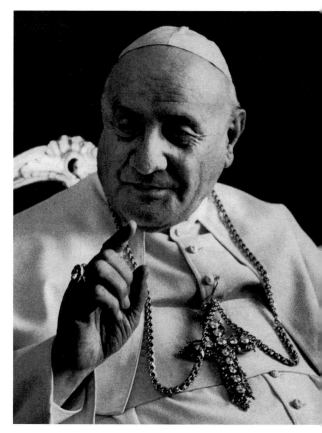

extraordinary piety. Surely will it be for the citizens of the present and for those yet to come a strong and encouraging reminder that, in the midst of the waves of earthly vicissitudes, they must keep their eyes fixed with a lively hope on things heavenly and eternal and that they must likewise reflect that the cause of any human progress worthy of the name is the religion founded by Jesus Christ; by that religion nations flourish and stand steadfast, based on solid foundations, namely on reverence and fear of the most high God, on justice and zeal for charity, on the true principle of liberty which adheres always to moral precepts and is not in conflict with tranquil order."

Hardly anyone in the vast congregation appreciated the significance of the Shrine's dedication on a more personal level than the guest of honor who occu-

pied a reserved place (along with two other previous directors, Msgrs. O'Connor and Reilly) in the chancel during the dedication liturgy — Msgr. Bernard A. McKenna. Now in failing health, the Shrine's first director returned to the spot where he had toiled with fervent devotion alongside the Shrine's founder, Bishop Thomas J. Shahan, to revel in the noble fulfillment of his early efforts.

The doors of the National Shrine of the Immaculate Conception were now opened to the nation and world. What had culminated in the Church's highly stylized and ancient ritual celebration of Catholic devotion, generosity and soli-

(above) An honor guard from the Knights of Columbus and a military escort for the procession of ecclesiastical and government dignitaries.

(right) Attired in princely splendor, Cardinal Francis J. Spellman pauses on the front steps of the National Shrine after performing the dedication ritual, Nov. 20, 1959.

(left) Among the prelates present on the Day of Dedication are Cardinal José Garibi y Rivera of Guadalajara, Mexico; Cardinal Joseph E. Ritter of St. Louis; Cardinal Spellman; Cardinal Thomas Tien Kenhsin of Peking, China, who had been exiled by the Chinese communist government; and Cardinal Richard J. Cushing of Boston.

(below) A grand procession on the Day of Dedication.

darity of purpose could only be regarded as a prelude to the ordained task of forging a clear and decisive path for continued Catholic influence within all sectors of American society. In many ways, the completion of the superstructure of the National Shrine marked the end of one era and the beginning of another. Although no one could reasonably dispute the indelible mark that Catholics had made on American society through the erection of schools, hospitals, churches and formation of fraternal organizations committed to accomplishing innumerable charitable activities, circumstances were changing fast. In just a few short years, Pope John XXIII would convene the Second Vatican Council, forever altering how Catholics defined their faith and its implementation in everyday life. The 1960s would usher in an era of irresistible adventure, vision and hope, as well as incomparable tragedy and division. Catholics who relied merely on traditional formulaic expressions of their faith would encounter increasing difficulty in dealing with the turbulence that would arise in the years immediately following the Shrine's dedication.

For a majority of American Catholics, the completion of the National Shrine provided irrefutable evidence that their faith played a vital role in shaping American life. Now the question that presented itself with increasing urgency was how Catholics in America would utilize their growing influence to address the pressing moral and societal concerns of the day. Catholics across the nation, and those gathered for the majestic ceremony within the newly completed National Shrine, had every reason to celebrate that Day of Dedication. It was not so much an occasion to rest in the work completed but to prayerfully contemplate and gather strength for the even more challenging work now before them.

AMERICA'S CHURCH

ADORNED AND ADORED

THE SHRINE'S ROLE IN THE MODERN WORLD

1959 – 1975

With the scaffolding finally removed and the formal blessing and dedication of the National Shrine of the Immaculate Conception accomplished, the immediate challenge facing Msgr. Grady and his skeleton staff was to figure out what to do with the many thousands of pilgrims who now filled its vast spaces day after day. The nationwide publicity generated by the dedication did much to transform the Shrine into one of the most visited sites in the nation's capital. In the year following the Day of Dedication, approximately 1.25 million people visited the Shrine, eager to voice their prayers and devotion and to leave some evidence that they were included in this monumental expression of Catholic faith. Msgr. Grady later recounted the chal-

lenge of keeping up with the demands of the Shrine's early pilgrims:

"In order to try to keep up with the crowds, we had boxes of candles stacked up on the wall opposite the picture of Our Lady [located in an alcove in what later became the entrance to the Blessed Sacrament Chapel]. One day, I came through the Shrine, as I usually did, just walking around to see what was doing, and I found that people had torn open the cardboard boxes with the new candles and they had lit the candles right in the cardboard boxes."

With the exterior finished, the thoughts and energies of Msgr. Grady soon turned to the task of finishing the interior of the Great Upper Church (referred to at the time as the "Main Church"). Publicity was further enhanced by the live television broadcast of the Midnight Mass on Christmas in 1959 by

(right) The live televised broadcast of the Midnight Mass in 1959.

(below) Archbishop O'Boyle (in bishop's miter), Msgr. Grady (fifth from right) and representatives of the Catholic Daughters of America gather in the north apse for the dedication of the five apsidal chapels given by the organization.

ABC-TV (CBS Radio aired the Mass in part). The new Shrine cafeteria opened early in 1960, and a Shrine store, offering a wide selection of religious articles, prayer books and photographic reproductions, opened at the west front entrance of the crypt level.

Further construction during the months immediately following the dedication involved the Confessional Chapel (later the Chapel of Our Lady of Hostyn) and the addition of pews in the Crypt Church. Work was also begun on the massive baldachin intended for the main

altar of the Great Upper Church and was completed by Easter 1960. Gradually, plans for the extensive interior ornamentation were beginning to come together. There were regular appeals in the pages of *Mary's Shrine* to attract prospective donors who would contribute to the costs of additional sculptural work and other interior adornments. The architectural plans approved by the nation's bishops in 1952 did not include the east and west lateral nave chapels. Provisions were now underway to add them in the near future.

Once again, Catholic women assumed a leading role in the completion of the National Shrine. During their 27th Biennial National Convention on July 10, 1958, representatives of the 209,000-member Catholic Daughters of America (CDA) approved a $250,000 gift to pay for the five chapels of the north apse that would depict the Glorious Mysteries of the Rosary. John De Rosen designed the mosaics that adorn each altar alcove. Archbishop O'Boyle consecrated the altars on Nov. 12, 1960.

Prior to the Shrine's dedication in December 1958, Cardinal Spellman, archbishop of New York and head of the military ordinariate, had promised to donate the main pipe organ of the National Shrine, designated for the south

(above) South gallery (prior to installation of "Universal Call to Holiness" sculpture in 1999) within which the "Voice of the Military" Möller organ resounds. A tuner makes final adjustments to the largest of the organ's 9,138 pipes. The organ represents a gift of the Catholic chaplains and Catholic military personnel, dedicated in honor of deceased chaplains and members of the Armed Forces.

gallery, as a gift of the Catholic chaplains of the U.S. military. Archbishop O'Boyle related the rather matter-of-fact way in which this substantial gift came to pass: "One day, when Cardinal Spellman was in Washington, we were riding together to the U.S. Catholic bishops' conference. I turned to him and said, 'You know, the Shrine needs an organ.' So, he asked me,

'What did you have in mind? How much will it cost?' I told him it would cost $250,000 and it could be called 'The Voice of the Military.' He didn't make any commitment until some months later at a dinner [when] he asked me, 'By the way, about that organ, how much did you say it would cost?' '$250,000,' I said. 'You got a deal,' he said."

J.B. Welk

ne wel-
visitors,
Montini,
Montini,
Paul VI,
visit the
li, later
ing the
ed state
, a new
priests
recalled
Cardinal

"At the time there still wasn't much in the Upper Church. But he commented on the details that he saw in the pews, the way they were carved. He said, 'If your work is as perfect elsewhere in the Shrine as the carvings of the ends of these pews — this will be a magnificent building.' "

In 1960, the Shrine received its second papal gift from the Vatican's mosaic studios — this one depicting Titian's painting of "The Assumption of the Virgin," which hangs in the Church of Santa Maria Gloriosa dei Frari in Venice. The mosaic had been promised by Pope Pius XII, who proclaimed the dogma of the Assumption in 1950, and was even-

tually completed in 1958 at the direction of his successor, Pope John XXIII.

In the year following its dedication, the Shrine's identity as a national symbol of Catholic prominence in the United States continued to be enhanced by the thousands of religious pilgrims and curiosity seekers who were eager to experience the largest Catholic church in the Western Hemisphere. It was a tribute to the vision of Bishop Thomas J. Shahan and his able and indefatigable assistant, Msgr. Bernard McKenna, that so many wished to adopt the newly completed National Shrine as *their* church — a summation of *their* faith and devotion.

After a long and fruitful life of priestly service, the Shrine's dutiful servant and first director, Msgr. McKenna, died at

Archbishop O'Boyle (left) and the apostolic delegate, Archbishop Amleto Giovanni Cicognani (right), with the visiting papal secretary of state, Cardinal Giovanni Battista Montini, the future Pope Paul VI, during Cardinal Montini's visit to Washington, which included a tour of the Great Upper Church.

the age of 85 on July 20, 1960. Perhaps as divine recompense for his tireless effort, Msgr. McKenna had lived to see the fulfillment of what his mentor, Bishop Shahan, had often referred to as a "great hymn in stone."

∞

A CATHOLIC PRESIDENT

Less than two months after the Shrine's celebrated dedication, the mood among Catholics in America at the dawn of a new decade was one of boundless optimism. With the election of John Fitzgerald Kennedy as the nation's 35th president and its first Roman Catholic chief executive, one of the last remaining barriers to Catholics contemplating the ultimate mantle of political prestige and power had been overcome. Even as America was embarking on a "new frontier" ushered in by the youngest president in 60 years, the grandfatherly Pope John XXIII was preparing to throw open the windows of the Church Universal in

a new spirit of collaboration and openness to the non-Catholic and secular world by convening the Second Vatican Council.

In 1961, construction was begun on the first chapel to be added since the north apse Glorious Mysteries chapels. The Redemptorist Fathers of the United States pledged $145,000 for a chapel to Our Lady of Perpetual Help in the north side of the east transept. By February 1962, a new phase of construction was underway. The ambitious five-year construction plan devised by Msgr. Grady and Archbishop O'Boyle evidenced a clear intent to continue the momentum

of national support toward the ultimate completion of the National Shrine.

The plan included the completion of the east and west lateral nave chapels, the east and west apses, the transept chapels and the great organ, as well as the addition of a carillon of 56 cast bells to the Knights' Tower.

(left) America's first Roman Catholic president, John F. Kennedy.

(below) Chapel of Our Lady of Perpetual Help, a gift of the Redemptorist Fathers.

A CARILLON OF BELLS

~~

During the annual Knights of Columbus' Fourth-Degree Banquet in the fall of 1961, Supreme Knight Luke Hart raised an issue that had long been on the minds of those who gazed upon the soaring, albeit silent, Knights' Tower of the National Shrine. In his after-dinner remarks to the attending Knights, and in the presence of Cardinal Joseph E. Ritter of St. Louis, Hart suggested somewhat casually that if the American hierarchy were to express a desire to complete the Knights' Tower with chimes or a carillon of bells, the Knights would readily agree to the additional gift. Hart further emphasized that he had no intention of allowing a donor other than the Knights to place bells in "their tower." Cardinal Ritter relayed Hart's remarks to Archbishop O'Boyle, who, characteristically, moved swiftly in claiming the Knights' pledge. Hart reiterated his earlier comments that "the Knights of Columbus will be ready to

install the bells whenever the hierarchy is ready for us to do so."

The 56 bells of the Knights' Tower carillon were cast in the foundries of Les Fils De Georges Paccard in Annecy-Le-Vieux, France, and at Petit and Fritsen Ltd., Aarle-Rixtel, Holland, over a period of nine months. They arrived in Baltimore aboard the *President Adams* on July 10, 1963, and were inspected there by Msgr. Grady and Father Robert Kilroy, an Oblate of Mary Immaculate who was an associate at the Shrine. Archbishop O'Boyle presided over the ancient rite of consecration of the bells on July 15, when they were blessed with holy water, anointed with oil and incensed. On July 23, the bells were hoisted into the galleries of the Knights' Tower through an opening made in its north wall at approximately the 50-foot level. Once inside the tower, the bells were further hoisted an additional 200 feet to

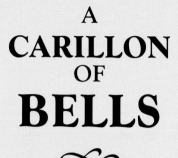

(above) Fourth-Degree Knights gather for the dedication of the carillon of bells, July 14, 1963.

(top right) Msgr. Grady, Auxiliary Bishop Philip Hannan and Archbishop O'Boyle stand between the Mary and Christopher bells.

Christopher, St. Michael, St. James, St. John the Evangelist, St. Edward, St. Martin of Tours, St. Francis of Assisi and St. Luke — the last named for the Knights' leader who made possible both the tower and its carillon.

The carillon bells — ranging from Mary, which sounds the note B-flat, down to the handbell-sized top G — are played from the traditional "baton" manual keyboard and pedal clavier (located in the "playing cabin" between the two bell chambers, at about the 200-foot level of the 329-foot tower).

Three of the largest bells — the lowest B-flat, D and F — also function as pealing bells, to which four stationary bells with "simulated peal" strikers may be added for a seven-bell peal. The Mary bell also sounds the hours. The Angelus is rung following the noon and the 6 p.m. hour strikes; Mass peals are rung before the 12:10 and 5:15 p.m. daily Masses and for the weekend Masses.

In 1989, the carillon was renovated by the Verdin Company of Cincinnati, Ohio, with new playing and practice consoles.

The Knights' Tower carillon and the peal of seven bells may be heard on the CD recording *Carols for Carillon*. ∞

(left) A crane hoists one of the largest bells through an opening made in the north wall of the Knight's Tower. From this position, they were again hoisted more than 200 feet to their final position in the galleries, July 23, 1963.

(below) Archbishop O'Boyle consecrates the largest bell, Mary. The bells were formally dedicated on Sept. 8, 1963, when the first carillon concert was performed by Princeton bellmaster Arthur Bigelow.

their final position. The formal dedication of the bells took place on Sept. 8, 1963, the feast of the Nativity of the Blessed Mother. A "Dedication Concert," attended by some 8,000 people, was performed by Arthur Lynds Bigelow, bellmaster of Princeton University, who also designed the Knights' Tower carillon. The concert opened with the National Anthem and included the ringing of the three largest bells to demonstrate the full and solemn peal which would hence mark the passing of time for all within their hearing.

After the larger bells had demonstrated their impressive tone, each of the 56 bells was sounded from the keyboard to demonstrate the full range of the carillon. In keeping with the ancient custom of assigning names to church bells, the largest bell, weighing 7,200 pounds, was inscribed: "Mary is my name, Mary is my sound, Beloved Mother, Queen of Heaven and Earth, Queen of this dear land, For Knights to God and Country bound, And all who hear my voice I sing the praises of God." The other larger bells were named St.

DEATH OF A POPE AND A PRESIDENT

The year 1963 brought incomparable loss for Catholics throughout the world. In just six months, the world's two most prominent Catholics would both be called from this world. The beloved Pope John XXIII, whose humble and affable manner had endeared him to Catholics and non-Catholics alike, died in the papal apartments on June 3, 1963.

Archbishop Egidio Vagnozzi, apostolic delegate to the United States, celebrated a Pontifical Requiem Mass in the Great Upper Church, which was filled with Catholics of all ages. Representatives of the U.S. government were also in attendance, including Robert F. Kennedy, attorney general; Dean Rusk, secretary of state; and Anthony Celebrezze, secretary of health, education and welfare. Archbishop O'Boyle preached the sermon before a congregation that also included some 100 non-Catholic religious leaders and representatives from nearly every foreign embassy in Washington. The main portal of the Shrine was draped in black cloth, and a mock catafalque was positioned in the chancel among six large candle stands with a bishop's miter ceremoniously placed at the head. The Chair of Peter was vacant, and Catholics throughout the world and at America's patronal church were in official mourning.

On June 21, 1963, Cardinal Montini, a familiar figure at the Vatican for most of his priestly life, assumed the throne of St. Peter. One week later, on June 30, 1963, the apostolic delegate returned to the Shrine to celebrate the Coronation Mass of the new Pope Paul VI. Nearly 3,000 attended, again with the diplomatic corps present and various leaders of the

U.S. government. The Shrine was proving its capacity to bring together both the Church and the nation in moments of joy and sorrow.

On Nov. 22, 1963, Americans were stunned to learn that their youthful and dashing president had been gunned down while traveling by motorcade through the streets of Dallas, Texas. The tragedy of John F. Kennedy's assassination was magnified for Catholics in the United States, who only a thousand days

Several top officials of the Kennedy administration attended the Pontifical Requiem Mass, including Attorney General Robert F. Kennedy (far right), in addition to representatives from nearly every foreign embassy in Washington.

(left inset) President and Mrs. Kennedy moments before the fateful gunshots in Dallas, Texas.

(center) A young John F. Kennedy Jr., whose own death 36 years later would stun the nation, offers a final salute to his father.

(right inset) Cardinal Richard J. Cushing of Boston, treasurer of the Shrine Episcopal Committee, presides over the funeral of President John F. Kennedy at Washington's St. Matthew's Cathedral.

before had reveled in the election of the first Roman Catholic to the nation's highest office. Once again, thousands of Catholics streamed into the National Shrine to be consoled in their loss. The Shrine was filled to capacity, even though there had been no public notice of the Mass.

A CROWN OF SILVER AND GOLD
FOR THE WORLD'S POOR

There were a number of significant highlights in the life of the Shrine during 1964. Cardinal Léon Joseph Suenens of Malines-Brussels, Belgium, a leading figure of the Second Vatican Council, visited on May 8. The double episcopal consecration of Bishop William J. McDonald, rector of The Catholic University of America, and Bishop John S. Spence, a priest of the Archdiocese of Washington, as auxiliary bishops in the Washington archdiocese took place on May 19, 1964. Ten days later, on May 29, Irish President Eamon de Valera attended a memorial Mass for President Kennedy. Beginning on Nov. 30, 1964, daily Mass in the Crypt Church was offered for the first time with the celebrant facing the congregation. The crypt was uniquely suited for this major change in the liturgical life of the Church, given the central location of the main altar.

Two days later, on Nov. 13, 1964, Pope Paul VI made a dramatic gesture that would serve to forever link him to the National Shrine. During deliberations of the Second Vatican Council on poverty in the world, the Pope placed his coronation tiara, given to him by the faithful of his archdiocese in Milan, on the altar

Pope Paul VI is crowed with the silver-and-gold tiara, a gift of the people of the Milan archdiocese, on the day of his coronation at St. Peter's Basilica, June 30, 1963.

of St. Peter's Basilica as a symbol of his special concern for the poor of the world. Later, it was announced that the tiara would be a gift to the Catholics of the United States. The tiara was eventually entrusted to the custody of New York's Cardinal Spellman, who "smuggled" it past customs officials at New York's Kennedy Airport. (When asked what was inside the white leather covered box, Cardinal Spellman replied simply, "An ecclesiastical ornament." No further questions were asked, and the Cardinal was permitted to pass with the historic papal headpiece.)

The 10-pound tiara was displayed at St. Patrick's Cathedral and then at the World's Fair in New York. It was soon made available for display within any

The apostolic delegate, Archbishop Luigi Raimondi, presents the Shrine's sixth director, Msgr. William McDonough, with the tiara of Pope Paul VI on Feb. 6, 1968, for permanent display at the National Shrine.

Cardinal Spellman's reply proved true. Between 1964 and 1968, Pope Paul's tiara helped raise over $35,000 at a time when its value was estimated at $10,000. Today, contributions made at its permanent exhibit at the north end of Memorial Hall are submitted annually to the Vatican for disbursement to the poor, in keeping with the wishes of Pope Paul VI.

On Feb. 6, 1968, the tiara was finally presented to the Shrine's sixth director, Msgr. William McDonough, by the apostolic delegate, Archbishop Luigi Raimondi. The tiara of Pope Paul VI is the only papal tiara permanently on display outside the Vatican. In 1994, the tiara was carried by then-associate rector Father Paul deLadurantaye to Denver, Colo., for a special exhibit of Vatican treasures in conjunction with the visit of Pope John Paul II for World Youth Day.

GROWING IN LEAPS AND BOUNDS

The year 1965 saw tremendous progress in the ongoing completion of the Shrine's vast interior space. Four new chapels were added: the Chapel of Mary, Queen of All Hearts, a gift of the Montfort Missionaries; the Chapel of Our Mother of Good Counsel, a gift of the Augustinian Fathers; the Chapel of Our Mother of Sorrows, a gift of the First Catholic Slovak Union of the United

diocese or archdiocese that requested it. The National Shrine was eventually designated as the permanent place of exhibition. To critics who maintained that the Pope's wishes of giving away his tiara to benefit the poor of the world had been subverted by "simply moving one expensive ornament from a church in Rome to a church in Washington," Cardinal Spellman's office rejoined: "Exhibition of Pope Paul VI's tiara will raise a far larger sum for the poor than outright sale of it would have earned."

States (*Jednota*); and the Chapel of Our Lady of Guadalupe, a gift of Cardinal Richard Cushing and the Archdiocese of Boston. The great organ and chancel organ were installed, as were the chancel clerestory windows as a gift of the Sisters of Mercy. Nine other stained-glass windows were also installed, and the permanent pulpit, carved of Botticino marble and ornamented with discreet bas-relief sculptures, was positioned in the Great Upper Church and used for the first time by Msgr. Grady on Sept. 5, 1965. It was indeed a year of constant construction, an indication that the work of completing the National Shrine was an all-consuming task. Not only were the physical dimensions and adornments of the Shrine being enhanced, but millions of visitors had distinguished the Shrine as one of the most popular destinations in a city known for its majestic monuments.

Mary's Shrine of August 1965 published a running tally of events held at the Shrine since the Day of Dedication. Over 7 million people had visited the Shrine, thousands of young men had received minor and major orders to the priesthood in the Upper Church, 75,000 Masses had been offered, over 200,000 confessions had been heard, more than 1.5 million people had received Holy Communion, 200 carillon concerts had been played since Sept. 8, 1963, and five major organ concerts since April 25, 1965, attracting over 20,000 people.

Officers of the First Catholic Slovak Union (Jednota) gather for the dedication of the Chapel of Our Lady of Sorrows.

Newsweek
AUGUST 15, 1966 40c

White
House
Wedding

(above and right) Joined by Fathers William Kaifer and John Kuzinskas, Archbishop O'Boyle presides over the wedding of the president's daughter Luci to Patrick Nugent at the Shrine's high altar. The "family wedding" and the Shrine made national news as an estimated 55 million watched television coverage of the wedding.

(opposite) President and Mrs. Lady Bird Johnson pause with their 19-year-old daughter, Luci, at the main entrance to the Shrine prior to the nuptial Mass.

Described as the social event of 1966, the marriage of President Lyndon B. Johnson's 19-year-old daughter, Luci Baines Johnson, to 23-year-old Patrick Nugent at the National Shrine was remembered by Msgr. Grady as the greatest publicity coup in the Shrine's history. Indeed, the wedding focused the eyes of an entire nation, as well as the national and international news media, on the Shrine as never before. According to Msgr. Grady, the wedding "gave the Shrine a much broader kind of publicity than anything before because it became something beyond just a church service, or something related to church. It was an event that involved the President's daughter."

This was the first and last wedding to take place in the Great Upper Church of the Shrine. Since the Shrine keeps no baptismal or matrimonial records, as a parish church or cathedral would, these sacraments are not performed without consent of the resident archbishop. The White House petitioned Cardinal O'Boyle directly. After conferring with Msgr. Grady, the cardinal felt he could hardly refuse.

As publicity mounted, the location of Luci Johnson's wedding gained as much mention as the wedding itself. *The New York Times* declared the National Shrine the perfect choice for the presidential wedding. "There is no place in Washington, including the White House, that could offer a setting for a bridal spectacular like the National Shrine of the Immaculate Conception" (Feb. 19, 1966).

Msgr. Grady's major preoccupation was to ensure the completion of the chancel dome mosaic and the removal of scaffolding in time for the much-publicized nuptial Mass. It should be noted that the east and west apses were also under construction, as was the Chapel of Our Lady of Siluva. All were completed in time for the wedding — a heroic achievement worthy of presidential honors!

The day of the Johnson-Nugent wedding, Aug. 6, 1966, was a typically sweltering day in Washington. Mobile air-conditioning units, normally used to cool airplanes, were obtained from United Airlines to force air through the ducts of the Shrine's ventilation system. Secret Service agents were posted on the parapets of the Knights' Tower and above the main portal of the Shrine. The 90-minute ceremony was closed to the print and broadcast media, in keeping with the Johnson family's hopes for a small "family" wedding. But the nation's attention could not be diverted. Detailed reports of the wedding preparations and the actual ceremony at the Shrine appeared on page one of all the major newspapers and graced the covers of *Life, Time, Newsweek, Look* and *Motion Picture* magazines. *U.S. News & World Report* likewise covered the nuptial celebration. The only interruptions to the "simple, deeply moving ceremony," were picketers at the Shrine and the White House, who chanted their opposition to continued U.S. involvement in the Vietnam War. ∞

A
WEDDING
∞

(above) Two Claretian provincials, Fathers Patrick J. McPolin (left) and Eugene N. Grainer, present their order's final check to Msgr. Grady for the Immaculate Heart of Mary Chapel, 1965.

(right) The Venetian-glass mosaic of the chapel (far left) was designed by John De Rosen and depicts Pope Pius XII consecrating the world to the Immaculate Heart of Mary on Oct. 31, 1942.

∞
IMMACULATE HEART
OF MARY CHAPEL

In November 1958, Father Patrick J. McPolin, provincial secretary of the Eastern Province of the Claretian Order, wrote Msgr. Grady to inquire about donating a statue of the order's founder, St. Anthony Mary Claret. Msgr. Grady readily agreed, with expressions of gratitude and assurances that he would be in contact as soon as the iconography for the statue was worked out.

In 1962, however, Claretian Father Michael Cecere, provincial superior of the California Province, visited the Shrine to investigate the possibility of donating the much larger gift of a chapel. After the visit, Msgr. Grady reserved two adjoining chapels in the Crypt Church across from the Founder's Chapel and Pope St. Pius X Chapel for the Claretian Order. By Sept. 6, 1963, both the Western and Eastern Provinces agreed to the plan to establish a chapel dedicated to the Immaculate Heart of Mary and St. Anthony Mary Claret as a gift of the Claretians. The chapels were completed in 1966 and dedicated in a Mass celebrated by Bishop Joseph Querexeta, a Claretian and bishop of Isabella, Philippines, on July 16, 1967.

∞
COMPLETING THE EAST APSE

Among the most ambitious projects undertaken following the Shrine's dedication was the completion of the east and west apses that flank the "Christ in Majesty" mosaic.

Given the scope of such an undertaking and the considerable costs involved, Archbishop O'Boyle appealed to Msgr. Donald Hoag, provincial of the Holy Name Province of the Franciscans, in September 1961 and offered the "Franciscan family" the opportunity to donate the east apse to the National Shrine. The Iconography Committee had already determined the theme of the apse — namely, St. Joseph as Protector of the Church, with the five apsidal chapels below dedicated to the Sorrowful Mysteries of the Rosary. It was suggested, however, that Franciscan saints of the order's choosing could be designated for the columns between the chapels. The

estimated cost was $500,000.

The committee's original design for the apse, however, was later altered to commemorate the Second Vatican Council, which was already underway by the time financial circumstances made it possible to complete the east apse. St. Joseph's newly appointed role as patron of the council was emphasized in the revised design. The leading council fathers were incorporated into the mosaic along with other key non-Catholic observers. The mosaic thus captures the spirit of open dialogue among faiths that the council fathers encouraged in this era of ecumenism. Along the bottom of the mosaic are depicted various workers to illustrate the theme of St. Joseph as

The five chapels depicting the Sorrowful Mysteries of the Rosary within the east apse, designed by Austin Purves. The entire east apse represents the gift of the American Franciscans.

patron of laborers, which was one of the early ideas proposed by several of the U.S. bishops for the east apse.

Within the mosaic is an imposing figure of St. Joseph holding the Christ Child in his arms. Below and to the right of St. Joseph is a tree near running water, an allusion to the description of the "just man" of Psalm 1:3. To his left is a family consisting of father, mother, son and daughter to symbolize Joseph's position as foster father of the Holy Family and the model for fathers and family life. Beneath St. Joseph is a series of figures representing the working men and women of the world; and to the right, a representation of Pope John XXIII and

(below) Detail of east-apse mosaic depicting an ecumenical group of fathers and observers who participated in the Second Vatican Council. Pope John XXIII is pictured at center.

(right) East apse of the Great Upper Church.

the major fathers and observers of the Second Vatican Council.

The artist for all the east-apse mosaics was Austin Purves Jr. He began sketching the mosaic in 1964, had his renderings executed by the Venetian Art Mosaic Company beginning in late 1965 and completed the mosaics by December 1966. In all, the mosaics cover 3,570 square feet.

The east apse was blessed and dedicated as a gift of the Franciscan community of the United States by Cardinal O'Boyle on Dec. 9, 1967.

THE FIRST MOSAIC DOME

In 1967, the first of the great domes of the interior of the National Shrine was completed in mosaic. "The Triumph of the Lamb" actually was the second gift of Polish Americans, since it resulted from the surplus collected for the Chapel of Our Lady of Czestochowa. Designed by internationally acclaimed artist Millard Sheets of Los Angeles, the mosaic was manufactured by the Ravenna Mosaic Company of St. Louis. As in previous instances, the Iconography Committee had selected the theological motif for the dome years before. The Apocalyptic Lamb of John's vision in the fifth and sixth chapters of the Book of Revelation is featured prominently in the mosaic's center and was designated for its symbolism of the central mystery of Christ in the Eucharist. The Apocalyptic Lamb is also depicted on the altar front of the Our Lady of Czestochowa Chapel to symbolize the indomitable faith of the Polish people through centuries of persecution.

Mary's Shrine of May 1967 provides a thorough rationale for the mosaic's iconography:

"[T]he representation of the Lamb is focal. Directly above the main altar is pictured the mysterious vision given to John of the full paschal mystery of Christ. The Lamb of God

is the one foretold in the Old Testament: the lion of the tribe of Judah and the Root of David; the One who was slain but who yet lives and will live forevermore; the Lamb whose wisdom can penetrate the mystery of the scroll and whose eyes are the seven spirits of God sent into all the world; he is a Lamb gentle, bleeding, slain yet he is Lord of Lords and King of Kings, proclaimed to the holy people of God by the four evangelists, worshiped by the elders and angels of heaven; the one who had experienced life and death and is beyond time; the one on the throne, veiled with poetic language in mystery, revealed to us as a lamb, the pasch of the Jews, the gentle victim of Calvary, the mysterious one ruling the universe and waiting for us in the land of everlasting vision."

Mosaic artist Millard Sheets and a small-scale cartoon of his "Triumph of the Lamb" mosaic, intended for the main sanctuary dome as a gift of Polish Catholics throughout the United States.

(above) The west apse of the Great Upper Church, depicting the "Woman of Revelation," crafted by Joseph L. Young.

(right) Archbishop O'Boyle dedicates the west apse, 1967.

WEST APSE — A GIFT OF THE SOCIETY OF JESUS

Unlike the "Christ in Majesty" mosaic in the north apse of the Great Upper Church — which necessitated the elimination of the vertical apsidal window to accommodate it — the mosaic of Mary as the "Woman of Revelation" was positioned to the right of the west-apse window and the seven-headed dragon to the left, thus enabling the image of Mary to be seen from the main body of the Church. This mosaic, measuring 3,570 square feet, was designed by architect Eugene Kennedy, crafted by Joseph L. Young and manufactured by the Ravenna Mosaic Company of St. Louis. It was installed in 1957 as a gift of the Society of Jesus.

Shortly after the Day of Dedication in 1961, Archbishop O'Boyle invited the Society of Jesus to complete the west apse in mosaic. Cardinal Joseph E. Ritter of St. Louis made a second pitch when he addressed the Jesuits' annual meeting in his archdiocese on May 1, 1961. Nine days later, on May 10, Jesuit Father Joseph P. Fisher wrote Archbishop O'Boyle on behalf of the Jesuit provincials to accept the invitation, agreeing to donate $500,000 to complete the west apse. The Jesuits emphasized, however, that the gift would represent not only the solemnly professed men of the order, but the students and alumni of Jesuit schools, the

THE THREEFOLD GIFT OF THE DOMINICANS

∞

Determined that no religious community be denied an opportunity to be represented at the National Shrine, Archbishop O'Boyle wrote to Father Joseph M. Agius, provincial of the Dominicans' Holy Name Province in San Francisco, in November 1960 to suggest that his order step forward to complete the west apse of the Great Upper Church. The appeal, although untimely given the ever-increasing challenges confronting religious communities to support their apostolates, was not one the Dominicans could easily dismiss. The Dominicans, like the other religious communities that ultimately came forward, could not pass up an opportunity to be represented prominently in the nation's patronal church.

Ultimately, Dominican Fathers J.E. Marr of the Chicago province and W.D. Marrin of the New York province met with Msgr. Grady at the Shrine in April 1961. The Dominicans insisted that any representation of their order include a depiction of the Blessed Mother presenting St. Dominic with the rosary. Msgr. Grady expressed strong doubt that the Iconography Committee would consider altering the apocalyptic theme already established for the west apse. After considerable discussion, it was agreed that that the Dominicans would best be represented by a separate chapel to Our Lady of the Rosary. Archbishop O'Boyle later suggested that the Dominicans establish not one, but three, chapels — to Our Lady of the Rosary, a minor chapel dedicated to St. Dominic, and a second minor chapel to St. Catherine of Siena. The threefold gift of the Dominicans, with an estimated cost of $700,000, was designated for the east lateral nave.

To provide for the considerable gift, the Dominicans extended the invitation to religious women of their order. By September 1961, Mother M. Justin, prioress general of the Congregation of the Holy Names and president of the Conference of Dominican Mothers General, wrote to Archbishop O'Boyle to pledge $350,000 for the Dominican chapels. In May of the following year, the Dominicans agreed to a 10-year payment schedule for the chapels. Joined by the Dominican provincials of the United States, Cardinal O'Boyle dedicated the three Dominican chapels on May 17, 1970. ∞

faithful of Jesuit-run parishes and all who benefited from the Jesuits' many apostolates.

The west apse — depicting the apocalyptic "woman clothed with the sun" and the Joyful Mysteries within the five chapels below — would not, however, be completed for another six years.

Beneath the mosaic, five Jesuit saints were selected in the same way the Franciscan saints were chosen to adorn the lower east apse. The five saints depicted are: St. Francis Xavier, St. Aloysius Gonzaga, St. Alphonsus Rodriguez, St. John Berchmans and St. Stanislaus Kostka.

The three apsidal windows were designed to represent Mary's role as humanity's true hope as the one who precipitated victory over Satan and evil. The north window is enscripted: "I am the Mother of the Gift of Love, of the Fear and Knowledge of God, and of the Just Man's Hope" (Ecclesiasticus [Sirach] 24:24, Douay-Rheims Bible). The center window reads: "Victorious are you, Holy Virgin Mary, and Worthy of All Praise. You are the Virgin Who Crushed the Head of the Serpent" (feast of Our Lady of Lourdes). The south window reads: "I was Watching Satan Fall as Lightning from Heaven. Behold I have Given You Power Over All the Might of the Enemy" (Lk 10:18-19).

A POLISH CHAPEL

Conceived as a memorial of the 1,000th anniversary of Poland's conversion to Christianity being planned for 1966, the idea of establishing the Chapel of Our Lady of Czestochowa was actually the brainchild of an Irishman, Archbishop O'Boyle. Ever eager to ensure the completion of the Shrine's vast interior spaces, the archbishop relayed his idea to Auxiliary Bishop Henry T. Klonowski of Scranton, Pa. (the archbishop's hometown), who eagerly enlisted the aid of the other American bishops of Polish ancestry.

Given the proposed chapel's estimated cost of $375,000, there was little doubt that a national collection among the nation's Polish parishes would be necessary to fund the project. A committee of Polish bishops met to plot their strategy on Nov. 16, 1960, during the U.S. bishops' meeting in Washington. Once again, it became necessary to seek the permission of every bishop before proceeding with the national collection. The Episcopal Committee for the Chapel of Our Lady of Czestochowa included Archbishop John J. Krol of Philadelphia, Bishop Klonowski, Auxiliary Bishop Roman R. Atkielski of Milwaukee,

Auxiliary Bishop Aloysius J. Wycislo of Chicago, Bishop Stephen S. Woznicki of Saginaw, Mich., Auxiliary Bishop

(above) Archbishop O'Boyle accepts a check from Philadelphia Archbishop John J. Krol and other bishops of Polish descent for the chapel. From left, the prelates include Auxiliary Bishop Alexander M. Zaleski, Detroit; Bishop Stanislaus V. Bona, Green Bay, Wis.; Archbishop O'Boyle; Archbishop Krol; Auxiliary Bishop Henry T. Klonowski, Scranton, Pa.; and Auxiliary Bishop Aloysius J. Wycislo, Chicago.

(left) Archbishop Krol, center, with Archbishop O'Boyle and several Polish-American bishops, presides over the dedication of the Chapel of Our Lady of Czestochowa in the presence of 10,000 pilgrims, May 3, 1964.

the surplus would go toward the creation of the "Triumph of the Lamb" mosaic intended for the sanctuary dome.

Archbishop Krol formally dedicated the Chapel of Our Lady of Czestochowa on May 3, 1964, in the presence of over 10,000 people who traveled across the country to take part in this celebration of Polish faith, devotion and culture. While the dedication planners had intended to hold a simultaneous Mass in the Crypt Church, with the main sermon broadcast through the Crypt Church sound system, it became necessary at the last minute to erect a makeshift altar on the east porch to accommodate the enormous crowd. In all, there were three simultaneous Masses offered at the Shrine for the Chapel's dedication.

The celebration recalled the tragic situation of modern Poles, whose faith and basic liberties were oppressed by the atheistic communist system. Efforts to complete the superstructure of the National Shrine gained momentum in response to frequent proclamations against the atheistic tendencies of communism at the height of the Cold War. Similarly, Polish Americans used this occasion to reaffirm their faith and determination to prevail over the same forces unleashed in their ancestral homeland.

Alexander M. Zaleski of Detroit, Bishop Stanislaus V. Bona of Green Bay, Wis., and Bishop Thomas L. Noa of Marquette, Wis.

By August 1961, permission was granted. The national collection, held in October, drew an overwhelming response. Over $542,000 was collected, and the bishops were faced with the enviable dilemma of what to do with the extra $117,000. It was later decided that

In 1965, Msgr. Grady presided over several additional projects even while the liturgical and pilgrimage life of the Shrine continued to grow. During this period of constant activity, the Chapel of Our Mother of Sorrows was completed as a gift of the people of America from the First Catholic Slovak Union of the United States (*Jednota*); the Sisters of Mary gave three new stained-glass windows for the clerestory level along with a permanent pulpit of Botticino marble, adorned with bas-relief sculptures depicting St. Bernard, St. John Eudes and St. John Damascene; and construction was underway on the Chapel of Our Lady of Guadalupe.

∝
UNITING THE PEOPLE
OF THE AMERICAS

The Chapel of Our Lady of Guadalupe was completed in 1966 as a gift of Cardinal Richard J. Cushing and the people of his Archdiocese of Boston, although a committee had been formed as early as the mid-1950s to secure a representation of Our Lady of Guadalupe in the Shrine. Established as the *Comité Guadalupano del Santuario Nacional de la Immaculada Concepción, Washington, D.C.,* the committee's founder, Mrs. J.E. Anderlik of Chicago, promoted the eventual chapel and collected funds for its establishment. In 1961, a donor

Chapel of Our Lady of Guadalupe.

FUTURE HOPES

∞

In a January 1996 interview, Bishop Thomas J. Grady described his hopes for how pilgrims 100 years from his time might regard the National Shrine: "I hope they will say, 'This church says something to the world about God and about Mary and about the relationship of the American Catholic people to God and to Mary.' They might feel that in a land where scattered across the country there are so many churches named in honor of Mary that it was only appropriate that in the Capital there should be one monumental church to express the devotion of the Catholics of the United States. At that time they might possibly wonder that it could be possible to gather the funds for such a major project. If that is the case, it would be something like we view the cathedrals of Chartres or Rouen. We marvel at the faith of people from two small towns who could erect such beautiful and lasting monuments to their faith. Whatever they say, it will not be possible to ignore the Shrine. They will have to say something. It will be a challenge to their faith and to their devotion of Mary." ∞

pledged funds for the chapel's construction, only to later withdraw his pledge because of difficult financial circumstances. Cardinal Cushing, then-treasurer of the Episcopal Committee of the Shrine and chairman of the U.S. bishops' Committee for Latin America, stepped forward in 1963 to take up the cause as a "visible sign of solidarity between the people of the United States and the people of Latin America."

Throughout 1966, additional chapels were completed, making 1965-66 the most productive period of the Shrine's interior completion. Added were the Chapel of Mary Help of Christians, a gift of the Salesian priests and nuns of the United States; the Chapel of Our Lady of Siluva, a gift of Lithuanian Catholics of America and initiated by the exiled auxiliary bishop of Kaunas, Lithuania, Bishop Vincent Brizgys; and the Chapels of Immaculate Heart of Mary and St. Anthony Mary Claret, gifts of the Claretian Fathers.

∞

GRADY DEPARTS A BISHOP

On June 21, 1967, it was announced that the Shrine's fifth director, Msgr. Thomas Grady, had been named auxiliary bishop of the Archdiocese of Chicago. His hasty departure, necessitated by the Aug. 24 consecration ceremony in Chicago, made it difficult to arrange an appropriate acknowledgement of his many accomplishments during the nearly 11 years he spent as the Shrine's director. *Mary's Shrine* noted the tremendous progress achieved during Msgr. Grady's tenure, the result of his keen managerial skills and tireless dedication to completing the work he had inherited. Not only had Msgr. Grady overseen the construction of the Great Upper

Church, but 26 chapels had been added since the Day of Dedication, in addition to the south gallery's massive organ. Additionally, the two main chancel domes had been completed in mosaic as well as the east and west apses, and numerous stained-glass windows had been added. Bishop Grady would continue throughout the years to be an active presence at the National Shrine, frequently visiting for the Shrine's major liturgical celebrations and even dedicating several of the chapels he initiated with Cardinal O'Boyle during his tenure at the Shrine.

In 1974, Bishop Grady was named ordinary of the Diocese of Orlando, Fla., where he served until his retirement in 1989.

At the invitation of Msgr. Michael Bransfield, the Shrine's 10th director, Bishop Grady agreed in 1993 to serve as a member of the revived Iconography Committee to offer advice on proposed artwork for a new era of construction not seen since the period of his own directorship.

∽

THE SIXTH DIRECTOR
— Father William F. McDonough —

On Aug. 10, 1967, Father William F. McDonough was appointed acting director of the Shrine after only nine months

THE SIXTH DIRECTOR
∽

Msgr. William F. McDonough's seven-year tenure as director was marked by tremendous growth in both the physical and spiritual dimensions of the Shrine. He ushered the Shrine through a new and often difficult era in the wake of Vatican II reforms and the resulting criticisms of the "institutional" model of the Church which many considered the Shrine as representing. Msgr. McDonough established the Shrine's active pilgrimage ministry, which continues in the present day to draw capacity crowds from dioceses around the country. As a key participant in developing the U.S. bishops' pastoral letter "Behold Your Mother," He was instrumental in advancing a contemporary understanding of Marian devotion at a time when previously revered articles of Catholic faith were being discarded in favor of liturgical and theological experimentation. ∽

as the assistant director. On Nov. 12, 1968, it was announced that Father McDonough would become the Shrine's sixth director. Like his predecessor, Father McDonough became director without the experience of administering a major church or Catholic institution. He was confronted with challenges unlike those facing any previous Shrine director upon assuming responsibility for the Shrine's management.

As many in the Church continued to grapple with the changes brought about

Blessed Sacrament Chapel

by the Second Vatican Council, a growing number of Catholics — and a large segment of the American public — were beginning to call into question the basic premises of the social, political and religious institutions that had long defined their beliefs and way of life. Once again, the Shrine would have to assert its relevance in a changing and skeptical society, even while the work of completing the Shrine continued at a rapid pace.

During a November 1964 meeting of the Board of Trustees in Rome, plans had been initiated to complete the Blessed Sacrament Chapel as a gift of the priests of the United States. After considerable discussion about how to provide for the estimated $1 million cost of the chapel, it was decided that Archbishop O'Boyle would address the matter at the next general meeting of the U.S. bishops. Eventually, the Shrine petitioned the nation's 35,000 priests to contribute through their ordinaries for the chapel (approximately $30 per priest). Cardinal Joseph Ritter of St. Louis, chairman of the Shrine Episcopal Committee, wrote to the bishops in June 1965 requesting that each ordinary contribute 2.5 times his diocese's quota to the bishops' conference for the chapel.

Msgr. Grady and Eugene Kennedy collaborated closely on the design of the chapel to ensure that it would conform to the developing eucharistic theology emerging from the Second Vatican Council. Msgr. Grady insisted on a design that would facilitate concelebrated liturgies and an appropriate emphasis on the Liturgy of the Word.

The August 1970 edition of *Mary's Shrine* featured its first color cover depicting the newly completed chapel, acclaimed for its "daring" architecture, "brilliance in execution and breath-taking beauty." Cardinal O'Boyle (who was made a cardinal in 1967) presided over the dedication on Sept. 20, 1970, during a Mass commemorating the 50th anniversary of the foundation-stone laying.

∞
TIDES OF DISSENT

Also in 1967, the Shrine was host to the largest gathering ever for the celebration of the "Year of Faith" declared by Pope Paul VI for 1967-68. The Mass was celebrated by the apostolic delegate, Archbishop Luigi Raimondi, on the east porch of the National Shrine. Bishop Grady returned to concelebrate the Mass, attended by an estimated 58,000 people who filled the expanse between the university's Mullen Library and the Shrine.

The "Year of Faith" was initiated to counter what was then perceived as excessive secular influences and casual experimentation with liturgical norms by priests, religious and the laity. Unlike previous eras, when the Church represented a united front in counteracting the moral and spiritual challenges posed by secular society, the Church now was faced with a crisis from within, one brought on by its own members who sought to introduce new modes of religious and liturgical expression. Cardinal O'Boyle emphasized to the assembly the responsibility of those entrusted with teaching the faith:

> *"Granted that every competent teacher of religion has the right to speculate on those matters which have not been clearly defined by the Church; nevertheless, prudence and justice demand that his personal opinions do not damage the Church or scandalize the faithful."*

A crowd of some 58,000 gathers on the campus of The Catholic University of America for the Mass honoring the "Year of Faith."

Queen of Missions Chapel, a gift of the Oblates of Mary Immaculate.

PROGRESS CONTINUED

An ambitious construction schedule was implemented throughout 1967. In addition to the completion of the Blessed Sacrament Chapel, the Queen of Missions Chapel was established as a gift of the Oblates of Mary Immaculate; the west apse, with its five apsidal chapels depicting the Joyful Mysteries of the Rosary, was at last completed as a gift of the Jesuits, their students, alumni, parishioners of Jesuit-run parishes and supporters; 17 new stained-glass windows depicting prominent bishops and priests of American history were added to the upper sacristy; and the west chancel gallery screen and ambulatory with mosaic vaulting was completed. It was also in 1967 that Cardinal Francis J.

Spellman of New York, the nation's most prominent churchman who dedicated the Great Upper Church, died on Dec. 2.

CHANCEL MOSAIC COMPLETED

With the installation of the main chancel dome mosaic in 1968, all of the domes and apses of the northern end of the Great Upper Church were completed. The theme of this prominent dome directly over the newly positioned main altar was designated in the late 1950s by the Iconography Committee under the direction of John De Rosen. The dome, however, was particularly evocative of one of the central themes evoked by the Second Vatican Council: namely, the role of the Holy Spirit in the life of the Church.

Measuring 3,950 square feet and comprising 1.25 million mosaic tiles, the "Descent of the Holy Spirit" mosaic is the largest in the Shrine. It represents the birth of the Church through the descent of the Holy Spirit at Pentecost (Acts 2:1-4). The accompanying texts further elaborate the role of the Third Person of the Trinity as the fulfillment of Christ's promise to send a Helper to guide and sustain the Church until His return: "Jesus has poured forth this spirit you see and hear" (Acts 2:33); "In these days I will pour out my spirit upon all mankind" (Jl 1:2); "Send forth your spirit and renew

the faces of the earth" (Ps 104:30); "The spirit of the Lord fills the world and governs all" (Wis 7:24-8:1).

The mosaic depicts the apostles and the Virgin Mary receiving the Holy Spirit as described in the Acts of the Apostles. Within the mosaic, three diverse groups of individuals are seen receiving the Holy Spirit in keeping with the Second Vatican Council's central teaching that all of humanity is called to holiness. The theme continues into the four pendentives, where the tongues of fire fall upon representations of the four parts of the world: Europe (heir to the Mediterranean classical world), Asia (represented as a Buddhist monk), Africa (represented as a tribesman) and America (symbolized by an American Indian). The artist of the mosaic was Max Ingrand of Paris. The mosaic was manufactured by the Ravenna Mosaic Company of St. Louis.

Chancel mosaic depicting the "Descent of the Holy Spirit."

A SEASON OF TURMOIL

While it was by now clear that the National Shrine was representative of the diverse cultures comprising the Church in America, the Shrine was increasingly powerless to counteract the disenfranchisement that a large number of Catholics were experiencing. From its earliest beginnings, those responsible for the Shrine had attempted to cultivate a national character and an identity that appealed to the diversity of religious and cultural backgrounds that constituted the Catholic Church in the United States. For many, the Shrine remained a proud national symbol of the enduring elements of Catholic faith in the midst of the growing tensions of 1968. For others, however, the Shrine was a conspicu-

ous reminder of everything that was "wrong" with the Church.

Anti-war demonstrations were frequent occurrences at the National Shrine. At other times, demonstrators protested what they perceived as the Church's indifference to the injustices of war, poverty and racism. As the Shrine prepared to celebrate the 10th anniversary of the Great Upper Church's completion, a growing segment of the Catholic population was beginning to question the basic tenets of Catholic faith that justified the establishment of the Shrine in the first place. The more vocal opponents assailed the Shrine as representing a bygone era of ecclesiastical splendor, obsolete devotion and wasteful expenditure of Church resources. Many regarded the enhancements to the Shrine — the addition of new chapels, mosaics and marble cladding to the interior brick surfaces — as an affront to the impoverished neighborhoods located just a short distance from the Shrine's main doors.

The assassination of Martin Luther King Jr. on April 4, 1968, and the subsequent murder of Robert F. Kennedy on June 6, 1968, by yet another crazed gunman, caused large segments of the population to harbor serious doubts about the "rightness" of the American way of life. King's murder, which triggered racial violence in major cities throughout the country, was responsible for the rioting that all but shut down the city of Washington.

On April 7, 1968, Cardinal O'Boyle celebrated a memorial Mass in the Great Upper Church for the slain civil-rights leader that was attended by nearly 4,000 people. Then, on June 8, 1968, a memorial Mass for Robert Kennedy was cele-

Cardinal O'Boyle offers consolation to the thousands gathered at the memorial for Martin Luther King Jr. on April 7, 1968.

brated in the Crypt Church by Father George F. McLean, an Oblate of Mary Immaculate. Msgr. McDonough offered a second Mass for Kennedy in the Great Upper Church the next day. The Shrine demonstrated once again that in the midst of turmoil at home, wars abroad and widespread moral and spiritual decline, it was still a vital force for comfort and healing.

INDEPENDENCE

The more than 50-year effort to define the National Shrine as a distinctly separate institution from Catholic University and assert its national character reached a defining moment in June 1968 when a new and separate Board of Trustees was established. Owing to the Shrine's increasing influence as the major liturgical center for the Church in the United States, it was finally determined that a

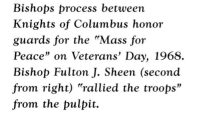

Bishops process between Knights of Columbus honor guards for the "Mass for Peace" on Veterans' Day, 1968. Bishop Fulton J. Sheen (second from right) "rallied the troops" from the pulpit.

more efficient process should be established to direct the Shrine's year-round activities and to consider the future of the Shrine's ministry in light of the fast-changing climate of the postconciliar era. The Shrine's long struggle for independence, which had resulted in the resignations of the Shrine's original Building Committee chairman, Cardinal Dennis Dougherty, and Msgr. Bernard McKenna, in addition to the unhappy cohabitation of several other directors and university officials, had at last been won.

'MASS FOR PEACE'

As the 10th anniversary of the National Shrine's dedication approached, those involved with celebratory preparations were intent on using the occasion to rejuvenate Catholics' faith in their Church and to make a strong statement in support of the United States government as it struggled to resolve America's ongoing involvement in the Vietnam War.

Characterized as a "Mass for Peace," the Shrine's 10th anniversary was celebrated at the closing Mass of the meeting of the National Conference of Catholic Bishops (NCCB — formerly the National Catholic Welfare Conference). It also served to celebrate the nation's observance of Veterans' Day. The church-state liturgy was attended by seven American cardinals, the apostolic delegate and some 175 other bishops, including Bishop Grady. An original work for organ, titled "Solemn Mass for Peace," was composed especially for the celebration by Jean Langlais, the renowned organist of St. Clotilde in Paris. Esteemed Catholic orator Bishop Fulton J. Sheen delivered a stirring sermon, during which he insisted that "peace is [achieved] from the inside out, not from the outside in."

A military presence was particularly conspicuous as the colors were presented prior to the start of Mass. Cadets and midshipmen of the Holy Trinity Chapel Choir of West Point, the U.S. Naval Academy Catholic Chapel Choir and the U.S. Air Force Academy Catholic Choir joined the National Shrine Chorale and the Catholic University Choir in singing the various parts of the Mass. Additionally, representatives of the U.S. government, various branches of the U.S. military and foreign embassies were in attendance for what must have seemed a veritable church-and-state pep rally. During the Mass, a lively protest ensued on the front steps of the National Shrine, resulting in the highly publicized arrest of six Washington-area Catholics, including a suspended priest of the

PRAY THE ROSARY FOR PEACE

Archdiocese of Washington.

Bishop Sheen, who himself had openly opposed America's involvement in the Vietnam War earlier, now warned against "the delusion" that the cessation of the war would guarantee peace. He challenged those in attendance to consider not only the political and economic revolutions underway but also the moral, spiritual and personal revolutions as well.

The May 1971 cover of Mary's Shrine offered a poignant reminder of America's cost of involvement in the Vietnam War.

In his characteristic dramatic style, Bishop Sheen noted with irony the abandonment of tried-and-true expressions of devotion, which he claimed resulted in the moral and spiritual afflictions gripping the nation. "As we drop the Rosary, the hippies put beads around their necks; as nuns drop the long habits, the young women wear maxi-coats, and as we drop dying to self, or mortification, youth mortifies and does violence to those who differ with them," he said. "Unless there is a spiritual unburdening of guilt and egotism in the heart of man, all that an economic revolution will do will be to transfer money from one man's pocket to another; and all that a political revolution will do will be to transfer power from the shaved to the hirsute —

(right) An impassioned Bishop Sheen.

(below) "One giant leap. . . ." The crew of the Apollo 11 — (left to right) Neil A. Armstrong, Michael Collins and Edwin E. Aldrin Jr.

from those with short hair to those with long hair."

∞

A QUEST FOR PEACE: 'REFLECTIONS ON THE MOON WALK'

Seeking to chronicle and provide a spiritual interpretation of the significant events of the nation and world, even as it reported on the Shrine's physical advancements, the August 1969 edition of *Mary's Shrine* featured on its cover the three astronauts of the Apollo 11 moon mission — Neil Armstrong, Michael Collins and Edwin "Buzz" Aldrin Jr. Beneath their photograph, the caption read: "Astronauts leave for the moon on the feast of Our Lady of Mt. Carmel." In

an article titled "Reflections on the Moon Walk," the unnamed author, obviously referring to the Vietnam War, pondered the deeper implications of scientific and technological progress: "This far-reaching scientific achievement is an indication of the evolution and development of the human mind. Christ beckons us gently to explore the wonders of all creation. . . . Will this initial conquest of the moon help man conquer himself? Will it bring us closer to world peace? Many think it will. Peace and space have similar spellings. May the success of our peace program equal the success of our space program! Not to live in peace with our brother is, in reality, not to live."

∞

DETERMINED GROWTH

At the beginning of the 1970s, the Shrine's Board of Trustees looked forward to the completion of all the chapels planned for the Great Upper Church and to the continuing transformation of the Shrine's unadorned brick interior with marble veneer.

The chapels of Our Lady of the Rosary, St. Dominic and St. Catherine of

(above) Cardinal O'Boyle sprinkles the Blessed Sacrament Chapel with holy water during the dedication liturgy, Sept. 20, 1970.

(left) Msgr. McDonough and Theodore Cooley observe Louise Cooley as she stitches an explanatory appendium to the tapestry of the Chapel of Our Lady of Czestochowa. Both appendium and tapestry were designed by French artist Max Ingrand.

(above) Archbishop Franjo Kuharic of Zagreb (center) dedicates the Croatian Chapel of Our Lady of Bistrica, Oct. 7, 1970.

Siena were completed in the east lateral nave of the Great Upper Church as a gift of the more than 1,000 priests and brothers of the three American provinces, 35,000 sisters and thousands of tertiaries of the Order of Preachers (Dominicans). These chapels were designed by Eugene Kennedy; Dominican Sister Thoma Swanson designed the mosaics that adorn the chapels.

The Croatian chapels of Our Lady of Bistrica and Our Lady Queen of Peace by the Croatian Catholic Union of the United States were established to memorialize not only the heroic perseverance of the Croatian people in their centuries-old faith, but the beloved figures of Croatia's past and present who embodied the highest ideals of Croatian nationalism and Christian discipleship. On June 21, 1970, in the presence of some 20,000 Croatians gathered in Rome for the ceremony, Pope Paul VI canonized Blessed Nicholas Tavelic, a Franciscan

A second Croatian chapel, honoring Our Lady Queen of Peace.

priest who was martyred in the Holy Land in the 14th century.

The memory of Croatia's modern-day unofficial saint, Cardinal Aloysius Victor Stepinac — the former archbishop of Zagreb who died in 1960 after enduring years of harassment in occupied Croatia during World War II and imprisonment by communists after the war — further inspired the determination of Croatian Catholics to establish a Croatian presence at the Shrine. Renowned Croatian sculptor Ivan Mestrovic, who produced the figures of Mary Immaculate above the main portal of the Shrine and at the exterior north apse, had ensured a special relationship between the Croatian people and the National Shrine. With the erection of two Croatian chapels on either side of the entrance to the crypt, this relationship became even stronger. The Croatian Catholic Union of the United States agreed in 1966 to establish two chapels — one in honor of Our Lady of Bistrica and the other in honor of Our Lady Queen of Peace. Both altars were consecrated by Archbishop Franjo Kubaric of Zagreb on Oct. 17, 1970. Over 3,000 people of Croatian descent joined in the celebration.

∞

A WORLD PREMIERE AT THE NATIONAL SHRINE

On March 19, 1972, the Shrine secured what *The New York Times* described as a "footnote in musical history" with the world premiere of "Meditations on the Holy Trinity" by one of the 20th century's foremost composers and organists, Olivier Messiaen.

The Shrine's organist, Joseph Michaud, met Messiaen in Washington during a composition symposium held at American University in 1971. Their discussion afterward led to a tour of the Shrine and an inspection of its Möller organ in the south gallery. Messiaen was immediately impressed with the Shrine as a truly "modern church" and expressed a desire to premiere a work which he was in the process of completing.

The eventual premiere of Messiaen's composition proved a defining moment in the musical life of the Shrine. Nearly 3,000 people, including several prominent music critics, came from many parts of North America and Canada. The 85-minute performance gained high critical acclaim, *The Washington Post* reported:

Program of the March 20, 1972, world premiere concert by Olivier Messiaen.

THE NATIONAL SHRINE OF THE IMMACULATE CONCEPTION
WASHINGTON, D.C.

Premiere Performance

MÉDITATIONS SUR LE MYSTÈRE DE LA SAINTE TRINITÉ

Olivier Messiaen

MARCH 20, 1972

"As for the great and small of the organist's profession, they were there as if on a welcome pilgrimage. When the long work, containing about an hour and a quarter of music, was over, it was clear that only Messiaen's expressed wish against applause prevented an enthusiastic outburst. Even so, shortly after the music ended, as he walked down the long aisle to the front of the church to accept an honorary doctorate from Catholic University, his audience seized the opportunity to applaud vehemently. . . .

"It was an extraordinary evening filled with new, and now and then a little old, familiar beauty recalled from his famous earlier works such as 'The Ascension' and 'The Nativity.' No other man could have accomplished any part of it."

The occasion was equally satisfying and poignant for Messiaen, a devout Catholic. Catholic University conferred an honorary doctorate in music on Messiaen following the concert. Messiaen was likewise generous in his praise of the Shrine, describing it as a "perfect church by virtue of its architecture, its symbolism, its admirable mosaics and glass." He went on to conclude: "I consider myself fortunate in having played the magnificent and complete instrument of this beautiful edifice."

The world premiere of a major work by such a noted composer set a modern precedent for the use of the nation's largest Catholic church as an appropriate space for nonliturgical musical events.

The south-gallery Möller organ, with its four manuals, six divisions, 100 stops and 119 ranks, served as the main attraction for this historic musical occasion, However, there are actually four impressive organs at the Shrine in the present day. The west chancel gallery also includes a Möller organ with three manuals, four divisions, 40 stops and 48 ranks.

Maestro Messiaen is awarded an honorary doctorate following his Shrine concert by Clarence C. Walton, president of Catholic University.

Although a city block apart, the two organs are played simultaneously during the noon choral Mass, usually joining together during the entrance and recessional hymns and acclamations. The two organists communicate via intercomphone headsets. Video monitors on both consoles enable the organists to view the nave and the choral conductor's podium located within the rear of the chancel. The south-gallery organ may be heard on the CD recordings *The Mystic Organ, In Dulci Jubilo* and *Times and Seasons.* Both organs are featured on the CD reissue *Maurice and Marie-Madeleine Duruflé.*

The Crypt Church organ (positioned to the right of the Mary Memorial Altar) was built by the Schudi Organ Company and installed in 1987, a gift of Jerome

The Schudi organ of the Crypt Church.

on two CD recordings, *A Child is Born* and *I Sing of a Maiden.*

The Blessed Sacrament Chapel of the Great Upper Church includes a Möller cabinet organ, with two ranks of pipes (flute and principal). Since it is mobile, it also serves in the Upper Church chancel as a continuo instrument for use with orchestral and choral ensembles.

Originally acquired for the Crypt Church, this cabinet organ was moved to the Blessed Sacrament Chapel after the Schudi organ was installed in the Crypt Church in 1987.

In addition to Oliver Messiaen, many of the most prominent organists of the 20th century have performed at the Shrine in recital and for major liturgical events. They include Marcel Dupré, Flor Peeters, Maruice and Marie-Madeleine Duruflé, Jean Langlais, Simon Preston, Heinz Wunderlich, Virgil Fox, E. Power Biggs, Daniel Roth (artist-in-residence for two years), Pierre Cochereau, Gillian Weir and Marilyn Keiser (at the Crypt Church organ dedication), among others.

On Sept. 11, 1976, the LaScala Opera Company, under the direction of maestro Romano Gandolfi, performed Verdi's "Requiem" at a special Mass celebrated by Cardinal William W. Baum, who by then was archbishop of Washington. In 1997, the National Symphony Orchestra, under

and Grace Murray. It features two manuals, three divisions, 23 stops and 25 ranks and includes mechanical key and stop actions with a parallel solenoid-controlled combination action, inspired by the Silbermann organs of Bach's time. This beautifully encased organ is played for weekday Masses, on Sunday and for a variety of special liturgies throughout the year. It can be heard in performance

the direction of Leonard Slatkin, performed Hector Berlioz's "Requiem," with the Choir of the Basilica and members of Washington's Choral Arts Society. Renowned tenor John Aler was the soloist.

Then, on Feb. 7, 1998, the legendary St. Thomas Boys' Choir of Leipzig, Germany, under the direction of Georg Christoph Biller, performed for an immense crowd of some 7,000 in the Great Upper Church. The history of the choir spans more than 780 years and has been led by many of history's most renowned musicians — the most notable being Johann Sebastian Bach, who directed the choir from 1723 until his death in 1750.

'BEHOLD YOUR MOTHER'

Early in 1971, Msgr. McDonough and Cardinal John J. Carberry of St. Louis began a discussion that would eventually result in the first pastoral letter of the U.S. bishops on the appropriateness of Marian devotion in contemporary Catholic faith. The two sought to clarify and reassert Mary's role in the Church for a new generation of Catholics less familiar with the Marian-centered spirituality which had given rise to the National Shrine nearly a century earlier. Surprisingly, the U.S. bishops had never before issued a pastoral letter with Mary as the primary subject.

The task of drafting the essential

Statue depicting "Our Lady of Mankind" within the present-day Memorial Hall.

Cardinal Carberry, who was asked to head the committee, explained the need for such a document during his homily at the NCCB Mass held at the Shrine on Nov. 14, 1973:

"Through our pastoral letter, we hope to set aside completely the report that Vatican Council II had de-emphasized love and devotion to Mary. On the contrary, Vatican Council II, in the Dogmatic Constitution of the Church, chapter VII, entitled 'The Role of the Blessed Virgin Mary, Mother of God, in the Mystery of Christ and the Church,' has given us, as Pope Paul VI has expressed it, 'A vast synthesis of Catholic doctrine' on the teachings of the Church about Mary. Our pastoral letter seeks to present for our beloved faithful, a careful study and amplification of the teachings on Mary which the fathers of the council so carefully prepared."

That it was regarded necessary for the bishops to reassert the importance of Marian devotion for American Catholics was evidence of how much the nature of Catholic faith and devotion had changed in the wake of the Second Vatican Council. Previous references to the essential role of Mary and the saints as intercessors gave way to an increased emphasis on personal spiritual development. For the Shrine, as a national sanctuary dedicated to fostering devotion to the Virgin Mary, this shift in contemporary spirituality had serious ramifications. Msgr. McDonough and others concerned

points to be included in the pastoral letter fell mainly to Msgr. McDonough, who, in turn, consulted 14 prominent Marian scholars. Eventually, a committee of bishops was appointed by Cardinal John F. Dearden, archbishop of Detroit and president of the National Conference of Catholic Bishops (NCCB), to develop the official draft of the pastoral letter, "Behold Your Mother," for formal consideration at the November 1973 meeting of the nation's bishops.

(left) *Then the assistant direc-tor and later the seventh direc-tor, Father John Murphy (left) gets a lesson in the intricate process of assembling mosaic tiles intended for the Byzantine-Ruthenian Chapel.*

(below) *The Byzantine-Ruthenian Chapel.*

with the Shrine's future harbored expectations that the first-ever American pastoral letter on Mary would inspire renewed interest in Marian spirituality.

∞

THE BYZANTINE-RUTHENIAN CHAPEL

Described erroneously as the "last chapel space in the National Shrine," the Byzantine-Ruthenian Chapel was first suggested by Byzantine Archbishop Stephen J. Kocisko of Pittsburgh in a telephone call to Msgr. McDonough in December 1971. The archbishop was later joined in his efforts to establish a chapel by Byzantine Bishop Michael J. Dudick of Passaic, N.J., Ruthenian Bishop Emil J.

(top) **Bishops representing the major rites of the Byzantine Catholic Church gather in the Great Upper Church for the dedication of the Byzantine-Ruthenian Chapel, Oct. 6, 1974.**

(above and right) **Hand-painted icons of the Virgin and Child and Christ that decorate the gate of the Byzantine-Ruthenian Chapel.**

Mihalik of Parma, N.J., and Philadelphia artist Christina Douchwat. The "Eastern-rite Chapel," as it is commonly called, was proposed as a fitting commemoration of the 50th anniversary of the first Byzantine-Ruthenian diocese in the United States. By March 24, 1972, the terms for donating the chapel were agreed upon and the Eastern Catholic bishops were set to campaign for the necessary funds in their parishes across the country during the following October.

On Oct. 6, 1974, the only chapel representing Byzantine Catholics at the National Shrine was dedicated in the presence of more than 6,000 people.

CARDINAL WILLIAM W. BAUM

In 1973, Pope Paul VI accepted Cardinal O'Boyle's resignation as Washington's archbishop and named Bishop William W. Baum of Springfield-Cape Girardeau, Mo., to succeed him.

Born in Dallas, Texas, on Nov. 21, 1926, William Baum and his family moved to Kansas City, Mo., in his early years. He entered St. John's Minor Seminary in 1940, and in 1947 continued his priesthood preparations at Kenrick Seminary in St. Louis. Following his ordination in 1951 and a brief parish and teaching assignment, he attended the University of St. Thomas Aquinas in Rome, where he obtained a doctorate in sacred theology.

Returning to Kansas City in 1958, Father Baum served as secretary of the diocesan tribunal and taught at Avila College in addition to doing parish work. In 1961, he was named a monsignor by Pope John XXIII. When the Second Vatican Council was convened in 1962, Bishop Charles H. Helmsing of Kansas City-St. Joseph, Mo., requested that Msgr. Baum accompany him to Rome as an adviser. He was assigned to work with the Secretariat for Christian Unity, during which time he participated in drafting the document *Unitatis Redintegratio*

(Decree on Ecumenism), which the council fathers approved in November 1964.

When the U.S. bishops formed a Committee for Ecumenical and Interreligious Affairs in 1964, they chose Msgr. Baum as its first executive director, a post he held for five years. Following this, he served as a member of the joint working group of representatives of the Catholic Church and the World Council of Churches. He was named chancellor of the Diocese of Kansas City in 1967.

In 1970, Pope Paul VI named Msgr. Baum the third bishop of the Diocese of Springfield-Cape Girardeau. The following year, the Pope appointed him an American delegate to the World Synod of Bishops at the Vatican.

On May 9, 1973, he succeeded Cardinal O'Boyle as the second resident archbishop of Washington. He was elevated to the rank of cardinal on May 24, 1976.

Archbishop William W. Baum receives congratulations from Cardinal O'Boyle after his elevation to cardinal by Pope Paul VI in 1976.

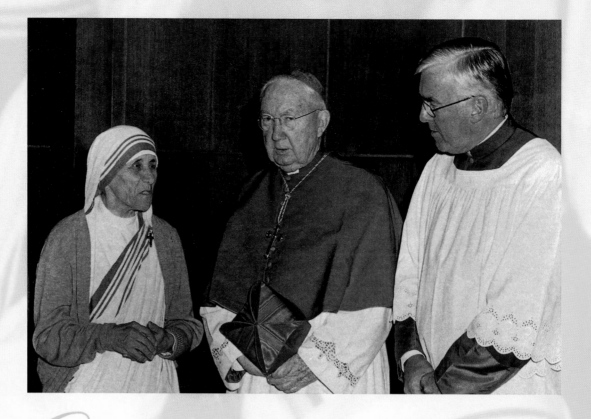

MOTHER TERESA

On July 10, 1974, Mother Teresa of Calcutta made what would be the first of many visits to the National Shrine. She was greatly moved by the majesty of the Great Upper Church and exclaimed, "How pleased the Father must be with this holy place!" During her next visit, at a special Mass marking the International Women's Year on Oct. 26, 1975, Mother Teresa was honored for her work with the poor and dying of the world and presented with a monetary gift collected at the display of Pope Paul VI's coronation tiara. Cardinal O'Boyle, by now retired as Washington's archbishop, introduced Mother Teresa as a great woman "who sees Jesus in every human creature, especially those in the distressing disguise of leprosy, extreme poverty or abandonment."

On the feast of the Immaculate Conception, Dec. 8, 1979, Mother Teresa was awarded the Patronal Medal at the National Shrine. Mrs. Frank Collins of the Co-Workers of Mother Teresa in America, Inc., accepted the award on behalf of Mother Teresa. The Patronal Medal is bestowed annually by The Catholic University of America and the National Shrine on individuals who have advanced the cause of Marian devotion and whose lives mirror Mary's example of faithfulness.

In succeeding years, Mother Teresa regularly journeyed to the Shrine to attend the solemn profession of her sisters into the Society of the Missionaries of Charity, which she founded in 1948. Mother Teresa's last visit occurred on Dec. 8, 1995, when she attended the profession of 15 Missionaries of Charity in the Great Upper Church. Although in failing health, the 86-year-old Nobel Peace Prize laureate recounted with characteristic enthusiasm her order's expansion into 129 countries, and singled out the rapid growth of her order in her native Albania.

Shortly after her death on Sept. 6, 1997, a stained-glass window depicting Mother Teresa was commissioned and installed in the crypt sacristy to honor her long association with the Shrine as well as her inspiring service to the "poorest of the poor." ∞

(above) Mother Teresa is surrounded by members of her Missionaries of Charity and Cardinal James A. Hickey of Washington, Dec. 8, 1995.

(left) A stained-glass depiction of Mother Teresa within the Crypt Church sacristy.

(bottom left) Mother Teresa addresses the congregation from the lectern in the Great Upper Church during her last visit to the National Shrine on Dec. 8, 1995, for the solemn profession of 15 Missionaries of Charity.

(opposite) Mother Teresa, Cardinal O'Boyle and Msgr. Murphy discuss the work of the Missionaries of Charity following a Shrine Mass honoring her order's service to the poor, dying and dispossessed, Oct. 26, 1975.

THE SEVENTH DIRECTOR

Msgr. John J. Murphy's 14 years of service at the National Shrine — first as assistant director shortly after the Shrine's dedication, and then as director beginning in 1973 — were marked more by the development of programs to reflect the catechetical and liturgical changes brought on by the Second Vatican Council than by new building projects. The greatest challenge for the Shrine in the postconciliar age was how to reassert the role of Mary as model of faith and intercessor for a new generation of Catholics unfamiliar with traditional expressions of Marian devotion that justified the Shrine in its early years. Msgr. Murphy put special emphasis on the Shrine's "cultural outreach" programs, represented primarily by an active music ministry, as a means of attracting to the Shrine those who otherwise might not come for purely "religious" reasons. Along with the traditional devotions of the Rosary and Angelus, the Shrine under Msgr. Murphy initiated a series of Marian "dialogues" and Vespers as part of the vigil celebration of each solemnity and feast of the Virgin Mary.

In keeping with the Church's renewed emphasis on the proper initiation of adults into the Catholic faith, more than 80 people received instructions as catechumens and were received into the Church at the National Shrine. In many ways, the Shrine under Msgr. Murphy functioned very much like a parish church. This was due in large part to the desire of so many Catholics to become more intimately involved in the liturgical and ministerial functions of their faith. ∞

THE SEVENTH DIRECTOR
— Msgr. John J. Murphy —

In May 1973, Msgr. McDonough returned to the Archdiocese of Philadelphia as pastor of Mother of Divine Providence Church, King of Prussia, Pa. He regularly visited the National Shrine and later served on the special committee of the Board of Trustees to promote Marian devotion at the Shrine. He continued in faithful service to the Philadelphia archdiocese until his death in 1995.

Msgr. John J. Murphy was the first priest of the Archdiocese of Washington to serve as Shrine director. A native of Boston, Mass., Msgr. Murphy was ordained on May 1, 1954, by Archbishop O'Boyle. Prior to his appointment as the Shrine's seventh director by Archbishop Baum on June 1, 1973, Msgr. Murphy had served as the Shrine's assistant director from December 1959 to May 1966.

The beginning of his directorship had a good deal in common with that of other Shrine directors who suddenly found themselves responsible for the nation's largest Catholic church with little or no preparation. Soon after Msgr. Murphy's appointment, St. Joseph Sister Joan Noreen, the first woman to serve on the staff of the National Shrine, was named assistant to the director.

TOWARD THE THIRD MILLENNIUM

1975 - Onward

When Pope Paul VI declared the year 1975 a Holy Year, he used the word "jubilee" to characterize this special period set aside as a time of reconciliation and renewal for the entire Church. The Holy Father's choice of the term "jubilee" was borrowed from the practice of the Israelites of the Old Testament, who observed a jubilee year of emancipation and restoration every 50 years as prescribed in the Book of Leviticus (25:10).

In Christian tradition, the celebration of a jubilee serves to mark a profound religious experience among the people of God. The ritual expression of Christian celebration of a jubilee is the act of making a pilgrimage. The National Conference of Catholic Bishops' designation of the National Shrine as a "place of pilgrimage" in the United States during the Holy Year helped reinforce the importance of the Shrine as the pre-eminent pilgrimage site of the country.

❧

A BICENTENNIAL CELEBRATION

America's bicentennial year in 1976 provided a unique opportunity to reiterate the National Shrine's importance as the patronal church of the nation.

In an article titled "Our National Expression of Gratitude," by the Shrine's assistant director, Father Richard J. Shmaruk, the establishment of the National Shrine was characterized as a dutiful gesture by Catholics in America who rightly comprehended not only their material advantage, but the freedom to exercise their spiritual vision:

More than 10,000 worshipers gather at the Shrine on July 4, 1976, for a Mass for children and young people during the nation's bicentennial celebration. The Old Guard Fife and Drum Corps, 3rd Infantry, Fort Meyer, Va., led the flag-presentation ceremony prior to the liturgy.

"The National Shrine has been erected by the Catholic people of this nation as a memorial, and as an act of thanksgiving for the many blessings God has bestowed on the Church in America: his gift of salvation, his protection and guidance, the freedom to worship and practice the faith, and especially, the generous gift of his Mother who, under the title of Immaculate Conception, is patroness of the United States of America. It is a church where the Eucharist, the great banquet of thanksgiving, is offered to God every day in response to his loving generosity. And it is a place of pilgrimage in the tradition of God's pilgrim people in biblical times, as well as in the history of Catholicism in America."

During this period, a spirit of ecumenism permeated the Church. At the National Shrine, the emphasis on Christian unity resulted in several ecumenical celebrations during the year. The first took place during the Week of Prayer for Christian Unity on Jan. 18, 1976. The dean of Washington National Cathedral, the Rev. Francis B. Sayre Jr., delivered a sermon at the Shrine that emphasized the parallel history these two great churches shared in the capital city as well as the need for closer collaboration in prayer and works of charity:

"Sometimes, as I step outside the door of the Protestant Cathedral on Mount St. Alban and see the dome and campanile of this Catholic Shrine across the city, I think of St. Dominic and St. Francis and how once they came together, Christ between them.

"Not many of you may know that these two great churches were actually built in part by the same honest hands of mason and bricklayer. Years ago, I used to climb up on the scaffolding about our vaulting to visit with the men who, when we were idle, were borrowed here and who, when this great work was done came back to us again.

"Emblems are they of what we, too, are about this afternoon, they whose labor served the one God over there and over here."

On Feb. 1, 1976, the Hebrew Congregation of Washington met with Catholics and other Christians at the Shrine to celebrate a Judeo-Christian "Festival of Psalms." Archbishop Baum and Rabbi Joshua O. Haberman, senior rabbi of Washington Hebrew Congregation, jointly presided. This was the first time that a Jewish-Catholic program was held at the National Shrine.

(left) President Gerald R. Ford honors the contribution of Spanish-speaking peoples to America's heritage in remarks delivered in the Shrine's Memorial Hall during Spanish Heritage Week, Sept. 16, 1976.

(below) President Ford with Msgr. John Murphy and Auxiliary Bishop Patrick F. Flores of San Antonio.

On Aug. 16, 1976, Gerald R. Ford became the second American president to visit the National Shrine when he attended a Mass in celebration of Hispanic American Heritage Week. Afterwards, he addressed the congregation in Memorial Hall and posed for photographs with members of the Shrine staff.

The National Shrine's bicentennial observance culminated on Sunday, July 4, 1977, with a day of liturgical, devotional, patriotic and musical celebration. More than 16,000 people attended what was billed as a celebration of "The American Experience." The Old Guard Fife and Drum Corps, 3rd Infantry, from Fort Meyer, Va., led the flag-presentation ceremony at the start of the noon "Mass for Children and Young People."

(above) Cardinal Karol Wojtyla of Kraków, Poland, elevates the host during a Mass in the Shrine's Great Upper Church on Aug. 9, 1976.

(left) The future pope gathers in the Chapel of Our Lady of Czestochowa with a delegation of Polish priests, bishops and young people in traditional costumes following Mass. Cardinal Wojtyla is flanked by (from left) Bishop James S. Rausch, executive director of the National Conference of Catholic Bishops, Cardinal Baum, and Archbishop Joseph Bernardin of Cincinnati, president of the United States Catholic Conference.

⸎
A POLISH POPE — A LASTING
FRIENDSHIP FORMED

The International Eucharistic Congress, held in Philadelphia in 1976, brought thousands of pilgrims from around the world to the National Shrine. Groups from Australia, Japan, Italy, Africa, England, Canada, Latin America, Portugal, Mexico, Korea and many other nations visited the Shrine in the three weeks before, during and after the Congress during the month of August. Most notable among the many ecclesiastical visitors was the Archbishop of Kraków, Poland, Cardinal Karol Wojtyla, who led 19 Polish bishops to the Eucharistic Congress and journeyed to the Shrine after the Philadelphia gathering concluded. During his Aug. 9 visit, Cardinal Wojtyla celebrated Mass before a sizable Polish delegation and prayed in the Chapel of Our Lady of Czestochowa.

(This was the second visit of the future pope to the National Shrine. The first took place in 1969 during the directorship of Msgr. McDonough.)

In May 1978, the Shrine's relationship with the future pope was further solidified when Msgr. Murphy, Cardinal Baum (who was elevated to cardinal in 1976) and the cardinal's secretary, Msgr. James Gillen, conducted a 10-day tour of Poland as guests of Cardinal Wojtyla and Cardinal Stefan Wyszynski, primate of Poland. Together with Cardinal Wojtyla, they toured the Nazi death camp of Auschwitz, placed flowers in the cell of Blessed Maximilian Kolbe (later proclaimed a saint by Pope John Paul II) and visited the revered Shrine of Our Lady of Czestochowa.

The tour afforded Msgr. Murphy and Cardinal Baum a unique opportunity to experience the fervent piety and devotion of Polish Catholics with the two leaders who best symbolized the Church's uncompromising posture toward the prevailing communist regime. During their visit, Cardinal Baum, Msgr. Murphy and Msgr. Gillen were invited to participate in the eucharistic procession on the feast of Corpus Christi, during which a throng of 300,000 people lined the main streets of Warsaw. They also attended the annual celebration of Our Lady of Piekary for laborers, at which Cardinal Wojtyla delivered a homily evoking themes that would later rally the Gdansk shipyard workers of the Solidarity movement. Cardinal Baum

(left) The Shrine's sixth director, Msgr. William McDonough, greets Archbishop Karol Wojtyla on the occasion of the Polish prelate's first visit to the National Shrine in 1969.

(below) The newly installed Pope John Paul II is joined by Cardinal Baum (left) as he bestows the apostolic blessing on Msgr. Murphy and the cardinal's secretary, Msgr. James Gillen, for the benefit of pilgrims to the National Shrine, Oct. 28, 1978.

Polish Ambassador Romuald Spasowski and his wife (far left) attend the Shrine's Mass of Thanksgiving for the election of Pope John Paul II, celebrated by Msgr. Eugene G. Bilski (second from right), Oct. 22, 1978.

and Msgr. Murphy's experiences in Poland, virtually on the eve of Cardinal Wojtyla's election to the papacy, served to establish lasting bonds of friendship between the Shrine and the first Polish pope.

Just six days after the Investiture Mass of Pope John Paul II on Oct. 22, 1978, Msgr. Murphy and Cardinal Baum reunited with their esteemed "tour guide" in a private audience at the Vatican. According to Msgr. Murphy, the Holy Father recalled their visit to Poland and his previous visit to Washington. "He made a particular point to ask for the prayers of all who visit the National Shrine that his pontificate would reflect Christ's vision for the world. He then asked Cardinal Baum to join him in giv-

ing a blessing for me to take back to all who pilgrimage to the Shrine." On the same day as the Pope's Investiture Mass in Rome, a special Mass of Thanksgiving was offered at the National Shrine by Msgr. Eugene Bilski, then an assistant director. Heading the list of distinguished guests who attended the Mass were Romuald Spasowski, Poland's ambassador to the United States, and his wife. Both later defected in the wake of the communist crackdown in Poland. Ambassador Spasowski eventually converted to Catholicism and was a frequent visitor to the Shrine.

The Shrine would again welcome Karol Wojtyla on Oct. 7, 1979, during his historic first apostolic pilgrimage to the United States, one year after his election as Pope John Paul II.

❦

OUR LADY OF CHARITY

On Sept. 4, 1977, an 11-foot, 8-inch-high Botticino marble statue of "Our Lady of Charity, Patroness of Cuba" was installed and blessed at the National Shrine, a gift of Cubans of the United States. The statue represented the people whose faith, like the faith of so many others represented at the Shrine, had prevailed against the forces of atheistic communism. The statue was blessed by Bishop Edward Boza-Masvidal, exiled

(left) Cuban pilgrims crowd the Great Upper Church for the blessing of the statue of "Our Lady of Charity, Patroness of Cuba," Sept. 4, 1977.

bishop of Havana. The week that the statue was installed permanently near the chancel in the Great Upper Church, the Carter administration initiated efforts to re-establish relations with Cuba.

The Cuban Madonna was the first statue to be commissioned at the Shrine as a result of artistic competition. Cuban sculptor Manuel Rudolfo Tardo of New York, with his wife, Gilesa, and sculptor Rene Benevides, were responsible for the statue's design. Renowned for his "totemic tropical sculptures," Tardo was the former director of the Cuban School of Plastic Arts and founder of the Art Gallery of Mantanzas. He emigrated to the United States in 1961.

A
PAPAL
VISIT
∞

Early on the morning of Oct. 7, 1979, the National Shrine experienced what was described as its "finest hour" as the 263rd successor to the Apostle Peter ascended its granite stairs and entered the Great Upper Church.

The historic visit of Pope John Paul II to the National Shrine provided the ultimate affirmation for this church, which from its beginnings had sought the approval and encouragement of every pope of the 20th century. This was not Karol Wojtyla's first visit to the National Shrine. but it was the first time that a reigning pope had come to pray beneath the Shrine's great dome.

Early in his papacy, Pope John Paul had emphasized that he did not intend to follow the example of his predecessors — "prisoners of the Vatican" — whose excursions took them scarcely beyond the 108.7 acres of Vatican City State. Rather, he would be known as the "Pilgrim Pope," traversing the globe in witness to the Gospel of Christ and to his role as "Universal Shepherd."

The Pope's visit to the National Shrine, less than a year after his election, had as its primary purpose a major address to women religious of the United States following the ancient Morning Prayer liturgy of the Church. As the Holy Father's motorcade turned into the main entrance of the Shrine from Michigan Avenue at approximately 8:30 that morning, the great bells of the Knights' Tower pealed in joyful celebration. A banner affixed high on the exterior of the tower bearing the Pope's coat of arms with his chosen motto, *Totus Tuus* ("Totally Yours"), was visible from far and wide. As the Pope disembarked his limousine with the apostolic delegate, Archbishop Jean Jadot, at his side, he was met by Msgr. Murphy, the Shrine's director, and two assistant directors, Msgr. Bilski and Father Donald E. Leighton. The thousands who had assembled to welcome the Holy Father cheered wildly and shouted "Long live the Pope" — John Paul II, we love you!" He paused briefly at the top of the steps of the Shrine to speak to the many students and others who had spent the night in an outdoor prayer vigil in anticipation of his visit. At the main doors, the women religious of the Shrine staff presented the Pope with a bouquet of flowers.

In his address to the gathered religious women, the Pope reaffirmed the Shrine as an important national sanctuary which represents the diverse modes of faith and devotion that constitute the Catholic Church in the United States. In part, he proclaimed:

"This Shrine speaks to us with the voice of all America, with the voice of all the sons and daughters of America, who have come here from the various countries of the Old World. When they came, they brought with them in their hearts the same love for the Mother of God that was characteristic of their ancestors and of themselves in their native lands. These people, speaking different languages, coming from different backgrounds of history and tradition in their own countries, came together around the heart of a Mother whom they all had in common. While their faith in Christ made all of them aware of being the one People of God, this awareness became all the more vivid through the presence of the Mother in the work of Christ and the Church."

As Pope John Paul II concluded his visit to the National Shrine, he paused once again at the top of the Shrine's main stairs to offer a prayer for the benefit of those not permitted inside the church, but who waited patiently nonetheless outside the church, hoping for a glimpse of the pilgrim Pope:

"I leave you now with this prayer: that the Lord Jesus will reveal himself to each one of you, that He will give you the strength to go out and profess that you are Christians, that He will show you that He alone can fill your hearts."

'TU ES PETRUS'

Mary's Shrine of November 1979 captures the joy and enthusiasm which Pope John Paul II's visit inspired among the thousands in attendance at the National Shrine on this memorable October morning:

"Once inside, the Great Organs, the brass instruments and 150 voice choir burst into the glorious sounds of 'Tu Es Petrus — You Are Peter.' At the same time the thundering applause and voices of 7,000 people, most of them sisters, reverberated from dome to dome mixing with the music, echoing all of it back to the happy crowd.

"The Pope electrified the atmosphere and seemed in turn to be charged by it. The sisters clamored to reach beyond their lengths — to touch this man. It was obvious that something was going out from him and many struggled to make contact with it.

"After stopping at the communion rail to greet the handicapped sisters, the Pope went to the Blessed Sacrament Chapel for private prayer. The shouts subsided, the great Shrine was still except for the voices of the choir softly singing 'Ubi Caritas — Where There Is Love.' It was the Pope's moment to pray, privately and quietly.

"Returning to his chair, the Holy Father began morning prayer. . . . At the conclusion of the ceremonies the Pope went directly to the Chapel of Our Lady of Czestochowa for a brief period of private prayer. From there he went to the Crypt Church and Memorial Hall to greet the religious brothers of the Archdiocese; staff members of the United States Catholic Conference; the special committee responsible for the planning of the papal visit to Washington, and, finally, those who work in the various agencies of the Archdiocese of Washington."

A SECOND NATIONAL CAMPAIGN

By the mid-1970s, the National Shrine's financial health began to show signs of deterioration. A number of factors contributed to the need to once again appeal to the goodwill of American Catholics through a national collection.

The City of Washington, like other large urban centers of the country that had experienced the strain of political protest and urban violence, struggled to regain the confidence of tourists. Pilgrimages to the National Shrine had declined steadily in the years following Washington's widely publicized riots of 1968. And since it had yet to establish its pilgrimage program that fills the Shrine most weekends in the spring and fall with organized diocesan pilgrimages, the Shrine was beginning to recede from the consciousness of Catholic America. With the emergence of the Catholic renewal movements in the United States, there was a greater emphasis on involvement at the local parish level. Marriage Encounter, Cursillo and the Charismatic Renewal movements all reinforced the need to develop a strong personal spirituality as well as a commitment to rejuvenating one's own parish community.

Between 1974 and 1979, income at the

National Shrine increased a mere 8 percent while, during this same period, operating expenses increased 29 percent. The aggressive nationwide direct-mail program, which today sustains the Shrine's day-to-day operations, had not yet been developed. In short, the Shrine was living beyond its means. Once again, it was time to remind Catholic America that the Shrine was not a parish that could rely on a resident community to sustain its ministry and operations, but a national church for which such responsibilities were shared by all American Catholics.

On Aug. 13, 1978, the Shrine's Board of Trustees commissioned a two-month study by Community Counseling Services, Inc., to determine the feasibility and probable yield of a national collection. An intense review of the Shrine's internal fund-raising operation was initiated as well as a national survey aimed at measuring Catholics' perception of the Shrine. While the attitude of many of those surveyed was that of pride and was generally positive, the survey revealed that large segments of the Catholic population were not even aware of the Shrine's existence.

The Shrine had not prevailed as a dominant force in the life of Catholic America. Even after nearly 60 years, the Shrine struggled to carve out an identity among American Catholics that mirrored its claims of being the pre-eminent center for Marian devotion in the United States, and more significantly America's "patronal church." The Shrine's prognosis compelled immediate action on the part of the American hierarchy. If the trend continued, the consultants predicted, the Shrine would be incapable of continuing beyond the next 10 years.

A national collection would once again have to be accepted by the American bishops, this time with the ambitious goal of raising $10 million. Fortunately, there was little resistance among the bishops, who were well aware of how far the Shrine had come in six decades. They could not ignore the Shrine's progress since the late 1940s, when revived plans for its completion culminated in nearly 60 new chapels and oratories representing the collective achievements of America's religious and ethnic communities.

The Shrine's Board of Trustees and, in turn, the bishops of the nation, responded decisively. The one-time collection for the National Shrine was scheduled for Saturday, Dec. 8 and Sunday, Dec. 9, 1979, in conjunction with the 125th anniversary of the promulgation of the dogma of the Immaculate Conception.

As in 1953, bishops and pastors received parish kits containing suggested homilies, sample collection envelopes, news releases for use in local newspapers, a Marian hymn composed specially for the feast of the Immaculate Conception and a detailed fact sheet about the Shrine emphasizing its historical and spiritual significance to the Church in the United States. A separate appeal was extended simultaneously to all religious orders of men and women, Catholic fraternal and religious organizations, and to prominent members of the laity and charitable foundations.

Once again, a committee was appointed by the board to head the national campaign. It comprised some familiar faces as well as representatives of Catholic fraternal organizations who had previously seen the Shrine through difficult periods. Cardinal O'Boyle was appointed honorary chairman of the campaign. Also included were Bishop Grady of Orlando, Fla.; Bishop Joseph T. Daley of Harrisburg, Pa.; Virgil C. Dechant, supreme knight of the Knights of Columbus; Mrs. Anthony P. Hillemeier, president of the National Council of Catholic Women; Mary Murray, national regent of the Catholic Daughters of America; Dominican Father Gilbert Graham and Sister Mary Clare Hughes, provincial superior of the Emmitsburg Province of the Daughters of Charity.

In conjunction with the campaign, the first promotional film about the National Shrine was produced for nationwide distribution. Titled *To Him She Leads*, the 14-minute "documentary"

KEEPING VIGIL FOR AMERICAN HOSTAGES

Throughout the long ordeal of the Americans held hostage by Iranian extremists between 1979 and 1981, the bells of the National Shrine tolled each day following the noon Angelus in response to President Jimmy Carter's request that churches across the nation ring bells as a constant reminder of the 53 hostages. Additionally, prayers for the safe return of the hostages and a peaceful solution to tensions between Iran and the United States were offered at all Masses at the Shrine and during the twice-daily Rosary. Msgr. Murphy at the time noted that it was "the Blessed Mother's way of showing concern for her children who are being kept against their will from returning to their homeland." ❧

provided a walking tour of the Shrine by actress Helen Hayes and featured footage of the recent visit of Pope John Paul II. It was hoped that Hayes, a devout Catholic, and scenes of the Holy Father speaking from the chancel of the Great Upper Church, would spur renewed appreciation for the Shrine in its hour of need.

With only 139 dioceses (representing roughly 63 percent of the U.S. Catholic population) participating, however, the national campaign garnered just a little over $4 million — far short of its $10 million goal. While certainly not the success hoped for, the campaign achieved the primary objective of rescuing the Shrine from the brink of bankruptcy and forced the Shrine's administrators to conduct a re-examination of the Shrine's development program. What became all too obvious as a result of the national collection of 1979 was that the Shrine would have to continually reassert its role in the life of the Church in America and work for the support that it had come to take for granted.

Following the Shrine's dedication in 1959, religious communities and Catholics nationwide readily identified with the National Shrine as the "official" monument to the accomplishments of the Catholic faith in America. This outpouring of allegiance resulted in a nearly

uninterrupted construction schedule throughout the 1960s and early 1970s. Now, with the chapel areas of the Great Upper Church completed, the Shrine staff faced the more daunting challenge of sustaining national interest and support.

Catholics were becoming more focused on what was occurring in their own dioceses and parishes. Community centers needed to be built; parish churches needed to be renovated to

"The first lady of the theater," actress Helen Hayes, with Msgr. Murphy following the taping of her video tour of the Shrine, titled "To Him She Leads."

accommodate the liturgical reforms of the Second Vatican Council; a new emphasis on developing and supporting programs to address social concerns was underway. In short, the challenge facing the Shrine was how to perpetuate a compelling case for its existence and reassert its relevance for Catholics increasingly preoccupied with implementing their faith through bold action. No longer could the Shrine regard itself merely as an impressive ecclesiastical "monument"; rather, it would have to establish a new role as a living and vibrant national center for prayer and worship where faith and devotion were emphasized as the basis for action. In rethinking its mission, the National Shrine began to assert a new identity as both a reference point for the heroic accomplishments of Catholic America in the 20th century and as a point of departure for the equally ambitious work of accomplishing the work of faith in the years ahead.

Archbishop James A. Hickey

∞

CARDINAL JAMES A. HICKEY

The year 1980 signaled a significant change in the governance of the Shrine's administrative body, Pope John Paul II appointed Cardinal Baum to serve in the Roman Curia as prefect of the Sacred Congregation for Catholic Education. Succeeding him as archbishop of Washington was Bishop James Aloysius Hickey of Cleveland.

Born in Midland, Mich., in 1920, James Hickey graduated from Sacred Heart Seminary College in Detroit in 1942. He completed graduate studies in theology at The Catholic University of America in 1946 and was ordained a priest of the Diocese of Saginaw that same year. Shortly after Father Hickey's ordination, Bishop Stephen S. Woznicki dispatched him for doctoral studies in canon law at the Pontifical Lateran University in Rome. He later earned a doctorate in theology at Rome's Pontifical Angelicum University.

Returning to the United States in 1957, Father Hickey served for nine years as Bishop Woznicki's secretary. In February 1967, Pope Paul VI named him auxiliary bishop of Saginaw. A little over a year later, Bishop Hickey became administrator of the Diocese of Saginaw after Bishop Woznicki retired. In 1969, Bishop Hickey was appointed rector of the Pontifical North American College in Rome. On June 5, 1974, he was named bishop of Cleveland, where he was responsible for 951,000 Catholics in northeastern Ohio.

On June 17, 1980, Pope John Paul II appointed Bishop Hickey the third archbishop of Washington. Archbishop Hickey was elevated to the College of Cardinals by Pope John Paul II on June 28, 1988. As archbishop of Washington, Cardinal Hickey continued the tradition of serving as ex officio chancellor of Catholic University and chairman of the Board of Trustees of the Basilica of the National Shrine. In succeeding years, Cardinal Hickey would preside over the board during one of the most ambitious growth periods in the Shrine's history.

OUR LADY, QUEEN OF IRELAND

On Nov. 9, 1980, a new oratory was dedicated in the west narthex of the Great Upper Church as a tribute to Mary as Queen and Protectress of the Catholic faith in Ireland, and to honor the unparalleled influence of Irish faith, devotion and culture on the Church in the New World. The gift of the Oratory of Our Lady, Queen of Ireland, was first announced by New York's archbishop, Cardinal Terence J. Cooke, in a June 5, 1976, letter to Msgr. Murphy:

"I am pleased to let you know that I have found a donor for the proposed Irish Oratory at the National Shrine. Mr. McShain of Philadelphia has indicated his willingness to cover the $177,000.00 cost."

Early in 1974, Cardinal Timothy Manning of Los Angeles had engaged Msgr. Murphy in a discussion about designating a suitable place within the Shrine for an "Oratory of Irish Saints." In February 1976, Cardinal Cooke, another member of the hierarchy who shared a personal interest in an Irish memorial at the Shrine, entered the discussion about the proposed iconography for such an oratory. Cardinal Cooke had in mind a donor whose love of the Shrine and Ireland was equaled only by his own: John McShain. The gift of an Irish orato-

ry by McShain served as the last gesture of devotion by the man "who built Washington," to the church he characterized as the "fulfillment" of his life's ambition. The Iconography Committee — which now consisted of Cardinal Baum; Father Frederick R. McManus, Dominican Father Frederick M. Jelly and Father Eamon R. Carroll, all of Catholic University; Shrine assistant Sister Noreen, architect Eugene Kennedy, Msgr. Murphy and Bishop Grady — labored at great length to arrive at an iconographic scheme that articulated the rich tradition of Irish Catholicism without succumbing to sentimentality or dubious claims of popular devotion.

As a personal tribute to McShain and his family, it was decided that the McShain family coat-of-arms would be inscribed over the entrance (as seen from within the oratory). This pleased McShain very much and ensured that as long as the Shrine stood, the McShain name would be a permanent fixture on the walls he erected as builder and benefactor.

Bishop Grady referred to a 1974 publication titled *The Book of Kells: Reproductions from the Manuscripts in Trinity College, Dublin* as a starting point for considering the oratory's design and iconography. He encouraged the "style, coloration, sense of intricacy and mystery" found in *The Book of Kells* as the basis for developing a modernized adaptation of these qualities. Bishop Grady suggested the choice of green marble; the crystal mobile that hangs over the sculpted figure of the Madonna and Child; the inclusion of the four evangelists, symbolizing Irish fidelity to the Gospels; and the incorporation of the "Breastplate of St. Patrick" in the texts chosen for inscription within the chapel:

"Christ be with me, Christ within me,
Christ behind me, Christ before me,
Christ beside me, Christ to win me,
Christ to comfort and restore me,
Christ beneath me, Christ above me,
Christ in quiet, Christ in danger,
Christ in hearts of all that love me,
Christ in mouth of friend and stranger."

Within the oratory, the first of two fountain pools was established (the other is within the Chapel of Our Lady of Hope). The architect, Msgr. Murphy and McShain hoped to create a "refreshing resting place where one can stop and pause and sit." In this regard, the Irish Oratory was unlike any other Shrine chapel. There would be no altar; the seated Madonna and Child instead would be central. Benches would be placed along the perimeter of the oratory to allow visitors to sit in quiet reflection.

Throughout the long and involved

Builder and benefactor John McShain.

process of determining the final iconography of the oratory and producing architectural drawings, McShain followed the progress from his Kilarney House estate, located on the Lakes of Kilarney in County Kerry, Ireland, which he purchased in 1960. It was here in his beloved "Irish home" that McShain retired permanently in 1987 with his wife, Mary. On Sept. 9, 1989, John McShain died peacefully at Kilarney House at the age of 89.

THE EIGHTH DIRECTOR
— Msgr. Eugene G. Bilski —

On Dec. 18, Msgr. Murphy left his post as the Shrine's seventh director to assume new duties as pastor of St. Joseph's Parish on Capitol Hill. Msgr.

THE EIGHTH DIRECTOR

∞

After his appointment as director on March 19, 1981, Msgr. Eugene G. Bilski explained the new challenges facing the National Shrine:

"The Shrine has entered a new era. Prompted by an expression of needs from the thousands of pilgrims who travel here yearly, the Shrine seeks to respond, challenged by Pope Paul VI who, in the document 'On Evangelization In the Modern World,' calls upon the Church to 'see by every means of study how we can bring the Christian message to modern man.' "

Msgr. Bilski continued the emphasis on evangelization and catechesis as part of the Shrine's ministry. In the effort to further promote the bishops' 1973 pastoral letter "Behold Your Mother: Woman of Faith," the Shrine's board authorized the preparation of catechetical guidelines for distribution to families, schools and educational institutions throughout the country. Eventually, a catechetical-liturgical kit was developed in consultation with the National Catholic Education Association, the Conference of Diocesan Directors of CCD, the Office of Liturgy of the U.S. Catholic Conference and the Federation of Diocesan Liturgical Commissions. Authored by Chicago priest Father Louis J. Cameli, director of spiritual life at St. Mary of the Lake Seminary in Mundelein, Ill., and titled "Mary's Journey: A Kit for Marian Catechesis," the resource included Father Cameli's book and six catechetical booklets designed to provide instruction about Marian feasts and solemnities for various age groups, beginning with ages 6-8. Msgr. Bilski promoted this instructional tool in order to help pastors and parishioners across the country to gain a renewed and informed appreciation for the role of Marian devotion in the contemporary Church. ∞

Eugene G. Bilski, associate director of the Shrine since 1977, was named administrator by the Board of Trustees pending the formal selection of a new director. He was eventually named director on March 19, 1981.

Msgr. Bilski was a priest of the Diocese of Scranton, Pa., where he served as diocesan director of Christian doctrine. He was appointed a member of the Shrine's Board of Trustees by Archbishop Baum in 1976.

Just over a year later, Msgr. Bilski was appointed as an assistant director of the National Shrine to introduce a new catechetical and educational dimension to the Shrine's ministry. Through this new dimension, an outgrowth of the U.S. bishops' 1973 pastoral letter, "Behold Your Mother: Woman of Faith," the board sought to broaden the Shrine's appeal among a new generation of Catholics — who, in general, were less familiar with the tradition that had long justified the Shrine's existence and defined its identity.

Between 1981 and 1983, the "little journal" first begun by Bishop Shahan as *Salve Regina*, and changed to *Mary's Shrine* by Msgr. Grady in 1959, had its name changed again by Msgr. Bilski. The newly titled *To Him She Leads* was intended to reflect the Shrine's renewed emphasis on its mission to entice a steady flow of pilgrimages from across the nation. "Encouraged by the witness of Pope John Paul II who traveled to the Shrine as a pilgrim, the ministry here is becoming more sharply focused on that of pilgrimage as a contemporary experience of faith," wrote Msgr. Bilski in the September 1981 edition of *To Him She Leads*.

∞

CZECH NATIONAL CHAPEL OF OUR LADY OF HOSTYN

When the Confessional Chapel of Our Lady of Hostyn was dedicated in 1983, it was the culmination of 27 years of planning that began in 1956 when Benedictine Father Augustine Studeny, a prolific writer on Czech hagiography and history, first proposed the idea of a Czech chapel at the National Shrine. Father Studeny had been responsible for gathering 40,000 signatures of Czech Americans on behalf of the beatification of Bishop John Neumann in the late 1930s. Several others likewise attempted to encourage interest in a Czech chapel over the years, but abandoned their efforts due to a lack of sufficient coordination or interest.

In the early 1970s, an employee at the National Shrine, Eduard Fusek, revived the debate on the need for a Czech

chapel and gained the collaboration of several prominent churchman — most notably, Bishop John L. Morkovsky of Galveston-Houston, Texas; Archbishop Daniel W. Kucera, O.S.B., of Dubuque, Iowa; Bishop Jaroslav Skarvada of Rome, Bishop Alfred E. Novak of São Paulo, Brazil, and Cardinal John J. Krol of Philadelphia.

During a conference of Czech-American hierarchy, clergy and laity held on the occasion of the International Eucharistic Congress in Philadelphia on Aug. 9, 1976, it was decided that the Czech National Chapel of Our Lady of Hostyn should also honor Blessed John Neumann in light of his upcoming canonization, which was scheduled for the following year by Pope Paul VI.

Born in the Czech province of Bohemia, John Neumann emigrated to

the United States in 1836, and was ordained a priest for the diocese of New York on June 25 of the same year. He joined the Redemptorist Fathers in 1840, and was sent to serve in Baltimore from 1844 until 1851. There he was later named rector of his religious house and the church of St. Alphonsus. Baltimore Archbishop Francis P. Kenrick designated Father Neumann as his confessor and soon thereafter submitted his name to Rome for selection to the episcopacy. Father Neumann was named fourth bishop of Philadelphia by Pope Pius IX on

Bronze statue of St. John Neumann within the Chapel of Our Lady of Hostyn.

Feb. 1, 1852, and ordained the following month on Passion Sunday in his parish church of St. Alphonsus. He served in Philadelphia until his sudden death in 1860 at his cathedral parish.

A committee was formed in 1977 under the leadership of Bishop Morkovsky to raise funds and plan the architecture and iconography of the chapel. The Shrine's longstanding architect, Eugene Kennedy, designed the chapel and closely collaborated on all details. Early on, it was decided to include a statue of St. John Neumann in order to introduce an "intercontinental" focus. With the famed Madonna of the mountain church of Hostyn in Moravia positioned prominently behind the altar and the imposing bronze statue of St. John Neumann (created by sculptor Jan Koblasa, professor of the Academy of Arts in Kiel, Germany) just inside the entrance to the chapel, the two continents of Catholic Europe and Catholic America are brought together. Actual soil from Hostyn, from Prachatice (the birthplace of St. John Neumann) and from below the altar of St. Wenceslaus in the Cathedral of St. Vitus in Prague were encased in three containers and placed in a commemorative marble plaque affixed to the right wall within the chapel.

During his visit to the Shrine on Oct. 7, 1979, Pope John Paul II blessed the marble plaque symbolizing the first stone for the construction of the Czech Chapel. A relic of St. John Neumann is also contained within the chapel. Glass artist Isabel Piszek of Los Angeles executed the stained-glass entrance screen depicting episodes from the life of St. John Neumann — his missionary work, his love of children as one of the early founders of the parochial-school system, and his devotion to the Blessed Sacrament.

Described as the three "greatest days in the life of the Czechoslovak community of the United States and in all America," the dedication events of June 24-26, 1983, began with a pastoral conference of members of the Czech Catholic hierarchy, clergy and laity at Washington's Hilton Hotel. In this context, a press conference was also held to discuss the release of a Public Declaration on the Infringement of Human and Religious Rights in Czechoslovakia. Later the same day, Cardinal Krol presided over a prayer vigil and placed the relic of St. John Neumann permanently within the chapel.

The following day, the altar was dedicated, and the first Mass was offered in the chapel by Washington Archbishop

Statue of Our Lady of Hostyn with the Christ Child.

James A. Hickey, followed by a penitential service and a testimonial dinner later that evening in honor of Cardinal Frantisek Tomasek, the exiled archbishop of Prague and primate of Bohemia. Jeane Kirkpatrick, U.S. ambassador to the United Nations, addressed the 1,200 individuals gathered for the dinner and received a standing ovation when she read a *Washington Post* account of police crackdowns on anti-Soviet demonstrators underway in Czechoslovakia. President Ronald Reagan personally received the Czech Chapel Dedication Committee on Aug. 11, 1983, when committee members presented him the first St. John Neumann Award in an Oval Office ceremony.

The solemn dedication of the chapel took place on June 26 in the Great Upper Church with Bishop Morkovsky presiding. Homilies were delivered in both Czech and in English. Many of the more than 8,000 gathered for the dedication Mass were attired in elaborate Czech and Moravian national costumes. Following the moving liturgy, 15 various dancing groups from across the United States and Canada entertained those in attendance with traditional folk songs and dance on the east side of the Shrine.

The Chapel of Our Lady of Hostyn, as the Shrine's confessional chapel, is one of the most frequently visited chapels in the National Shrine.

∞

THE KNIGHTS OF COLUMBUS IN THE LIFE OF THE NATIONAL SHRINE

Of the many hundreds of fraternal organizations, lay societies and religious orders that carry out the Church's numerous apostolates throughout the United States and world, none is recognized as having made a more lasting mark on so many sectors of society than the Knights of Columbus. Always ready to assist with any cause that promotes the Catholic faith and makes possible new opportunities for fulfilling the Christian requirement of service, the Knights have been among the Shrine's strongest advocates from its earliest days.

When the site of the intended Shrine was originally blessed by the apostolic delegate on May 16, 1920, some 1,500 Knights of Columbus and 600 Daughters of Isabella traveled by chartered train from New Haven, Conn., to attend the significant occasion. Just four months later, the Knights of Columbus were again prominently represented as honor guard and escort to Cardinal James Gibbons during the cornerstone laying on Sept. 23, 1920. In 1957, as the superstructure of the National Shrine finally began to take form, it was the Knights of Columbus, under the direction of Supreme Knight Luke Hart, that ensured its intended form with a gift of $1 million for the construction of the 329-foot campanile tower. Just a few short years later, the Knights provided for the casting and installation of a 56-bell carillon to complete their gift of the tower, appropriately designated as the Knights' Tower.

By 1989, the Knights' Tower was in need of a thorough cleaning and restoration. Once again, the Knights of

Columbus stepped forward and contributed the considerable costs associated with the project. On Sept. 10, 1989, the Knights' Tower was rededicated by Cardinal Hickey in the presence of several thousand Knights and Ladies. Honoring Supreme Knight Virgil Dechant's devotion to the National Shrine, one of the carillon's large bells was named after his patron, St. Virgil.

On Sept. 12, 1982, the Knights of Columbus inaugurated a new era of service to the National Shrine when 231 knights assumed formal responsibility for the Shrine's Ministry of Usher Program. With no regular parish community from which to draw a staff of ushers to assist with crowds during the Shrine's many liturgies, Msgr. Bilski approached

Dechant to request his assistance in devising an usher program carried out by area Knights. All active members of the Knights of Columbus in the District of Columbia and the surrounding areas of Maryland and Virginia were invited to participate in the new usher program. From that time to the present, the Knights have fulfilled this vital ministry of hospitality at all Sunday Masses and at the many special Masses and events that constitute the Shrine's busy liturgical schedule.

In 1989, the Knights, again under Dechant's leadership, established an endowment to fund a schedule of national broadcasts of the Shrine's liturgies through the Eternal Word Television Network (EWTN). The broadcasts had

On the steps of the National Shrine, 231 Knights of Columbus and their spouses gather in preparation for a ministry of hospitality as the Shrine's ushers following their formal installation, Sept. 12, 1982.

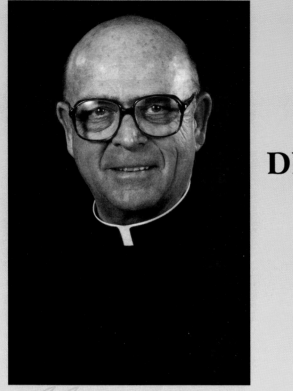

THE NINTH DIRECTOR

∽

Msgr. Harrold A. Murray brought the valuable experience of many years as a parish priest. He was readily at ease among the thousands of pilgrims who annually journeyed to the Shrine and was all too willing to extend "pilgrim" status to cover even members of the animal kingdom. Following the annual Mass commemorating the feast of St. Francis of Assisi, Msgr. Murray offered a special blessing to various animals, birds, reptiles and even fish who were brought by the faithful to the front steps of the National Shrine. It was a popular event that greatly amused the other staff priests, even as it caused understandable frustration for the maintenance staff charged with cleaning up after the pilgrims. ∽

begun the previous year at the request of the Shrine's 10th director and first rector, Msgr. Michael J. Bransfield, and the apostolic pro-nuncio, Archbishop Pio Laghi.

Founded in 1981 by Mother M. Angelica, EWTN continues to be perhaps the most successful religious network in America, reaching cable systems in nearly every state and throughout the world. During EWTN's first season of broadcasts from the National Shrine, 18 liturgies were transmitted across the nation via satellite. Since then, the number of broadcasts has expanded to over 30 annually. These broadcasts, now made possible by the ongoing generosity of the Knights of Columbus, have opened the doors of the Shrine to a new generation of pilgrims. For those who might never enjoy an opportunity to journey on pilgrimage to the National Shrine, EWTN has brought the Shrine to them, ensuring that all who wish to participate in the life of the America's patronal church have the opportunity to do so.

∽

THE NINTH DIRECTOR
— Msgr. Harrold A. Murray —

In the fall of 1984, Msgr. Harrold A. Murray took over the administration of the National Shrine as the ninth director. Msgr. Murray, a priest of the Archdiocese of Newark who was ordained just as forces were combining to resume construction on the National Shrine, assumed his new post after 10 years as an associate pastor in Summit, N.J. His previous assignments included serving as secretary of the United States Catholic Conference (USCC) in the Department of Social Justice and World Peace, director of the National Association of Catholic Chaplains, and director of the USCC's Department of Health Affairs.

Msgr. Murray's tenure as director was distinguished for his efforts to further enhance the Shrine's pilgrimage program. He sought to strengthen relationships with the American bishops, religious communities and ethnic groups represented at the Shrine by oratories and chapels they had donated. In doing so, he hoped to ensure a steady stream of organized pilgrimages to the Shrine from across the country.

Msgr. Murray's concern for the well-being of pilgrims once they were at the Shrine was evidenced by his requirement that the Shrine staff be trained in cardiopulmonary resuscitation (CPR) techniques. Maintaining that "we strive to render the highest quality of health care to the whole person — body, mind and spirit," he appointed a full-time registered nurse to the staff who offered a weekly blood-pressure clinic for Shrine employees and produced periodic fact sheets on pertinent health issues. Although this full-time position was later eliminated, there is presently a nurse on duty whenever large pilgrimages or other major events occur at the Shrine.

In 1986, as the Shrine prepared to celebrate the 25th anniversary of the Day of Dedication, Msgr. Murray advocated the appointment of Father Roger C. Roensch as the Shrine's first director of spiritual programs and pilgrimages. Originally a priest of the Archdiocese of Milwaukee, Father Roensch was later incardinated into the Archdiocese of Washington, where he was eventually named a monsignor.

Father Roensch had previously served as the director of the Office of Visitors to the Vatican with the North American College in Rome. His years in Rome occasioned numerous acquaintances with many of the nation's bishops. These associations, in turn, assisted Father Roensch in securing commitments by the bishops to sponsor pilgrimages to the Shrine from their dioceses on a regular basis. The Shrine's diocesan-pilgrimage ministry has continued to flourish in recent years as evidenced by the more than 50,000 diocesan pilgrims who visit annually.

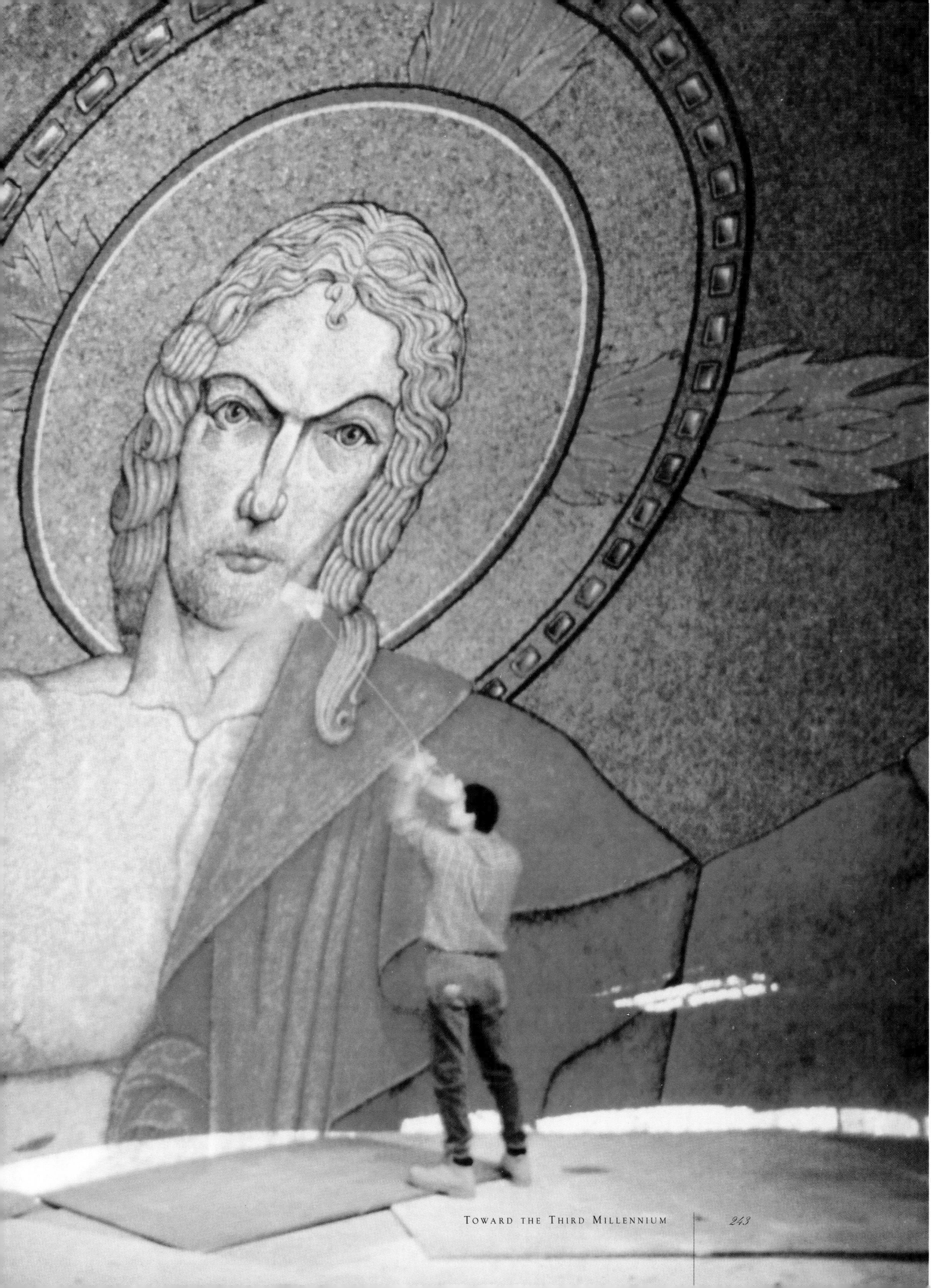

THE TENTH DIRECTOR

Father Michael J. Bransfield, ordained a priest of the Archdiocese of Philadelphia in 1971, was first introduced to the Shrine in the summer of 1970 while completing his master's degree in philosophy at Catholic University. Then a transitional deacon, he preached his first homilies at the National Shrine during the tenure of its sixth director, Msgr. William F. McDonough.

In 1980, Father Bransfield was appointed to the National Shrine by his archbishop, Cardinal John J. Krol, and served initially as director of liturgy. In 1982, he took on the added responsibilities as director of finance. It was in this capacity that Father Bransfield demonstrated his keen understanding of the practical considerations of managing the Shrine's ever-precarious financial state. His ability to quickly assess "the bottom line" and make the difficult choices avoided by others would serve to establish the strongest financial condition ever enjoyed by the National Shrine. Through prudent management of the Shrine's finances and the eventual expansion and reorganization of the Shrine's direct-mail program, which reaches hundreds of thousands of Catholics across the country, Father Bransfield helped establish new opportunities for expanding the Shrine's pilgrimage ministry while at the same time further enhancing its architectural and artistic beauty.

Father Bransfield was elevated to the rank of monsignor by Pope John Paul II on Jan. 11, 1987. ∞

TENTH DIRECTOR, FIRST RECTOR
— Msgr. Michael J. Bransfield —

In the fall of 1986, Msgr. Murray returned to parish life in the Archdiocese of Newark. He was succeeded by Father Michael J. Bransfield of Philadelphia as the 10th director of the National Shrine.

From his appointment on Oct. 1, 1986, Father Bransfield regarded his role as director as that of a faithful steward. The generosity of American Catholics was not to be taken for granted. To Father Bransfield, contributions both great and small were nothing less than a sacred trust. In addition to sustaining the Shrine's spiritual ministry, contributions provided for the practical concerns of paying the enormous electrical, heating and air-conditioning bills, making possible unexpected repairs and ensuring routine maintenance. As if to emphasize the necessary and costly requirements of maintaining the National Shrine, the announcement of Father Bransfield's appointment in *Mary's Shrine* in the spring of 1987 also featured a large photograph of workers repairing the Shrine roof with the caption, "Thank you — Your offerings helped us pay for the repairs."

This same issue of *Mary's Shrine* announced the Nov. 7, 1986, death of the

Shrine's longtime architect, Eugene F. Kennedy Jr. Appropriately, Bishop Grady offered a tribute to the "gentleman architect," noting his singular devotion to the "aesthetic integrity" of the church to which he devoted the majority of his professional years:

"He was committed to honesty and authenticity — to the use of the finest materials and the best available artists — nothing faked, nothing painted to look like what it was not. . . . Pervading all of his other qualities were Mr. Kennedy's faith in God and devotion to the Blessed Virgin Mary. His work as an architect at The National Shrine was more than a job. It was an expression of deep personal feelings — a commitment not only to aesthetic integrity, but also to his faith and to his love for Mary. His faith, like his talent, was honest, clear, sober, sensitive."

∞

A MARIAN YEAR

When Pope John Paul II designated 1987 a Marian Year, there was a new opportunity to again highlight the National Shrine as the principal pilgrimage destination for American Catholics. The Marian Year, extending from Pentecost Sunday on June 7, 1987, until the feast of the Assumption on Aug. 15, 1988, provided for a plenary indulgence for any and all who engaged in "a sacred ceremony connected with the Marian Year in their own parish church, in a designated Marian shrine or in another

sacred place." The staff of the National Shrine acted swiftly to encourage the nation's bishops to designate the National Shrine as an "official" Marian shrine at which the spiritual benefits associated with the Marian Year could be claimed.

On the eve of the Marian Year, several thousand Catholics from the Diocese of Arlington and the Archdiocese of Washington, as well as members of local chapters of the Knights of Columbus, filled the Great Upper Church to pray the Rosary with the Holy Father, whose image was projected by satellite on large-screen television monitors positioned on both sides of the chancel. The next day, Cardinal Hickey officially opened the Marian Year of Prayer at the National

Thousands pray the Rosary with Pope John Paul II, who was projected by satellite on large screens in the Great Upper Church, at the start of the Marian Year, June 7, 1987.

A MAN OF 'ORDINARY FAITH'

❧

On Aug. 10, 1987, Cardinal Patrick Aloysius O'Boyle, Washington's first resident archbishop and considered by many to be the Shrine's "second founder," passed from this world at the age of 91. He was remembered in a *Mary's Shrine* tribute, authored by Archbishop Philip M. Hannan of New Orleans (a former Washington auxiliary), for "his deep devotion to the Blessed Mother, his unwavering support of social justice, his loyalty to the Vicar of Christ as the expression of his faith." Archbishop Hannan further attested that Cardinal O'Boyle's "devotion to the Blessed Mother is memorialized in the building of the Shrine of the Immaculate Conception. He planned and plotted to secure the . . . collection that guaranteed its completion."

Cardinal O'Boyle remained close to the Shrine until his final day. In 1983, he was awarded the Patronal Medal by the National Shrine and The Catholic University of America together with the Shrine's two other prominent and devoted sons: architect Eugene Kennedy and builder John McShain.

In 1998, a bas-relief of Cardinal O'Boyle's profile was installed in the narthex in conjunction with the cladding of the narthex walls in Botticino marble. George Carr, sculptor of the "Universal Call to Holiness" relief, created the cardinal's likeness, which was carved in Pietrasanta, Italy. A window depicting Cardinal O'Boyle was also installed in the crypt sacristy along with one depicting the late Cardinal Krol of Philadelphia. ❧

Shrine during the Solemn Mass at noon.

Of the 25 diocesan pilgrimages to the National Shrine during the Marian Year, the largest by far was that of the Archdiocese of Newark. Archbishop Theodore E. McCarrick led nearly 7,000 pilgrims in 130 buses to the Shrine for a day of devotion and Marian reflection. Other pilgrims journeyed from Connecticut, New York, New Jersey, Delaware, Virginia, the District of Columbia and from every diocese in Pennsylvania.

The Marian Year provided a much-needed boost to the Shrine's pilgrimage program once again. It served to focus attention on the National Shrine as an accessible destination for American Catholics perhaps unable to journey to the world's other great pilgrimage sites. Many of the bishops who led their dioceses' Catholics to the Shrine during the Marian Year have continued to do so on a regular basis. The fruits of the Marian Year of 1987 are most evident during the Shrine's busy spring and fall pilgrimage seasons.

During this same time, two of the Shrine's most significant benefactors stepped forward to enhance the Shrine's accessibility for pilgrims who require special physical accommodations. Jerome and Grace Murray — who also donated the statue of St. Elizabeth Ann Seton in the Hall of American Saints in 1983 and the Crypt Church organ in 1987 — pledged funds for the installation of a new elevator, facilitating access to the Great Upper Church. They also provided for the installation of wheelchair ramps between Memorial Hall and the Crypt Church and for the renovation of the Shrine's restrooms at the south crypt-level entrance. In 1988, Mr. and Mrs. Murray, both graduates of The Catholic University of America, were honored with the Patronal Medal for their generosity to the Shrine and other Catholic concerns.

PAPAL HONORS: THE SHRINE BECOMES A BASILICA

In the autumn of 1990, an honor was bestowed on the National Shrine that served to underscore the unique character and significance of this national pilgrimage church. On Oct. 12, the National Shrine was designated a minor basilica by Pope John Paul II at the Vatican. The honor was officially communicated to the Shrine in late November 1990 in a letter from the Vatican's secretary of state, Cardinal Agostino Casaroli. Cardinal Hickey publicly announced the papal honor at the Noon Solemn Mass on the feast of the Immaculate

Conception, Dec. 8, 1990. The Mass, celebrated by Archbishop Agostino Cacciavillan, the apostolic pro-nuncio to the United States, was attended by a congregation of 3,000 and was televised nationally by EWTN.

Cardinal Hickey spoke about the special nature of the title of minor basilica and its meaning for both the church so honored and the Church Universal. He recalled the special relationship between the pope and the great basilicas of Rome — St. Peter's, St. Paul's, St. John Lateran and St. Mary Major. He went on to explain that "the title of minor basilica is given to other great churches in Rome and elsewhere by reason of their special and unique qualifications as centers of Catholic worship and devotion and as an expression of a special union with the Holy Father."

Honored Sons Eugene F. Kennedy Jr. (second from left), Bishop Thomas J. Grady and Cardinal Patrick O'Boyle gather in a familiar place on the eve of the 25th anniversary year of the Shrine's dedication, Dec. 4, 1983. Kennedy, Cardinal O'Boyle and Shrine builder John McShain were presented with the Patronal Medal by Jesuit Father William J. Byron (far right), president of Catholic University, for their lasting contributions to the Shrine. Also present are the Shrine's director of development, Father Roger C. Roensch (far left), and its director of finance, Father Michael Bransfield (second from right).

In keeping with the Vatican's documents on the requirements of basilicas throughout the world, Msgr. Bransfield's title, and that of every succeeding priest appointed to oversee the Shrine, was changed to "rector."

∞

A NEW SEASON OF BUILDING

By the early 1990s, the National Shrine, under Msgr. Bransfield's leadership, was poised to enter a new phase of building and enhancements not attempted since the mid-1960s when most of the chapels of the Great Upper Church and crypt level were added. The National

Shrine had by now regained a sound financial foothold, due to the 1979 national collection and the Shrine's prosperous direct-mail program. Msgr. Bransfield was in a position to begin contemplating the completion of the crypt's remaining unfinished spaces.

The first major initiative involved the renovation of the area now known as the "Flight Into Egypt" vestibule, located at the northeast crypt-level entrance to Memorial Hall. Anna Hyatt Huntington's bronze sculptural interpretation of the Holy Family resting during their flight to Egypt was chosen as the centerpiece of

Anna Hyatt Huntington's "Flight into Egypt."

the renovation. Previously located on the "bridge" between Memorial Hall and the Hall of American Saints, the "Flight into Egypt" sculpture was relocated to the more visible position of the east vestibule as a welcoming symbol for arriving pilgrims. The renovation was made possible by the generosity of Albert J. and Jeanne Degnan Forte of Washington, D.C.

That same year, Msgr. Bransfield undertook the renovation of the National Shrine Gift Shop in response to the increased demand for of religious articles, devotional aids, books and National Shrine mementos. The religious store was established in the early 1930s as the Madonna Room, which then carried a large inventory of framed pictures of the Virgin Mary, Catholic Bibles and rosary beads.

Several years later, on June 6, 1995, Cardinal Hickey dedicated the Shrine Bookstore, which completed the newly renovated space of the old Shrine gift shop located inside the west front entrance of the crypt level. The bookstore was made possible by Mr. and Mrs. B. Francis Saul of Chevy Chase, Md., whose determination to provide greater educational resources for individuals interested in the Catholic faith inspired their substantial gift.

✂ OUR LADY OF MARIAZELL

During a diplomatic visit to Washington in the mid-1980s, the president of the Austrian Federal Assembly, Dr. Herbert Schambeck, made time to visit the National Shrine and was immediately struck by the prominent representation of so many European nations in the side chapels of the crypt level and Great Upper Church. What impressed him most was the manner in which stories of devotion and faith were depicted so poignantly through sacred art, and how the immigrant communities represented came together to establish these sacred memorials. He and his companion, Friedrich Hoess, Austrian ambassador to the United States, discussed the possibility of establishing an Austrian

Cardinal James A. Hickey visits with eager young readers following the dedication of the Shrine Bookstore, June 6, 1995.

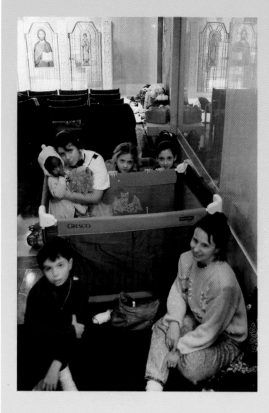

A PRAYER VIGIL FOR LIFE

∞

Ever since the Jan. 22, 1973, Supreme Court decision in *Roe vs. Wade* legalized abortion in the United States, the annual March For Life in Washington, D.C., has been the rallying point for thousands of Catholics, Protestants and non-Christians who seek to publicly state their opposition to abortion. Each year since 1981, on the anniversary of the Supreme Court ruling, Catholics have journeyed to the National Shrine as part of the March For Life activities to give thanks for the gift of human life, to pray for the protection of the unborn and for women contemplating the termination of their pregnancies.

The annual Prayer Vigil for Life at the National Shrine attracts several thousand high school and college students who spend the night in the Shrine's Memorial Hall in anticipation of a day of marching through the streets of Washington and lobbying their congressional representatives. The youthful pilgrims come not so much to argue their case as to bear witness to it by joining together in prayer and song at the Eucharist and the all-night Prayer Vigil for Life.

The festive and solemn occasion begins on the eve of the March For Life with a Mass in the Great Upper Church attended by a large contingent of cardinals, bishops and priests. It is followed by the Rosary, Night Prayer and an all-night prayer vigil in the Crypt Church. The vigil concludes with Mass in the Great Upper Church on the morning of the march, followed by breakfast in the National Shrine Dining Room. Nourished in spirit and body, the young and enthusiastic pilgrims then journey into the wintry streets of Washington to celebrate and bear witness to the "gospel of life." ∞

presence in the Shrine with a chapel honoring the centuries-old devotion to Our Lady of Mariazell.

Upon his return to Vienna, Schambeck immediately began lining up the support of colleagues in the Austrian Federal Assembly and gaining the cooperation of other prominent Austrians to realize his vision. Msgr. Bransfield traveled to Vienna to join Schambeck in meeting with top Austrian officials and to encourage support for the project. While Schambeck worked to gain funding in Austria, Hoess, with the aid of the Austrian community in this country, provided additional resources for establishing the chapel. Construction on the Chapel of Our Lady of Mariazell, located at the east side of the Crypt Church at the entrance to the crypt sacristy, was begun in the spring of 1992.

The 12th-century Benedictine monastery of Our Lady of Mariazell is located in the beautiful mountain village of Mariazell, southwest of Vienna. For centuries, devotion to Our Lady of Mariazell has drawn together the people of Austria and the Czech and Slovak provinces of Europe. In times of peace, and even more so in times of crisis, millions of the faithful throughout Bohemia, Moravia and Slovakia, as well as Hungary, Croatia, Slovenia and other German-speaking

(left) Chapel of Our Lady of Mariazell.

(below) Cardinal Hickey (left) joins Austrian President Thomas Klestil and Austrian Ambassador Helmut Tuerk (far right) for a tour of the Chapel of Our Lady of Mariazell during the president's visit in 1997. Msgr. Michael Bransfield (left) and Father Roger Roensch are seen in the background.

countries of Europe, have directed their prayers and devotions to Our Lady of Mariazell. As the *Magna Mater Austriae, Magna Hungarorum Domina*, and the *Magna Slavorum Gentium Mater*, the Shrine of Our Lady of Mariazell has been a potent force for peace and freedom in an area often divided by ethnic, religious and political strife.

Vienna architect Walter Son designed the thermal-finished charcoal granite chapel. The shape of the cross dominates the chapel's basic design and is repeated on the altar front and by the suspended brass framework that provides lighting within the chapel. The Austrian crest and coat of arms of each of the nine provinces of Austria adorn the east

An Austrian choir provides traditional hymns for the dedication of the Chapel of Our Lady of Mariazell, Sept. 27, 1992.

entrance wall of the chapel. The centerpiece is a 400-year-old replica statue of Our Lady of Mariazell, a gift from Bishop Eugen Kappelari of Carinthia, Austria.

The solemn dedication of the Chapel of Our Lady of Mariazell was celebrated on Sept. 27, 1992, by Cardinal Hickey. Bishop Kappelari, a large delegation from the Austrian Embassy in Washington and numerous Austrian government officials from Vienna attended the dedication Mass in celebration of Austrian faith, culture and devotion to the Virgin Mary.

On April 13, 1997, Schambeck, Austrian Ambassador Helmut Tuerk and many of those who attended the original dedication of the chapel gathered there for a second celebratory Mass to witness the blessing of new dedicatory plaques and bronze busts depicting two Austrian

saints, St. Leopold III and St. Clement Hofbauer. Once again, Cardinal Hickey, as principal celebrant, welcomed the distinguished Austrian pilgrims and commended those responsible for introducing this centuries-old Marian devotion at the National Shrine, thus enhancing the Shrine's identity by including this important and traditionally Catholic nation.

OUR LADY OF HOPE

Throughout its history, the National Shrine has attracted devoted Catholics of all ages, ethnic backgrounds, economic means and theological persuasions. The many side chapels and oratories provide abundant evidence of the Shrine's ability to draw together a multicultural "family" that is equally "at home" at the Shrine and speak the common language of faith in Christ and devotion to His Mother.

The Shrine has attracted many prominent government officials, foreign dignitaries, sports figures and celebrities from the stage and screen over the years. Few, however, have left a more lasting impression within the Shrine than entertainment icon Bob Hope, even though not a Catholic himself. Hope's wife, Dolores, had remained a devout Catholic all her life and frequently expressed special pride in having attended the Shrine's

Day of Dedication in 1959. Over the years, Mrs. Hope regularly visited the Shrine whenever in Washington.

During a visit in the mid-1980s, Mrs. Hope first contemplated a gift of a chapel to honor a cherished personal devotion of hers — Our Lady of Hope of Pontmain, France, a devotion that can be traced to the height of the Franco-Prussian War in 1871. During a later visit in 1989, Msgr. Bransfield led Mrs. Hope to the location within the Crypt Church that adjoins the stained-glass wall of the Chapel of Our Lady of Hostyn. The area's east-side counterpart, located directly in front of the crypt sacristy, had already been claimed by the Austrians for the Our Lady of Mariazell Chapel. Mrs. Hope immediately realized the possibilities for the significant space and agreed to proceed with plans to establish a chapel honoring Our Lady of Hope.

Several attempts to arrive at an architectural design and artistic interpretation of the late-19th-century French devotion failed to satisfy Mrs. Hope. Finally in 1991, she discussed possible design concepts with a South Dakota sculptor, Dale Claude Lamphere, who at the time was involved with creating bronze busts of Bob and Dolores Hope for the Mutual of Omaha headquarters in Omaha, Neb. Soon, Mrs. Hope's confidence in

Dolores and Bob Hope are greeted by Cardinal Hickey following the dedication of the Chapel of Our Lady of Hope, May 29, 1994.

Lamphere was sufficient to proceed with small-scale "sketches" of the sculptural figures intended for the chapel as well as preliminary architectural drawings of the chapel itself. Mrs. Hope remained constantly engaged in the design process, even insisting on putting her signature to construction documents prior to their execution.

The day before the chapel's dedication, Dolores and Bob Hope arrived at the Shrine to inspect their newly completed gift. Onlookers were amazed by the sight of the legendary comedian strolling casually through the Shrine to view the numerous chapels of the Crypt and Great Upper churches. Mr. Hope marveled at the enormity of the Shrine and the dedication required of so many to ensure its completion. He was reminded by Msgr. Bransfield that he and

Chapel of Our Lady of Hope.

Dolores were likewise part of the legacy of generous benefactors responsible for the Shrine's beauty.

On May 29, 1994 — Bob Hope's 91st birthday — the Chapel of Our Lady of Hope was consecrated by Cardinal Hickey during a solemn Mass on the afternoon of Trinity Sunday. Dolores and Bob Hope attended the Mass with a large contingent of family members and friends. An overflow congregation of more than 600 filled the Crypt Church during the Mass while millions more took part in the celebration via EWTN. Cardinal John J. Krol — Philadelphia's archbishop emeritus, who was integral in the creation of another chapel within the National Shrine, Our Lady of Czestochowa — concelebrated the Mass

along with Bishop Robert E. Mulvee of Wilmington, Del.; Archbishop Theodore E. McCarrick of Newark, N.J.; Bishop John J. Glynn of the Archdiocese of the Military Services, U.S.A.; and Msgr. Jean Rivain, rector of the Basilica of Our Lady of Hope in Pontmain, France.

ORATORY OF OUR LADY OF PEACE AND GOOD VOYAGE, ANTIPOLO

Following the passage of the 1965 Immigration Law which allowed for the reunification of families separated from one or more family members who had emigrated to the United States, Filipino migration to the U.S. increased dramatically. Determined to acquire enhanced educational, economic and employment opportunities, Filipinos came to the United States in record numbers. To this day, they represent the largest Asian American group in the United States.

In 1992, the local Filipino community first approached the National Shrine about the prospect of establishing a chapel for Filipino devotion. After choosing the alcove within the crypt where the Shrine's foundation stone is displayed, they obtained the episcopal sponsorship of Auxiliary Bishop Alvaro Corrada del Rio, S.J., of Washington, and enlisted the participation of Noemi M. Castillo, a staff member of the U.S. bishops' Office for Pastoral Care of Migrants and Refugees, and Eddy Caparas, whose additional contacts and associations proved an important asset.

A vast network of Filipino Catholics worked diligently to establish the necessary organization to raise funds nationally and even internationally. Appealing to the Philippine bishops, the committee received confirmation that the image of Our Lady of Peace and Good Voyage (Our Lady of Antipolo, as the devotion is also known) was the particular devotion to be represented at the National Shrine. A prominent family in the Philippines, Socorro and Pacita Mota, donated the 70-year-old replica image of Our Lady of Antipolo for the oratory. The Philippines' national artist, José Blanco, painted the oratory's murals — which he and his family also donated — tracing devotion to Our Lady of Antipolo throughout the centuries.

On May 20, 1997, over 5,000 Filipino Catholics from across the United States and the Phillipines gathered at the National Shrine for the solemn dedication of the Oratory of Our Lady of Peace and Good Voyage, Antipolo, by Cardinal Hickey. The names of individuals, families and Filipino organizations were deposited in the marble base that supports the image of Our Lady of Antipolo.

Filipino Catholics finally claimed their rightful place within the Shrine that honors the proud and heroic struggles of immigrant Catholics determined to pass on their faith and lively devotion to future generations.

Oratory of Our Lady of Peace and Good Voyage, Antipolo.

ASIAN INDIAN ORATORY OF OUR LADY OF VAILANKANNI

Not long after the Filipino Catholic community coordinated the national campaign to establish their oratory, rep-

Young Indian women present aromatic floral and incense offerings during the dedication of the Asian-Indian Oratory of Our Lady of Good Health, Aug. 16, 1997.

resentatives from the Indian American Catholic Association (IACA) in Washington, D.C., led by Joyce D'Souza, requested a meeting with Msgr. Bransfield to discuss an oratory representing Indian devotion to Our Lady of Good Health, Vailankanni.

The IACA was first incorporated in the District of Columbia to serve as a liaison between the Indian Catholic community and the U.S. bishops to address their unique pastoral and religious needs. The association also exists to assist members of their community in the process of assimilation in the United States while promoting the perpetuation of Indian culture and spiritual values.

The first letter of appeal to the Indian community in the United States for their oratory — which was designated for the crypt's northwest alcove, opposite the

Filipino oratory — explained the selection of the 16th-century devotion to Our Lady of Good Health, Vailankanni, for representation. Located on the Bay of Bengal (150 miles south of Madras in Tamil Nadu), the Shrine of Our Lady of Vailankanni, also known as the "Lourdes of the East," is the most visited Shrine in all of India. To this day, the feast of the Nativity of the Blessed Virgin Mary is celebrated as a nine-day festival, drawing more than 1.5 million pilgrims. Not only do vast numbers of Catholics journey to Vailankanni throughout the year, but many non-Christians visit as well. The festival of Our Lady of Vailankanni is another annual celebration that lasts 10 days and draws nearly 2 million pilgrims. The original modest chapel at Vailankanni, erected on the site where the Virgin Mary is said to have appeared on three separate occasions in the mid-16th century, was replaced by a modern and spacious church in 1933. The Shrine of Our Lady of Vailankanni was elevated to a basilica on Nov. 3, 1962, by Pope John XXIII.

The Board of Trustees of the National Shrine requested letters of support from the Indian Catholic hierarchy prior to soliciting funds for the oratory. The principal concern of the board was whether the Vailankanni devotion sufficiently appealed to all the various Catholic rites of India. In response to an inquiry by Cardinal Hickey, the Indian hierarchy gave its clear and enthusiastic support to the project. Cardinal Simon I. Pimenta of Bombay, Syro-Malabar Cardinal Anthony Padiyara of Ernakulam, Archbishop Joseph Powathil of Changanacherry, Syro-Malankar Bishop Geevarghese Timotheos Chundevalel of Tiruvalla; and Archbishop Packiam Arokiaswamy of Tanjore sent letters commending the project. Ukrainian Archbishop Stephen Sulyk of Philadelphia, metropolitan of Ukrainian Catholics in the United States, was instrumental in gaining the necessary assurances from the Indian hierarchy and further agreed to serve as the project's episcopal sponsor. Among the most influential advocates of the project was Archbishop Agostino Cacciavillan, apostolic pro-nuncio to the United States, who had previously served in the same capacity in India.

The basic design of the oratory was suggested by Bijoy Isaac, a Washington-area architect who was active in the IACA. Working with a committee appointed by the larger project committee, Isaac and the Shrine's architect, the Leo A. Daly Company, developed a simple design that relied on vibrant color and traditional Indian iconography.

Featured prominently within the cruciform oratory is a replica statue of Our Lady of Vailankanni holding the infant Christ, the original of which is enshrined in the Basilica Church of Vailankanni. Two bas-relief wall carvings of Carerra marble, created by Washington sculptor Robert Liberace, depict the apparitions and the healing miracles attributed to Our Lady of Vailankanni. Various architectural details reflect traditional Indian art; most notably, the multi-colored marble floor patterned after an Indian carpet and featuring a design of India's flag at its central axis.

On Saturday, Aug. 16, 1997, in conjunction with the 50th anniversary of India's independence from British rule, nearly 3,000 pilgrims of Asian Indian

Indian Archbishop Packiam Arokiaswamy blesses the Oratory of Our Lady of Good Health with holy water during the dedication liturgy.

descent made a daylong pilgrimage to the Basilica of the National Shrine to celebrate the dedication of the Oratory of Our Lady of Good Health, Vailankanni. Attired in the richly embroidered and multicolored costumes of their native India, the congregation rivaled the splendor of the Shrine's mosaics. They processed to the beat of traditional Indian ceremonial drums and beneath bejeweled Indian temple umbrellas as the Dedication Mass began. Archbishop Cacciavillan served as principal celebrant and was accompanied by three prominent members of India's Catholic hierarchy: Archbishop Arokiaswamy of Tanjore, rector of the Basilica of Our Lady of Good Health of India, Vailankanni; Cardinal Padiyara of the Syro-Malabar Catholic Church of India; and Syro-Malankar Chorbishop Yoohanon Chrysostom Kalloor.

Ed Dwight's bas-relief panel provides a panoramic depiction of the struggles and triumphs of Africans and African-Americans throughout history.

CHAPEL OF
OUR MOTHER OF AFRICA

In early 1994, the formal campaign to raise funds on a national level for the establishment of the chapel of Our Mother of Africa in the National Shrine was initiated. On numerous occasions, Msgr. Bransfield and Bishop Joseph Francis of Newark, N.J., had discussed the prospects for a chapel representing the experience of African American Catholics. The challenges, it was agreed, would be unique in that the chapel would have to summarize not only the devotional life of African Americans, but represent their unparalleled experiences — their enslavement, emancipation, the advancements in civil rights and the ongoing struggle against racism in contemporary society.

Given Washington's predominantly

African American population, Msgr. Bransfield had long felt that the Shrine did not adequately speak to the experience of African American Catholics who regularly attend Mass at the Shrine or who journey on pilgrimage from across the nation. There were by now nearly 60 oratories and chapels throughout the Shrine representing virtually every ethnic and Catholic tradition. With the African American Catholic population totaling approximately 2 million in the United States alone, the time had come to fill the persistent void. Baltimore Auxiliary Bishop John H. Ricard, S.S.J., was designated by the group of African American bishops to coordinate the project.

At the U.S. bishops' meeting in November 1993, Bishop Ricard presented plans for a national campaign to finance construction of the Chapel of Our Mother of Africa and to establish a sizable endowment for catechetical and educational programs to make the truths of the Catholic faith more relevant to young African Americans. The theme of the chapel campaign was "A National Call to Serve." Five objectives were identified that would serve to carry out the mission of the chapel beyond the Shrine and unite African American Catholics in the work of the Church: vocations, evan-

gelization, lay ministry, ministry to youths and religious education. Throughout the campaign, these areas of apostolic action would be underscored as the basis for establishing the Our Mother of Africa Chapel. In this sense, the chapel would function not merely as a memorial to past struggles and accomplishments but as a rallying point, a catalyst for a national call to serve both the Church and the community.

Ed Dwight's bronze statue of Our Mother of Africa and Christ Child engage pilgrims in a sacra conversazione.

Chapel of Our Mother of Africa. Note the incised depiction of the 17th-century slave ship Henrietta Marie *within the floor at the chapel's entrance.*

cussion of the proposals, Colorado sculptor Ed Dwight was commissioned to create the sculpture of Madonna and Child as well as his proposed bas-relief panel depicting the progression of Africans and African Americans through the centuries.

The three sculptural components — the crucifix, the statue of Our Mother of Africa and the bas-relief panel of the chapel — constitute a *sacra conversazione* ("sacred conversation") in which the spectator participates with Our Mother of Africa, her crucified Son and their African American children in the sacred drama enacted within the chapel. According to Dwight, the greatest challenge involved creating a black Madonna to articulate Mary's role as an intermediary in the African American experience rather than merely depicting the Blessed Mother as "somebody black for black's sake."

With the national campaign underway, the next task involved the selection of a reputable artist to execute a large statue of a Madonna and Child, dressed in African attire; as well as the other artwork for the chapel. Five prominent African American artists were identified and invited to submit small-scale conceptual models for consideration. Following an extensive review and dis-

Determining the exact style of clothing for the Madonna posed a particular challenge. Dwight wanted to avoid the European interpretation evident in most traditional depictions of the Virgin Mary. On the other hand, he was concerned that a reliance on distinctive African tribal dress might make it difficult for most pilgrims to recognize his statue as depicting the Mother of Christ. The bas-relief panel, which conveys a panoramic history of African Americans, was regarded by Dwight as a unique opportunity to educate black and white Americans alike about the struggles and triumphs of the people of African descent.

The crucifix, which hangs directly behind the altar, was created through the collaboration of Tanzanian sculptor Juvenal Kaliki and New York sculptor Jeffrey Brosk. Kaliki carved the solid ebony figure of Christ, and Brosk designed the cherry-wood cross. A bronze abstraction of the *Henrietta Marie* — a 17th-century slave ship that was discovered in 1972 on the ocean floor 34 miles west of Key West, Fla. — was inlaid in the floor at the chapel entrance.

The Aug. 30, 1997, dedication of the Chapel of Our Mother of Africa by Cardinal James Hickey included all 12 African American bishops of the United States and many participants of the National Black Catholic Congress, underway that week in Baltimore. Bishop Wilton D. Gregory of Belleville, Ill., presided at the dedication Mass, and Bishop Ricard, the episcopal sponsor of the chapel, offered the homily. The dedication liturgy was also attended by Archbishop Cacciavillan and Cardinals Bernard Law, William Keeler and Anthony Bevilacqua.

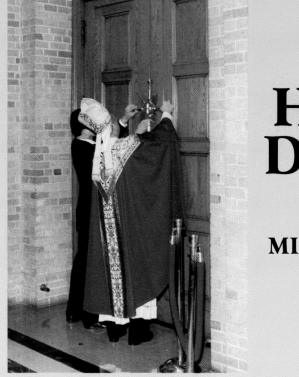

THE HOLY DOOR
TO THE NEW MILLENNIUM

"Bless this door, O Lord, which we consecrate to this time of preparation. Each day we pass this place, draw us more deeply into your presence and the wonders of your love for us."

With these words, Archbishop Agostino Cacciavillan, apostolic pronuncio to the United States, blessed and formally sealed the "National Holy Year Door" of the Basilica of the National Shrine of the Immaculate Conception on Nov. 30, 1997.

The sealing of a Holy Door has been a feature of Holy Year celebrations since 1350. In anticipation of the Great Jubilee of the Year 2000, Pope John Paul II invited churches around the world to designate and seal a Holy Door, to be ceremoniously reopened on Christmas Eve 1999, in union with the traditional Holy Doors at the four major basilicas of Rome. ∞

AMERICA'S CHURCH

THE UNIVERSAL CALL
TO HOLINESS

In 1994, Msgr. Bransfield and Cardinal James Hickey first discussed the possibility of completing the last unfinished brick wall within the Great Upper Church — the wall at the rear nave of the church that supports the south gallery. Cardinal Hickey, however, did not envision a treatment similar to what the architects had designed for the east and west nave walls (low bas-relief figures and Botticino marble cladding outlined by mosaic). Instead, the cardinal imagined a "triumphal arch" through which Christians on pilgrimage to the Shrine would pass on entering and departing. He was eager to explore the possibilities for making a bold architectural and iconographic statement in sculpture about the fundamental objective of the Christian life — the pursuit of holiness.

Cardinal Hickey originally suggested renowned sculptor Frederick Hart as the artist for the monumental task. Hart's previous experience in creating "*Ex Nihilo*," a sculptural interpretation of the Genesis account of creation at the west facade of Washington's National Cathedral, distinguished him as the ideal candidate. The Shrine approached the sculptor, only to discover that, while

intrigued by the prospect of producing a sculpture of such monumental proportions, Hart was unavailable for a prolonged assignment. Hart recommended George Carr, a lesser-known but highly talented realist sculptor from Silver Spring, Md., with whom he had worked on several projects.

Carr was not intimidated by the project before him. With Cardinal Hickey's blessing, he set out to create three small "sketches" of the "universal call to holiness" theme for the cardinal's review. This was no easy task, given the complex and abstract subject matter to be carved. Carr began an intense reading of the documents of the Second Vatican Council, focusing on *Lumen Gentium* (Dogmatic Constitution of the Church) in particular. Cardinal Hickey provided the passages in the fifth chapter that he regard-

(opposite) The "Universal Call to Holiness" sculptural relief as viewed at the south nave wall of the Great Upper Church, summer 1999.

(above) Sculptor George Carr makes adjustments to his full-scale model at the Laran Bronze Foundry, Chester, Pa., in the summer of 1997.

Stone carvers near completion on the final marble carving of the "Universal Call to Holiness" in Pietrasanta, Italy, in the spring of 1998.

imagery as a descending dove. The sculptural figures, whose number and racial and ethnic designations had yet to be defined, represented the human family being drawn to the source of holiness, the Third Person of the Holy Trinity. Cardinal Hickey later suggested the addition of Mary among the figures of the sculpture as a reminder of her unparalleled role as the first person to whom God revealed His new covenant of salvation through Christ.

Carr was given the go-ahead to proceed with further refinements and the larger one-sixth-scale clay model for inspection by the full Board of Trustees at its November 1995 meeting. With the "difficult" part of arriving at a sculptural interpretation of the intended theme resolved, Msgr. Bransfield now faced the daunting task of figuring out how to pay for the monumental artwork.

ed as the clearest articulation of the theme:

> *"Therefore all in the Church, whether they belong to the hierarchy or are cared for by it, are called to holiness, . . . It is expressed in many ways by the individuals who, each in his own state of life, tend to the perfection of love, thus sanctifying others. . . . It is therefore quite clear that all Christians in any state or walk of life are called to fullness of Christian life and to the perfection of love, and by this holiness a more human manner of life is fostered also in earthly society"* (nos. 39-40).

Roughly six weeks after he was commissioned, Carr was prepared for the first review of his clay "sketches." The cardinal was immediately impressed by the artist's clay representation of the Holy Spirit at the center of the model with rays extending out and encompassing human figures gazing up and moving toward the Holy Spirit, depicted in the traditional

Dr. Joseph and Bertha Braddock had been longtime contributors to the National Shrine, primarily in response to the regular appeals that the Shrine's extended family of benefactors receives throughout the year. In the summer of 1995, the Braddocks requested an appointment with Msgr. Bransfield to discuss how they might become more actively involved with the Shrine and assist in a more substantial way. Msgr.

Bransfield detailed the many ongoing projects and needs of the Shrine, including the planned "Universal Call to Holiness" sculpture.

As patrons of the arts, the Braddocks recognized the potential of art to hold its appeal from one generation to the next. Given the intended sculpture's timeless message, they were confident that their investment would have a lasting effect. The fact that the chosen art form was seldom, if ever, executed in the present day on such a massive scale made the project especially intriguing. In time, the Braddocks were convinced that the "Universal Call to Holiness" sculpture was not only *the* project with which they desired to be associated, but was one that they wished to fund in its entirety.

Among the most challenging aspects of the project was planning for the addition of nearly 50 tons of marble to an area designed only to accommodate thin marble cladding. A comprehensive engineering study was commissioned to determine the capacity of the early foundational support footings beneath the crypt level that would ultimately carry the added weight. Since none of the early drawings was available, the team assembled specially for the project pored over whatever early documentation and photographs were available and reviewed construction specifications and materials of the early 1920s. In all of the discussions, Dr. Braddock, a physicist by training and a highly successful businessman, was both a willing participant in the planning stages and the driving force throughout the project.

Architect Anthony Segreti — who was selected by a competitive process to oversee the project — and his structural engi-

Workers hoist the first segment of the "Universal Call to Holiness" sculpture on the east side of the Shrine as they begin the delicate installation process within the Great Upper Church. The panel, weighing 8,840 pounds and measuring approximately 10 feet, 4 inches in height, is the second largest of the 16 panels comprising the massive sculpture.

neer, James Cutts, eventually decided on a "belts-and-suspenders" structural design to ensure that the monumental relief would remain in place for "a thousand years," a requirement insisted upon by Dr. Braddock.

Using three-quarter-inch stainless steel throughout, Segreti and Cutts determined that a shelf/angle system was best suited to transfer the enormous weight of the sculpture to the sub-basement foundations. While this approach was sufficient to support the weight of the sculpture, Dr. Braddock insisted that additional measures be taken. Cutts devised a method to tie the brick "screen" wall back to the choir gallery structural slab in order to eliminate the possibility of an "overturning" moment of the scultpure.

With the clay model complete and the necessary architectural design underway, Carr and the project team focused their efforts on identifying a space and team to accommodate the process of enlarging the model to full scale. Eventually, the Laran Bronze foundry in Chester, Pa., was identified as having adequate space on the third floor of what was formerly a shipbuilding factory. As the weeks and months passed, Carr's sculptural concept began to emerge from clay. He and three other artists worked

five days a week for nearly eight months to apply the 10,000 pounds of clay to the armature in order to replicate the figures as they had been defined in the one-sixth-scale model.

Upon completion of the full-scale clay model, the team at Laran Bronze began the tedious process of creating a plaster cast of the sculpture, made up of 24 separate panels. The final plaster model eventually served as the template for a team of stone carvers in Pietrasanta, Italy, who were contracted to translate the model into marble. Carr's challenge at this point was to ensure that there was no possibility that the figures would be interrupted by the eventual segmentation of the completed marble carving, necessary for the shipment and handling of the sculpture within the Shrine. Carr was further required to determine reasonable sizes of the segmented panels, since the eventual marble blocks would weigh considerably more than their corresponding plaster counterparts. The finished carved blocks would have to be delicately transported into the Shrine and hoisted some 17 feet above the floor of the Great Upper Church.

Carr's completed full-scale plaster model measured 52 feet in length by 15 feet high. Each of the 24 panels comprising the model was placed individually in a wooden crate. In September 1997, the 24 crates containing the sculpture were shipped to the carving studios of Franco Cervietti in Pietrasanta, Italy. Once the massive blocks of Botticino marble had been quarried, Cervietti and his team of a dozen carvers were entrusted with the skillful task of replicating Carr's sculpture with chisel and hammer. The process required that each block of marble be carved separately by individual stone carvers, rather than attempting to carve the sculpture as a whole. Carr, Msgr. Bransfield, Dr. and Mrs. Braddock and Segreti conducted regular inspection visits to Pietrasanta. Following the nearly yearlong carving process, the sculpted blocks were "dry set" to ensure that the pieces fit properly together without any interruption to the images. It was during this period that adjustments and refinements to the sculpture were made prior to granting final approval to the carvers' efforts and authorizing the sculpture's shipment to the National Shrine in February 1999.

As plans to complete the Shrine's last interior wall with marble and artwork progressed, Msgr. Bransfield realized the advantages of also completing the vestibule, narthex and west narthex stairwell with the intended Botticino and Travertine marbles in the process.

Inasmuch as the narthex is prominently viewed from the nave when departing the Shrine, it was feared that its unfinished brick facing would adversely affect the overall beauty of the completed rear-wall sculpture. The Board of Trustees authorized the additional expenditure of funds to acquire the necessary marble and further approved the completion of the narthex ceiling in mosaic to correspond with the adjoining east and west lateral nave aisle ceilings.

In conjunction with the "Universal Call to Holiness" project, a one-hour documentary was produced by Journey

(below) "Universal Call to Holiness" detail of Mary and young figures encompassed by rays of the Holy Spirit.

Films, Inc., for national distribution by New York City's Public Broadcast System (PBS) network, WNET-Thirteen. The documentary, funded also by Dr. and Mrs. Braddock, chronicles the origin, progress and completion of George Carr's sculpture, in addition to positioning the National Shrine in the context of the other prominent churches of the world.

The "Universal Call to Holiness" sculpture — completed and installed 40 years after the celebrated Day of Dedication, at which time the only artistic adornment in the Great Upper Church was the imposing "Christ in Majesty" mosaic — is a powerful symbol of the Shrine's ongoing relevance to the lives of ordinary Catholics who seek out reminders of the

prerequisites of their faith. Viewed at its prominent placement at the rear nave wall, the massive sculpture represents the primary objective of Christian discipleship without regard for age, gender, race, social or ecclesiastical distinctions. Though extended universally by a benevolent, patient and forgiving God, the sculpture is a reminder that holiness must nevertheless be sought and embraced. As both a pilgrimage site and a national symbol for a people compelled by their faith to change their society for the better, the National Shrine bears witness to the prospect that holiness is indeed attainable in the here and now — even as the journey toward human redemption marches on.

Viewing progress on the installation of the "Universal Call to Holiness" sculpture at the Shrine are (from right) Cardinal Hickey, benefactors Bertha and Dr. Joseph V. Braddock, and Msgr. Michael J. Bransfield.

CONCLUSION

There is, in fact, no end to the story of the Basilica of the National Shrine of the Immaculate Conception. Efforts to complete the Shrine will continue in years to come as funds become available to fill the three remaining interior domes of the Great Upper Church with mosaic artwork, as intended by the Shrine's original architect and the early Iconography Committee.

More important than physical improvements, however, is the ongoing work of fulfilling the mission of the National Shrine in a modern world. Admittedly, the Shrine has its origins in a mode of Catholic piety and understanding of faith quite different from what is widely shared by Catholics at the dawn of Christianity's third millennium. And yet, the motivations that sustained the Shrine in difficult times, ensured its completion, and continue to make it a vibrant center of faith and authentic spiritual expression are surely the same.

The Shrine's massive proportions remind us that we belong to a context much bigger than our own circumstances and preoccupations. One need only spend a few moments in the tranquil surroundings of the Crypt Church to appreciate the Shrine's ability to connect us to our earliest ancestors in faith who first contemplated the challenges of making known Christ's Gospel to the world from within the concealment of the Roman catacombs. The many side chapels and oratories located throughout the lower and upper levels of the Shrine transport us through time and provide a veritable prism through which we can more clearly see God at work in the long course of human history and in our individual lives. The Shrine then invites us to consider our response in light of a renewed perspective gained through prayer, meditation and celebration with other Christians likewise committed to a lifelong pilgrimage toward holiness.

If, at the end of our visit, we experience a longing to stay yet awhile longer, the Shrine will have succeeded in its purpose to inspire within all who journey here a yearning for the Kingdom of God not yet come, but glimpsed through the sacred and incomparable beauty of "America's church."

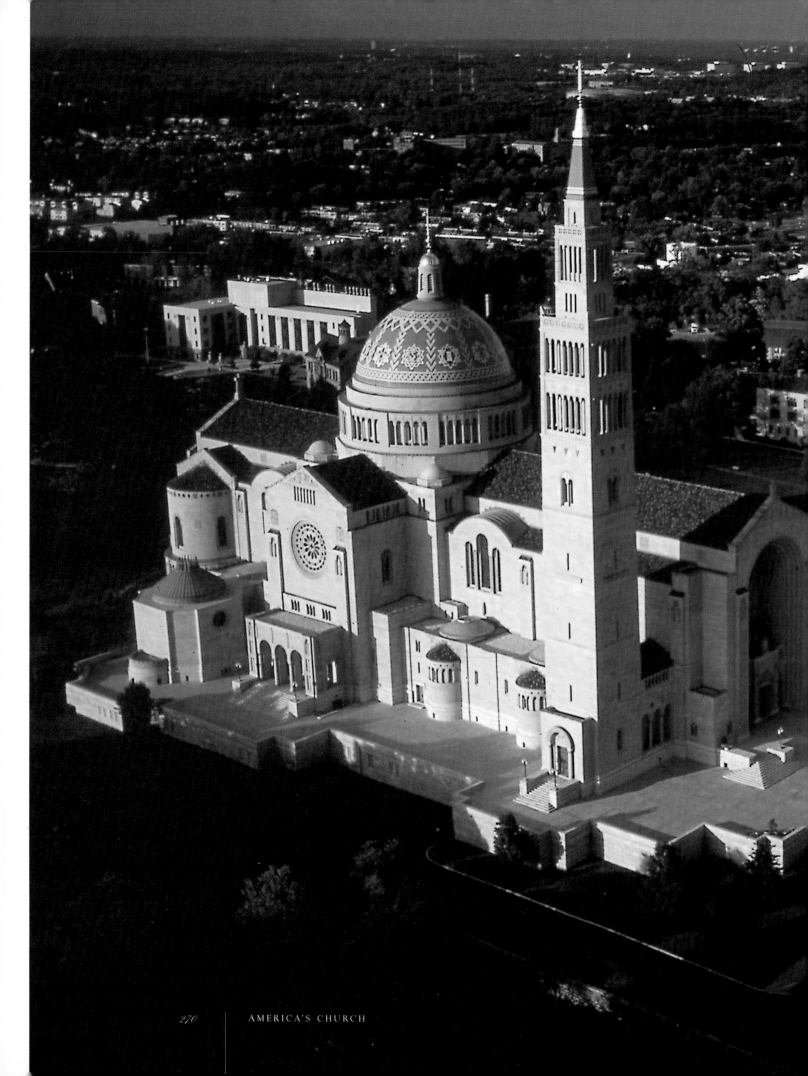

AFTERWORD

The story of Christianity, and of salvation history, is that of a pilgrim people in search of a deeper reality — one that conveys a profound truth about the events and circumstances of human experience as viewed through the prism of faith. The Basilica of the National Shrine of the Immaculate Conception is a monument to the generosity of Catholics in America, symbolizing their steadfast determination to share the gift of their faith in ways that have changed for better the society and world in which they live. Journeying as they do to the National Shrine on pilgrimage, Catholic pilgrims of today bear witness to their belief that human existence is itself not an end, but a long and often arduous journey, begun here and now, and only fully realized in the Kingdom of God.

The act of journeying on pilgrimage, however, long precedes the Christian experience. Early in the Jewish tradition, the pilgrimage was a common expression of the Israelites' worship of the one God. The annual religious feasts of the Hebrews were typically celebrated in the context of elaborate pilgrimages to the "shining city on a hill" — Jerusalem. The procession of the Ark of the Covenant to the Temple in Jerusalem is an example of the pilgrimage as a ritual expression of the determined faith of David and the Israelites to revere and celebrate God's presence made known in the midst of His people. Apart from the Judeo-Christian tradition, the Koran requires Muslims to make a pilgrimage to Mecca at least once during their lifetime. Throughout India, there are innumerable shrines in small villages and in major towns where Hindus regularly gather to make offerings and find meaning in the performance of routine activities of everyday life.

In the Gospel of Luke, the Holy

Family is recorded as participating in a yearly pilgrimage to Jerusalem to observe the feast of Passover, as prescribed by Jewish law and custom. "Each year, his parents went to Jerusalem for the feast of Passover, and when he was twelve years old, they went up according to festival custom" (Lk 2:41-42). Similarly, after Constantine ended their persecution in the fourth century, the early Christians customarily traveled to the Holy Land in order to walk in the footsteps of Christ and celebrate at the shrines erected to memorialize the divine manifestations of His earthly life. Since that time, Christians have traversed the globe to experience ordinary places made extra-ordinary by the presence of God.

Now as then, the Christian pilgrim proclaims to the rest of humanity that what the world offers is not sufficient to satisfy all of human longing. It is necessary to look elsewhere, even if the journey takes one far from the comfort of familiar surroundings to distant and unknown places. The very act of a pilgrimage reaffirms that while Christians are in the world, they are not of it: "We have here no lasting city" (Heb 13:14). And so a pilgrimage points one in a decisively new direction, one that enables the believer to discover God in any circumstance — if only one ventures to begin the journey.

The Basilica of the National Shrine, like other great Marian shrines throughout the world, is dedicated to the honor and devotion of the one who, in Christian tradition, first allowed the Word of God to take root and flourish. Mary, the mother of Jesus Christ, bridged the Old and New Covenants and defined for all future generations the perfect response to God, even when confronted with what seem to be unreasonable and desperate circumstances: "I am the handmaid of the Lord. May it be done to me according to your word" (Lk 1:38). Throughout the Gospels, hers is the clearest instruction for one seeking true discipleship: "Do whatever he tells you" (Jn 2:5). For this reason, Catholics seek her intercession and journey to shrines erected in homage to her enduring example.

The National Shrine's founders had ample justification for proposing the building of a monumental Marian shrine "after the style of the cathedrals of the Old World." Devotion to Mary Immaculate had long been regarded as a litmus test of orthodox Catholic belief and expression. Historical precedents abound: Columbus sailed to the New World aboard the *Santa Maria* in 1492; the city of St. Augustine, Fla., was founded on the feast of the Nativity of Mary in 1565; Catholics founded the colony of Maryland in 1634 and immediately built a chapel in honor of the Immaculate Conception; Father Jacques Marquette had dedicated his missionary work to the Blessed Virgin (and, incidentally, died on the feast of the Immaculate Conception in 1675); America's first bishop, John Carroll, chose Mary as patroness of the first and only diocese in the United States in 1782; and finally, eight years preceding the dogma of the Immaculate Conception by Pope Pius IX in 1854, the American bishops attending the Sixth Provincial Council of Baltimore designated the Immaculate Conception as patroness of the United States.

Revered by Christ's followers as early as the first century, the proper veneration of Mary has been a consistent, albeit often contentious, issue throughout the Church's 2,000-year history. Aside from the Gospels' account of the beginning and end of Jesus' life, little is known about Mary. A mere child herself when she was found to be with child, she is presented as the fulfillment of the prophecy of Isaiah: "The Lord himself will give you a sign. Behold, a young woman shall conceive and bear a son, and shall call his name Immanuel" (Is. 7:14).

Mary was bestowed with the popular title "Mother of God" during the second century, and the Council of Ephesus codified this distinction in A.D. 431 as both a doctrinal reassertion of Jesus' divine nature and a defining principle of Mary's unparalleled role in revealing the "new and everlasting Covenant." Gradually, the Church established individual Marian feast days: Mary's Purification, the Annunciation, the Assumption, and her own birth (the Nativity of Mary). These canonical feasts, established as part of the liturgical calendar in 799 by the Synod of Salzburg, served to perpetuate reverence for Mary and further exalt her status as "blessed among women."

Encouraged by the pietistic fervor of the Middle Ages, Mary assumed a new role: that of a consoling and compassionate mother pleading on behalf of her morally frail and sinful children to her Divine Son now seated in heavenly judgment. Questions concerning the Virgin Birth, her lifelong virginity and the Immaculate Conception occasioned differing views and eventual dissension among various sects within Christianity. The infallible dogma of Mary's Immaculate Conception, declared by Pope Pius IX on Dec. 8, 1854, was a turning point in Mariological history and debate. For many, the dogma of the Immaculate Conception was the supreme validation of their deep-seated devotion to the Mother of Christ. For others, it was a stumbling block that continues in the present day as a symbol of theological division among Christian believers.

Here at the church dedicated to the veneration of Mary and the perpetuation of her role as intercessor and model of faith, we do not seek to accentuate the unfortunate divisions that undermine the unity of Christian belief. Rather, we celebrate the fundamental truths of Christian and Catholic faith that have prevailed amid hostility, denial and persecution, and which persist as potent forces to bring about conversion in the hearts and minds of people everywhere. As a people marked with the sign of faith, Christian pilgrims are forever embarking on new adventures to discover and celebrate the evidence of God's presence among us. The Basilica of the National Shrine of the Immaculate Conception, as such, stands majestically before a modern world as a beacon of hope — both a destination and starting point — for those who can envision a better world, and who commit their lives to making it so.

"Lord, I love the habitation of thy house, the place where thy glory dwells" (Ps. 26:8).

MSGR. MICHAEL J. BRANSFIELD, RECTOR

CHRONOLOGY

1846 May 13 / Sixth Provincial Council of Baltimore designates the Immaculate Conception as patroness of the United States.

1887 / The Catholic University of America (CUA) established.

1895 July 22 / Bishop John J. Keane, rector, petitions faculty members of CUA for suggestions on need for a "University Chapel."

1903 October / Father Thomas J. Shahan suggests building a "suitable church" on the growing university's campus.

1909 May 27 / Father Shahan appointed to first full term as fourth rector of CUA; elevated to a domestic prelate.

1911 / "New Chapel Fund" established to solicit support for "University Chapel." National Organization of Catholic Women tapped by Msgr. Shahan to assist with fund raising for National Shrine.

1913 August 15 / Msgr. Shahan presents plans for National Shrine to Pope Pius X at Vatican with Cardinal James Gibbons.

1914 January / First issue of *Salve Regina* published.

1914 July 8 / First apostolic letter of support for National Shrine sent by Pope Pius X.

1915 June 5 / Father Bernard A. McKenna appointed secretary to Bishop Shahan with primary responsibility for Shrine effort.

1917 / Shrine Committee formed with Bishop Dennis Dougherty as chairman.

1917 December 8 / First public Mass offered for National Shrine in CUA's Caldwell Hall.

1918 / "First Pilgrims" arrive from St. Vincent Home for Orphans.

1918 November 20 / Cardinal James Gibbons, chancellor of CUA, appeals to all Catholics of America to cooperate in the erection of National Shrine as a "Victory Memorial."

1919 April 10 / Pope Benedict XV sends apostolic letter of support for National Shrine.

1919 June 15 / *Salve Regina* announces "Great Architects Obtained" to design National Shrine.

1920 May 16 / Archbishop John Bonzano, apostolic delegate, blesses site where National Shrine is to be built.

1920 July / Construction begins on *Salve Regina* offices on grounds of CUA to serve as Shrine "headquarters."

1920 September 23 / Cardinal Gibbons blesses foundation stone.

1921 March 21 / Cardinal Gibbons dies.

1922 April 25 / Pope Pius XI sends apostolic letter of support.

1922 September 18 / Bishop Shahan and Father McKenna turn first spadefuls of soil for National Shrine construction on northern section of crypt.

1924 April 20 / First Mass offered in National Shrine on Easter Sunday.

1924 December / Crypt Church of National Shrine completed.

1927 January / Mary Memorial Altar installed in Crypt Church.

1927 September 13 / Bishop Shahan announces retirement for following year.

1929 / Father McKenna appointed first director of National Shrine.

1929 December / Father McKenna elevated to domestic prelate.

1930 June 17 / Papal gift of Murillo mosaic arrives from Vatican mosaic studios.

1930 November 11 / Bishop Shahan petitions board to approve loan of $200,000 to complete southern foundations of crypt level.

1931 February 12 / First papal radio broadcast from Vatican heard in Crypt Church.

1931 September / Southern foundations of crypt complete.

1931 December 18 / First "Memorial Tablet" claimed for Cardinal John McCloskey, first American cardinal (New York).

1932 March 9 / The Shrine's founder, Bishop Shahan, dies.

1933 Spring / CUA Board of Trustees suspends construction on National Shrine.

1933 May 2 / Msgr. McKenna resigns as Shrine director.

1933 June / Msgr. David T. O'Dwyer appointed second director.

1935 / Publication of *Salve Regina* suspended.

1936 October / Cardinal Eugenio Pacelli (future Pope Pius XII) tours crypt.

1938 / Publication of *Salve Regina* resumes.

1940 / Msgr. John J. Reilly appointed third director of National Shrine.

1943 March 14 / Bishop John F. Noll and *Our Sunday Visitor* takes up Shrine cause.

1947 Mother's Day / First nationwide parish collection for National Shrine.

1947 May 16 / Death of Archbishop Michael J. Curley.

1948 January 21 / Archbishop Patrick J. O'Boyle installed as Washington's first resident archbishop.

1948 December 8 / National Shrine is incorporated separately from CUA.

1950 February / Msgr. Patrick "P.J." O'Connor appointed fourth director.

1951 / Archbishop O'Boyle commissions Eugene Kennedy Jr. to draw up plans for completing superstructure of National Shrine.

1953 December 6 / Nationwide collection appeal for National Shrine.

1954 November 15 / Archbishop O'Boyle presides over blessing of restart of construction.

1956 / Msgr. Thomas J. Grady appointed fifth director.

1956 July 31 / Archbishop Noll dies.

1957 / Knights of Columbus pledge $1 million for Knights' Tower.

1959 November 20 / Day of Dedication of National Shrine of the Immaculate Conception.

1960 June 9 / Archbishop Giovanni Battista Montini of Milan, the future Pope Paul VI, visits .National Shrine.

1960 / Five apsidal chapels of the north apse completed.

1960 / Baldachin over the main altar completed.

1962 April / Chapel of Our Lady of Perpetual Help completed.

1962 / Chapel of St. Pius X (crypt level) completed.

1963 May / Chapels of Our Lady of the Miraculous Medal, St. Vincent de Paul, St. Louise de Marillac completed in Great Upper Church.

1964 February / Marble facing of west chancel of Great Upper Church completed.

1964 March / Marble facing of south gallery of Great Upper Church completed.

1964 May / Chapel of Our Lady of Czestochowa completed.

1964 August / Chapel of Our Lady Queen of Hearts completed.

1964 September / Chapel of Our Lady of Mount Carmel completed.

1965 March / Chapel of Mother of Good Counsel completed.

1965 June / Chapel of Mary, Help of Christians completed.

1965 August / Chapel of Our Mother of Sorrows completed.

1965 September / Chapel of Our Lady of Guadalupe completed.

1965 / Great Organ installed; pulpit installed.

1966 August 6 / Wedding of Luci Baines Johnson and Patrick Nugent at Shrine.

1966 August / Chapel of Our Lady of Siluva completed. Sacristy of Memorial Hall completed.

1966 September / Chapels of Immaculate Heart of Mary and St. Anthony Mary Claret completed.

1966 December / "Triumph of the Lamb" mosaic and east apse mosaic in Great Upper Church completed.

1967 / West-chancel gallery screen and ambulatory of Great Upper Church completed.

1967 June / West-apse mosaic in Great Upper Church completed.

1967 June 21 / Msgr. Grady named auxiliary bishop of Chicago.

1967 Summer / West-chancel aisle completed.

1967 August / Chapel of Our Lady Queen of Missions completed.

1967 December / Sacristy of Great Upper Church completed.

1967 January / Sacristy of Crypt Church completed.

1967 February / East-chancel aisle completed.

1968 April / "Descent of the Holy Spirit" mosaic of Great Upper Church completed.

1968 November 12 / Msgr. William F. McDonough appointed sixth director.

1970 February / Chapels of Our Lady of the Rosary, St. Dominic and St.

Catherine of Siena completed.

1970 June / Blessed Sacrament Chapel of Great Upper Church completed.

1970 August / Chapels of Our Lady of Bistrica and Our Lady Queen of Peace completed.

1971 August / Chapel of Our Lady of Brezje completed.

1972 Summer / West-transept vault mosaic depicting "Last Judgment" completed.

1973 September / East-transept vault mosaic depicting "Creation" completed.

1974 November 14 / "Behold Your Mother," pastoral letter of the U.S. bishops, promulgated at National Shrine.

1973 June 1 / Msgr. John J. Murphy appointed seventh director.

1974 January 22 / First Prayer Vigil for Life at National Shrine.

1974 July 10 / Mother Teresa first visits National Shrine.

1974 Summer / Byzantine-Ruthenian Chapel completed.

1974 October / First section of north bay of Great Upper Church completed.

1975 Summer / Second section of north bay of Great Upper Church completed.

1976 August 9 / Cardinal Karol Wojtyla (future Pope John Paul II) visits Shrine with delegation of Polish bishops and priests following Eucharistic Congress in Philadelphia.

1979 October 7 / Pope John Paul II leads Morning Prayer for women religious in Great Upper Church of National Shrine.

1979 December 8-9 / Collection taken up in parishes nationwide for Shrine.

1980 Fall / Oratory of Our Lady Queen of Ireland completed.

1980 March 19 / Msgr. Eugene Bilski appointed eighth director.

1983 Spring / Chapel of Our Lady of Hostyn (Confessional Chapel) completed.

1984 Fall / Msgr. Harrold Murray appointed ninth director.

1986 Fall / Msgr. Michael J. Bransfield appointed 10th director.

1987 / Pope John Paul II designates Marian Year.

1987 August 10 / Cardinal O'Boyle dies.

1988 / Eternal Word Television Network begins Shrine broadcasts.

1990 October 12 / National Shrine designated a minor basilica by Pope John Paul II.

1992 / Spring east-entrance vestibule of crypt level completed in marble.

1992 September 27 / Austrian Chapel of Our Lady of Mariazell dedicated.

1994 May 29 / Chapel of Our Lady of Hope dedicated.

1996 July / Lighting of great dome completed.

1997 May 20 / Filipino Oratory of Our Lady of Peace and Good Voyage (Antipolo) dedicated.

1997 August 16 / Asian Indian Oratory of Our Lady of Good Health (Vailankanni) dedicated.

1997 August 30 / African American Chapel of Our Mother of Africa dedicated.

1999 Summer / "Universal Call to Holiness" sculpture installed.

1999 Fall / Marble cladding of narthex, addition of mosaics to narthex ceiling completed.

1999 November 14 / "Universal Call to Holiness" sculpture dedicated.

STATISTICS

DOME

Exterior Diameter: 108 feet

Interior Diameter: 89 feet

Height from main floor to interior dome to top of cross: 237 feet

Dome constructed of Guastavino tiles on which the polychrome tiles are attached.

HEIGHT

Eiffel Tower: 984 feet

Washington Monument: 555 feet

Knights' Tower: 329 feet

San Marco, Venice: 325 feet

Giotto's Tower, Florence: 275 feet

Leaning Tower of Pisa: 188 feet

DIMENSIONS OF THE NATIONAL SHRINE

Length, exterior measurement: 459 feet

Length, interior measurement: 399 feet

Width of nave: 58 feet

Width, exterior at transepts: 240 feet

CHURCH	AREA	LENGTH
St. Peter's Basilica, Vatican City	227,069 sq. ft.	718 feet
St. John the Divine, New York City	121,000 sq. ft.	601 feet
Nativity of Mary Cathedral, Milan	107,000 sq.ft.	500 feet
Christ Cathedral, Liverpool	101,000 sq. ft	619 feet
Mary of the Chair Cathedral, Seville	128,570 sq. ft.	430 feet
St. Peter's Cathedral, Cologne	91,464 sq. ft.	511 feet
Basilica of Our Lady of Peace, Ivory Coast	(statistics not available)	

Basilica of the National Shrine	**77,500 sq. ft.**	**459 feet**
Washington National Cathedral	75,000 sq. ft.	534 feet
Notre Dame Cathedral, Amiens	71,208 sq. ft.	521 feet
Santa Sophia, Istanbul	70,000 sq. ft.	350 feet
Notre Dame Cathedral, Chartres	68,260 sq. ft.	507 feet
Notre Dame Cathedral, Paris	64,108 sq. ft.	390 feet
York Minster, York, England	63,800 sq. ft.	486 feet
St. Paul's Cathedral, London	59,700 sq. ft.	460 feet
St. Patrick's Cathedral, New York City	57,768 sq. ft.	332 feet

The Shrine's foundation is of granite, quarried from Chelmsford, Mass. The upper walls are constructed of sandstone from Bedford, Ind.

The Shrine is constructed entirely of brick and stone. No wood or reinforced steel was used in its construction.

ABC-TV, 164

FRONT ELEVATION

0   10   20   30   40   50
SCALE IN FEET

INDEX

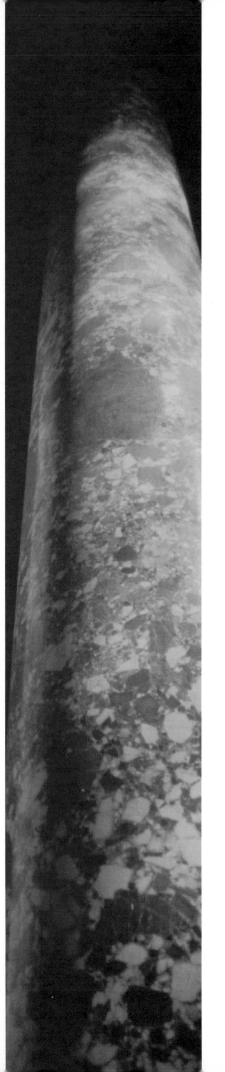

PHOTOGRAPHIC CONTRIBUTIONS